War after Death

War after Death

ON VIOLENCE AND ITS LIMITS

Steven Miller

FORDHAM UNIVERSITY PRESS *New York* 2014

THIS BOOK IS MADE POSSIBLE BY A COLLABORATIVE GRANT
FROM THE ANDREW W. MELLON FOUNDATION.

Library of Congress Cataloging-in-Publication Data
is available from the publisher.

Printed in the United States of America

16 15 14   5 4 3 2 1

First edition

For Barbara and Cleo

Only that historian will have the gift of fanning the spark of hope in the past who is firmly convinced that *even the dead* will not be safe from the enemy if he wins. And this enemy has not ceased to be victorious.

—Walter Benjamin, *Theses on the Philosophy of History*

One characteristic of hell is its unreality, which might be thought to mitigate hell's terrors but perhaps makes them all the worse.

—Jorge Luis Borges, *Emma Zunz*

In yet other cases one feels justified in maintaining the belief that a loss of this kind has occurred, but one cannot see clearly what it is that has been lost, and it is all the more reasonable to suppose that the patient cannot consciously perceive what he has lost either. This, indeed, might be so even if the patient is aware of the loss which has given rise to his melancholia, but only in the sense that he knows *whom* he has lost but not *what* he has lost in him.

—Sigmund Freud, *Mourning and Melancholia*

> Words dry and riderless,
> The indefatigable hoof-taps.
> While
> From the bottom of the pool, fixed stars
> Govern a life.

—Sylvia Plath, *Words*

CONTENTS

ACKNOWLEDGMENTS

I am delighted to acknowledge the wide array of debts that I have gathered in the process of writing this book.

The earliest formulations of the argument took shape in the beneficent atmosphere of the Cornell Society for the Humanities, where I was a postdoctoral fellow in 2003–4. Brett de Bary, then SHC director, deserves special mention for her graceful leadership and hospitality. I would also like to thank the wonderful students from my seminar "War, Technē, Religion," especially Josh Dittrich and Melanie Steiner who invited me back to Cornell the following year to give a plenary address at their conference on the "Aesthetics of War" (Spring 2005).

More recently, thanks to David Marriott's hospitality, I presented the section of Chapter 1 on the destruction of the Buddhas of Bamiyan to a wonderful audience from the History of Consciousness department at the University of California, Santa Cruz, a place that I long hoped to visit.

In Spring 2010, Inge Scholz-Strasser and Peter Nomaier were my hosts at the Freud Museum in Vienna where I spent a semester as Fulbright-Freud Scholar-in-Residence. Together with the incomparable Lonnie Johnson, the director of the Austrian-American Educational Commission, they provided for absolutely everything that I might need. The work that I undertook and the experiences I gained while in Austria contributed much to this project and will continue to nourish my projects long into the future. In addition, on my first day at the Freud Museum, I was fortunate to meet Christof Windgätter, an indefatigable coworker, ally, and friend.

I could only take advantage of this opportunity because the English Department at the University at Buffalo, SUNY, granted me release from my teaching duties. A junior faculty member could not hope for a more supportive department Chair than Cristanne Miller.

Both erstwhile and ongoing colleagues and students at the University at Buffalo, SUNY, have been invaluable mentors, examples, friends, and readers: Rachel Ablow, Sarah Bay-Cheung, Peter Degabriele, Rodolphe Gasché, Nate Gorelick, Danny Hack, Graham Hammill, Jim Holstun, Stacy Hubbard, Shaun Irlam, David Johnson, Lydia Kerr, Ruth Mack, Kalliopi Nicolopoulou, Neil Schmitz, Bill Solomon, Scott Stevens, Jim Swan, Roland Végsö, Hiroki Yoshikuni, Ewa Ziarek, and Kryzsztof Ziarek. But I would be remiss not to single out Joan Copjec and Tim Dean, my colleagues in the Center for the Study of Psychoanalysis and Culture, without whose militant support this book—or anything else—would never have had a chance of being written.

I also gratefully acknowledge the support of the Julian Park Publication Fund and the Technē Institute, both at UB, who provided subvention grants to cover the costs of producing this book.

Antony Gormley kindly gave permission to use the image of his sculpture *Still Feeling (Corner)*, 1993, which appears on the cover.

Helen Tartar and Thomas Lay at Fordham University Press and Tim Roberts at the Modern Language Initiative could not have been more supportive and responsive throughout the book's production process.

Gil Anidjar and Elissa Marder offered timely and generous reviews of the manuscript, for which I will always be grateful.

Finally, there a number of people that I would simply like to thank outright: Willy Apollon (who once said to me, "good, but you can still go further"), Danielle Bergeron, Ellen Burt, Lucie Cantin, Sara Guyer, Anna Kornbluh, Julia Reinhard Lupton, Juliet Flower MacCannell, Tracy McNulty, Jason Smith, and Andrzej Warminski.

First and last, now and always, this book is dedicated to Barbara Cole and Cleo Miller. Only for them, with them, and thanks to their angelic encouragement could it become a book at all.

Introduction

(i.e., the death drive)

War after Death: On Violence and Its Limits offers a philosophical reflection upon forms of violence that regularly occur in actual wars but do not often factor into the stories we tell ourselves about war. These stories—from Homer and Virgil to Kant, Clausewitz, Goya, Freud, Schmitt, and Derrida—revolve around killing and death. There is no way, it would seem, to capture the essence of war in word or image without linking it to death. Recent history demonstrates that body counts are more necessary than ever. I argue, however, that war-and-death is only part—a large part, certainly, but not necessarily the most important—of a much more bewildering story than is usually told. Despite tradition, this part of the story has little—if anything—to teach us about the psychic, ethical, and political meaning of war. Beyond the killing and death of human beings, everyone knows that war lays waste to the built environment, fragile ecosystems, personal property, works of art, archives, and intangible traditions. In addition, witnesses and researchers have amply documented that war provides a social framework that promotes the systematic perpetration of sexual violence. There is little question that the short- and long-term impact of such violence is more devastating than the loss of life on the battlefield (which is already horrible enough). There are ancient libidinal and cultural mechanisms designed to support the work of mourning the dead. But the aftermath of nonlethal violence against the living and nonliving remains more inchoate, improvised, and inarticulate. Sometimes this supposedly lesser violence is classified as "collateral damage." Most often, it is not even called violence because it poses no direct threat to the lives of human beings. In order to evaluate such violence, therefore, we need to rethink the critique of violence that structures the ethics and politics of war. It is necessary to take seriously, for example, the possibility that violence against the nonliving should rightfully be categorized as violence; that it can be (and perhaps always is) *more extreme* than killing; and, finally, that it is a constitutive dimension of all violence—including violence against the living.

Paradoxical as it may sound, killing becomes the exemplary as a use of force because of its economy and its self-restraint. The power of killing does not lie in its ability to possess or master life—which, in fact, it cannot do. If anything, killing lets life escape; it dispatches the soul of the enemy to the underworld. What matters is the finality and finitude of its act. The act of killing brings life to an end—finishes it off—and thereby brings itself to a conclusion without excessive expenditure. If all politics revolve around life—as theorists of biopolitics such as Michel Foucault and Giorgio Agamben teach us—this is because life underlies the primordial economy whereby power both extends its reach and holds itself in check. War-and-death, in turn, would be the narrative that at once maintains life at the center of an economy of power and upholds the power of economy. Killing is the use of force intended to end the use of force; it is war to end war.

Immanuel Kant opens his famous essay on perpetual peace upon a satiric note. The title of the essay, "Toward Perpetual Peace" (*Zum ewige Frieden*), is actually taken from an inscription on a Dutch innkeeper's sign depicting a graveyard. We can leave open, Kant writes, whether the inscription "applies to human beings in general, or specifically to the heads of state, who can never get enough of war, or to philosophers who dream the sweet dream of perpetual peace."[1] The satire suggests that the only peace worthy of the name would be the end result of a hyperbolic war to end all wars, the last war of the human race, the final war against war. At the same time, however, it reveals a fundamental and unquestioned supposition about the nature of war: that death—the peaceful and proper arrangement of the dead in a graveyard—is both the aim and the limit of war's violence.[2] The hope, for Kant, is that peace should become possible before the dead are the only people left to bury the dead.

The institution of war supposes that the end of life corresponds to an official, mutually recognized end to a given conflict and that the goal of violence corresponds to its limit. In order to understand the logic of biopower, therefore, it is not sufficient to analyze how sovereign power annexes life. It would also be necessary to examine how the relation between power and life itself founds a self-evident relation between violence and death. Agamben's analysis of biopolitics, for example, revolves around the construction of the originary politicization of bare life. "Not simple natural life, but life exposed to death (bare life or sacred life) is the originary political element."[3] To complete and complicate his analysis, however, it would be necessary to show that this politicization itself—which is inseparable from the reference to death—supposes a yet to be defined process whereby violence has been successfully reduced to killing. The same could be said of Foucault's construction of biopower in the final chapter of the first volume of *The History of Sexuality*, "The Right to Death and the Power over Life." This famous title does not only refer to the historical transition from a politics (of the people) that revolves around the death penalty to a politics (of population) that fosters and governs life; it also announces Foucault's philosophical analysis of the way in which the right to death lays the groundwork for biopolitics by making the life of the citizen into the subject of politics. But this historico-philosophical construction supposes an unanalyzed process whereby violence is reduced to killing. Life could never become a political issue unless the potential enormity of sovereign violence were captured, limited, and channeled toward death—the death of life.

War after Death presumes that the process whereby violence is folded into the narrative of war-and-death—which is nothing other than the politicization of violence itself—becomes most legible at moments, both historical and textual, when this narrative fails. Opting against an exhaustive historical survey, the method of this book is philosophical in that it privileges and seeks to reactivate selected moments of rupture at which the predominant narratives of war can no longer account for the extremity of war. More specifically, it selects moments at which the *nonlethal* or *extralethal* dimension of violence becomes the object of political discourse. Unlike killing, nonlethal violence against the living and the nonliving never encounters a natural limit upon its exercise. There are no criteria that allow one to judge whether such violence—an act of dismemberment, for example—stops short of death or continues after death; whether an attack situates its object as a living being or an inanimate object. Nor does such violence enact or prefigure the end of war; it possesses a specific finality—albeit difficult to define—that does not necessarily correspond either to the strategic aims or to the political telos of war. Both everywhere and rare, then, instances of such violence are most likely to raise essential questions about violence as such, the violence of violence, violence and its limits. In order to address some of these questions, I sometimes examine historical events and their immediate discursive aftermath: for instance, the destruction of the Buddhas of Bamiyan by the Taliban in March 2001 or the attacks of September 11, 2001. More often, I turn to textual events because they are more likely to be hospitable to the unreadability of war after death: Jean Genet's co-option of the liberal public sphere to stage himself as an inanimate decoy addressed to a hidden enemy; Goya's visionary testimony to the disasters of the Peninsular War; Samuel Beckett's attempt to imagine the worst beyond war; Jacques Derrida's experimentation with translation as a war of language against itself.

Through readings of these histories and texts, I demonstrate—against the intuitively satisfying tradition of Hobbesian political theory—that war is among the most important achievements of human culture; that it is a complex institution governed by a system of idealized conventions or rituals (what Lacan would call a "symbolic order"); and that killing is foremost among these rituals. Rather than undermine civilization, war-and-death, I argue, functions to consolidate its fundamental limits. Peace and survival are not merely a matter of saving life from death, protecting culture from nature; they depend, more primordially, upon the protection of death itself against forms of violence that disregard it as a limitation.

The institution of war represents—for soldiers and civilians alike, for everyone—the right to a specific form of death. The official burial of the dead and private rituals of mourning do not just occur in the aftermath of war; they are integral to the institution of war itself—perhaps even its most essential component. Despite the best intentions, protests against "the violence of war" or the "horror of war" do not necessarily amount to a struggle against war itself. Rather than promote peace, in fact, the struggle against war could very well begin with a struggle to defend the dignity of war-and-death against the incursion of violence worse than death. It is my contention that war itself—which is to say, the political economy of war-and-death—is founded upon such a defense of war. Precisely because war imposes and upholds death—celebrating it as both sacrifice and limit—philosophers and political leaders can claim it to be the elementary condition for eventual peace—or, at least, for a clean transition to a postwar world. It is only an apparent paradox that Barack Obama—whose administration has contributed as least as much as the Bush administration to the transformation and expansion of war around the world—was awarded the Nobel Peace Prize and that, in his lecture upon receiving this honor, he could resolutely affirm, "So yes, the instruments of war do have a role to play in the preservation of peace."[4]

Ultimately, however, I conclude that war's defense of war has never been effective. War has always been and will always be marred by forms of violence without internal limit that utterly disregard the distinction between the living and the dead, persons and things, combatants and noncombatants. This incontestable fact demands that we rethink the limits of violence and the role of violence in politics. The problem with war is not killing as such. Killing becomes a problem only if and when it fails to impose effective limits upon the use of force; if and when it becomes the means to restore limits where they have been breached, to restore death to war and thereby war to itself. The attempt to stop violence through killing achieves nothing but the atrocity of mass death. In a lecture offered within the framework of the Dictionary of War project, which I discuss at greater length in chapter 1, Saskia Sassen dares to raise an essential question: can we still take a stand against war in an age when war is no longer war? "'Anti-war' does not work any more as a word," she writes. "Is it that war itself is a situated historical something and that we've moved beyond that historical period? Is it that we are no longer positioned in a clear way so that we can identify war?"[5] To these questions, I would add a few more. Is not opposition to war predicated upon the authority of rituals and conventions that orient combat toward death's decision? In the name of what, therefore, could one struggle against war *after* death—if not war *and* death? The epochal legitimacy of this model of war derives from the fact that the aim of combat appears to coincide with its limit; and this limit appears to be unavoidable, immanent, and natural.

War after Death thus returns to an old question: Is there a substitute for war? If the function of war—on the most fundamental level—is to institute death as the officially recognized limit upon violence, could there be a limit upon violence beyond war? Is there a compelling and authoritative limit upon violence other than or beyond death? Is there a war to end war after death? Is war after death still war? Or does war after death demand a response to violence that breaks altogether with the paradigm of war and its vicissitudes? In order to respond adequately to this question, it will be necessary—at a minimum—to abandon the notion that the limit upon violence should correspond to its aim and end.

These considerations bring us to the Freudian theory of the death drive, for two primary reasons. First, the very drivenness of the death drive, which Freud aligned with primary masochism, bears witness to an agency of violence that structures the living being's relationship to its own existence; at the very heart of what is commonly called "death," is a disregard for the distinction between the living and the dead. Second, the psychoanalytic construction of the drive in general is predicated upon the refusal to align the aims of the drive with its limits. In fact, for Freud, the pathogenic effects of the drive can be limited only through what he called the "vicissitudes" or "destines" of the drive, which continue the work of the drive—beyond any putative object or aim—through various displacements or transformations. Indeed, it is precisely this limitlessness of the drive that founds—albeit upon ever shifting sands—the ethics of psychoanalysis and that ultimately distinguishes this ethics from morality and practical reason.[6] Psychoanalytic theory would thus be essential for thinking violence and its limits beyond the political economy of war-and-death.

The project of *War after Death*, then, is perhaps best encapsulated by the final parenthesis of the second chapter—the earliest written, containing the book's project *in nuce*—on Jean Genet's "open letter to the enemy": "(i.e. the death drive)." This almost ridiculously telegraphic evocation of the Freudian concept of the death drive was originally an impulsive insertion that I deleted and restored many times. The decision to insert it in the first place was based on the intuition—difficult to substantiate—that my entire reading of Genet was an allegory of the death drive and that, even in its elliptical form, this allegory would say more about the death drive than extensive theoretical elaboration. The decision to delete it was based on the conclusion that it can't be theoretically legitimate to throw in the death drive as final afterthought; that any mention of this notorious unruly concept must be rigorously justified and extensively elaborated. I would have to embed the Genet chapter within a larger project that elucidates how the questions of war and the politics of truth that it raises can only be evaluated in terms of the Freudian theory of the death drive or even be understood as an elaboration of this theory. Had I not decided to omit this parenthetical insertion, the remainder of the book might never have been written. Rather than theoretical elaboration, however, the book—perhaps inevitably—hazards a series of further allegories; and so I ended up restoring the parenthesis in order to punctuate this allegorical pattern.

Nonetheless, a very specific reading of Freud's *Beyond the Pleasure Principle* both generates and emerges from these allegories, and I would like to take the opportunity of this introduction to outline this reading. Freud's speculations on the death drive revolve around three theses that build upon one another:

1. An instinct is an urge in organic life to restore an earlier state of things.[7]
2. The aim of all life is death.[8]
3. Inanimate things existed before living ones.[9]

These theses clearly delineate the central enigma of the Freudian theory of the death drive. This drive does not hasten the living being forward toward the end of its life but rather backward to a state that preceded the emergence of life (and thus also of death). The death drive, in other words, is not true to its own name: rather than designate the living being's inner urge to die, it evokes the much more complex process whereby it seeks to nullify the fact of its own birth. Freud's representation of the unicellular life that becomes the unlikely hero of *Beyond the Pleasure Principle* might well have been animated by Job's lament:

> Why died I not from the womb? Why did I not give up the ghost when I came out of the belly?
>
> Why did the knees prevent me? Or why the breasts that I should suck?
>
> . . .
>
> Or as an hidden untimely birth I had not been; as infants which never saw light.[10]

If the death drive aims to reverse the course of time, to revert to the inanimate state that preceded birth, then it impels the living being to do more than die: it *cancels itself out*. Death is less cessation than dissipation:

> The attributes of life were at some time evoked in inanimate matter by the action of a force of whose nature we can form no conception. . . . The tension which then arose in what had hitherto been an inanimate substance endeavored to cancel itself out. In this way the

first instinct came into being: the instinct to return to an inanimate state [*zum Leblosen zurückzukehren*]. It was still an easy matter at the time for a living substance to die; the course of its life was probably a brief one, whose direction was determined by the chemical structure of the young life. For a long time, perhaps, living substance was thus being constantly created afresh and easily dying, till decisive external influences altered in such a way as to oblige the still surviving substance to diverge ever more widely from its original course of life and to make ever more complicated detours before reaching its aim of death. These circuitous paths to death [*Umwege zum Tode*], faithfully kept to by the conservative instincts, would thus present us today with the picture of the phenomena of life.[11]

James Strachey's translation of this passage is interesting: both off the mark and oddly to the point. Whereas Strachey's prose tells us, "The tension which then arose in what had hitherto been an inanimate substance endeavored to cancel itself out," Freud's German reads: "Die damals entstandene Spannung in dem vorhin unbelebten Stoff trachtete darnach, sich abzugleichen." Rather than "to cancel out," the verb, *sich abgleichen*—in keeping with the logic and tonality of the pleasure principle itself—means roughly "to equal itself out, "to level itself out," "to balance itself out," or perhaps "to settle down." The verb (whose root word *gleichen* refers to resemblance, equality, or *homoiosis*) thus underscores Freud's assumption that inanimate stuff exists in a state of unsullied equilibrium or selfsameness—that is, pure pleasure—that the birth of life will disturb. Freud's use of this word, then, bears an interesting relationship to his earlier citation of Nietzsche's concept of the "eternal return of the same" to designate the agency of the compulsion to repeat. On the one hand, the "same" would be the traumatic event or situation—the insuperable difference—that recurs in repetition. On the other hand, it would also be the compact sameness that precedes the upsurge of life. Read together, these references to the "same" clarify the paradoxical manner in which repetition supports the death drive. Repetition bears witness both to the living being's inability to escape trauma and to the ongoing endeavor to retract it once and for all, even if this means nullifying its own existence.

The etymology and dictionary definitions of the English verb, *to cancel*, carry a different—more violent—set of connotations. Strictly speaking, the *Oxford English Dictionary* informs us, cancellation is a matter of writing. First and foremost, *to cancel* means "1a) To deface or obliterate (writing), properly by drawing lines across it lattice-wise; to cross out, strike out . . . to annul, render void or invalid by so marking. 1b) To deface or destroy by cutting or tearing up. . . . 2a) To annul, repeal, render void (obligations, promises, vows, or other things binding) . . . 3a) To obliterate, blot out, delete from sight or memory. 3b) To frustrate, reduce to nought, put an end to, abolish." Next on the list, however, is an entry that approximates the sense of *Abgleichen*—although it remains articulated in terms of writing: "4a) To strike out (a figure) by drawing a line through it: esp. in removing a common factor, e.g. from the numerator and denominator of a fraction. 4b) To remove equivalent quantities of opposite signs, or on opposite signs of an equation, account, etc.; to balance a quantity of opposite sign, so that the sum is zero. 4c) To render (a thing) null by means of something of opposite nature; to neutralize, counterbalance, countervail. 4d) *Music.* To remove the effect of (a preceding sharp or flat), including an element of the key signature: marked by inserting a natural sign in the score."

Thanks to its misplaced reference to writing, the English translation of Freud's German helps to clarify the paradoxical logic of the death drive. Job, once again, reminds us that death can be understood in two related but ultimately divergent ways: as the negation of life and as the negation of birth. The fact that a person's life ends does not necessarily negate his birth. On the contrary, the event of death frequently provides the occasion to look back upon the entire span of his life from birth unto death. What Freud calls the emergent tension of life, *die entstandene Spannung*, is not necessarily resolved upon the end of life. To negate someone's birth, then, implies a very different process that would entail nullifying an entire life span. As Job's lament clarifies, it would entail nothing less than reversing the course of history. Beyond merely ending life—even prematurely—the negation of birth would retroactively impose death in place of life; to assert that there was—and, indeed, had always been—no one instead of someone. In spite of its name, then, the death drive goes beyond mere dying to the precise extent that it aims to impose death there where a singular life would have emerged; to restore the continuity of the death that didn't prevent this life from coming into being. A life may well return to the inanimate state that preceded its existence by balancing or equaling out the unbearable disequilibrium that resulted from its birth. However, if we do not relinquish the logic of Freud's thinking, we cannot fail to conclude that this *Abgleichung* is other than a biological or physical process. Even in life's most elementary form, it is always already more than a quantum of tension. No sooner is this tension evoked than it becomes the quality that allows life to enter into relation with itself. When the tension of life awakens, it awakens to itself. Even for the earliest aborted life-forms, to eliminate this tension is not the same as smothering a fire, for instance, or lowering blood pressure down to zero. Precisely because life is nothing other than tension or "span" (*Spannung*), for life to eliminate *it* amounts to revoking *itself*. Rather than eliminate tension in order to restore a previous state, the death drive brings about an event that consists in negating a previous event. Rather than eradicate the history of life, it ends up adding a "negative" or "destructive" event to this history. In this sense, as Freud clearly elaborates, the death drive turns out to be incurably positive. Indeed, it is this positivity of the death drive that radically expands the potential scope of its destructiveness beyond the bounds of an individual life.

This horrible positivity bears witness to a drive of destruction that opens beyond death and perhaps beyond the death drive. The best—or least worse—manner to conceive of this libidinal opening is in terms of the pragmatics of written signs and their cancellation. Once the tension of life arises, Strachey makes Freud say, it endeavors to "cancel itself out." As the dictionary definitions make perfectly clear, this means that the living being literally crosses itself out; that the death drive obliterates life by adding writing to writing, placing it under erasure; it effaces traces by multiplying them and then, in a supplementary turn, destroying the resulting accumulation of traces. The tension or span of life would be nothing other than a "written" trait that resists destruction—no matter how momentarily; and such a trait could only be neutralized by means of further traits. The return to the inanimate follows the itinerant path mapped out by the nonliving traces of life.

The agony of this circuitous itinerary plays a discreet but decisive role in Freud's brief reference to the narrative of Tancredi and Clorinda in Torquato Tasso's epic *Jerusalem Delivered* (*Gerusalemme Liberata*). In *Beyond the Pleasure Principle*, Freud adduces this narrative as the last in a series of examples that go to show that trauma can take the form of a complex situation that might develop over a long period and that, through repetition—repetition that might well define someone's entire lifetime—these situations assume the tragic character of fate. Freud provides examples of both active and passive versions of what, citing Nietzsche, he explicitly calls "the eternal recurrence of the same thing" (*ewige Wiederkehr des Gleichen*):

> Thus we have come across people all of whose relationships have the same outcome: such as the benefactor who is abandoned in anger after a time by each of his *protégés*, however much they might otherwise differ from one another, and who thus seems doomed to taste all the bitterness of ingratitude; or the man whose friendships all end in betrayal by his friend; or the man who time after time in the course of his life raises someone else into a position of great private or public authority and then, after a certain interval, himself upsets that authority and replaces him by a new one; or, again, the lover each of whose love affairs with a woman passes through the same phases and reaches the same conclusion. . . . There is the case, for instance, of the woman who married three successive husbands each of whom fell ill soon afterwards and had to be nursed by her on their death-beds. The most moving poetic picture of a fate such as this is given by Tasso in his romantic epic *Gerusalemme Liberata*.[12]

Like Oedipus who failed to escape fate through self-imposed exile, these are examples of the way in which repetition reduces supposed "life changes" to nothing. At the fatal moment when repetition appears—when the lover realizes she is caught in the same pattern, or the woman finds herself once again toiling over her husband's deathbed—it is as if nothing had changed; as if the subject never moved. Repetition cancels out both history and movement, always returning them to a point of no departure, subordinating them to the timeless logic of unconscious fantasy. Through the example of Tancredi and Clorinda, then, Freud turns from the war of the "war neuroses" to a literary or phantasmatic construction of war as a complex scene of misrecognition. Of particular interest is the way in which Tasso's tragic drama explores the role of identity, misrecognition, and simulation in combat. Freud's famous synopsis of the narrative stresses not only Tancredi's misrecognition of his lover for an enemy, but also of something immobile (symbolically speaking, inanimate) for a living being. In an initial moment, Tancredi fails to know his beloved because she is disguised in the armor of an enemy knight. Later, the warrior repeats the error because she is trapped in the body of a tree:

> [The epic's] hero, Tancred, unwittingly kills his beloved Clorinda in a duel while she is disguised in the armor of an enemy knight. After her burial he makes his way into a strange magic forest which strikes the Crusaders' army with terror. He slashes with his sword at a tall tree; but blood streams from the cut and the voice of Clorinda, whose soul is imprisoned in the tree, is heard complaining that he has wounded his beloved once again.[13]

To better grasp the stakes of repetition in this scene of war and sexual violence, then, I would like to return briefly to the text of Tasso's epic. The narrative, as Freud emphasizes, stages repetition. On the one hand, it is a story of "war and death." "'What are you bringing me,' she cried, / 'riding so fast?' 'War and death,' he replied. / 'War and death you shall have then, if you like. / I won't refuse you.' And she stood in wait."[14] The battle between Tancredi and Clorinda takes place at night, shrouded in darkness, but Tasso reminds us that the courage of the protagonists deserves a wider and brighter stage. The words of his epic poem will thus illuminate and keep safe what would otherwise be lost to memory:

> What they did now was unforgettable,
> deserving a wide stage, a brilliant sun.
> O Night, who shrouded such a great event
> in your deep darkness and oblivion
> let me bring it forth in the pure light of verse
> that every future age may look upon
> that famous pair, and let their glory be
> what makes your darkness shine in memory.[15]

But Tasso's narrative itself is double. The epic of great deeds also tells the romantic tale of star-crossed lovers. Glorious as it may be, it is predicated upon tragic misrecognition. The antagonists are not enemies at all. On the most basic level, then, the battle should never have happened; it represents a redundant and wasteful use of force. The more the contortions of battle approximate gestures of love, the more acute the misrecognition becomes; the more Tancredi's valiant deeds strive toward ultimate glory, the more they commit atrocity. Rather than achieve victory, violence systematically usurps the possibility of eros. At battle's end, the chance to replace blows with caresses is permanently lost: "Three times the knight gripped the young lady hard/ in his muscular arms, and three times she/ slipped herself out of those tenacious knots,/ no true love's, but the bonds of an enemy."[16] Recounting the moment of Clorinda's death, Tasso narrates what we know but Tancredi does not, sustaining the moment when his sword pierces Clorinda's armor to impale the female body hidden beneath it:

> But now the fatal moment has arrived
> Clorinda's life is hastening to the goal.
> Into her lovely breast he thrusts his blade,
> drowns it, eagerly drinks her blood. Her stole
> beneath the cuirass, sweetly lined with gold,

that held her breasts with light and tender pull,
now fills with a warm stream. She cannot stand;
her legs give way. She feels death at hand . . . [17]

Everything that happens in this battle happens two times at once. The fighting takes place between doubles, surrogates, effigies, or puppets; and everything that these figures do to one another happens to the lovers who animate them. But the point is not that war is a displaced form of eros. On the contrary, the function of this scene of misrecognition in an epic poem of war is to make visible the impersonal logic of war, to show that war has its own rhythm and its own emotions that have nothing to do with the protagonists' feelings for one another. Wrath, ire, rage, and furor are traditionally isolated as the defining affects of war—war reduced to itself, war as affect. From the *Iliad*'s first word (*menin*), the Western discourse of war is suffused with figures of wrath. In Tasso's epic, as in many other instances, wrath appears as a kind of élan or hyperbole that carries fighters beyond strategy, skill, and even strength toward unmitigated struggle. "Wrath seized their hearts and swept them up once more,/ weak as they were, unto the cruel fight,/ where strength is dead and art is used no more/ and fury fights in place of skill and might!"[18] In this instance, then, wrath explicitly leads to atrocity. Tasso exposes the inherent link between weakness and cruelty, and the sexual violence that always doubles the act of killing. When Freud reads this battle scene, in turn, it is precisely the sexual violence at the heart of war that becomes the trauma that gives rise to repetition.

The first iteration of the story is a drama of mistaken identity. Because of Clorinda's armor, Tancred tragically mistakes friend for enemy and is thus forced to confront the madness of war. Nonetheless, the moment of recognition also achieves reconciliation. When the enemy drops her mask, war ends and mourning begins. The second time around, Tancred's misrecognition is predicated upon a different kind of disguise. After her death, Clorinda's soul migrates into a new body—that of a tall tree. Tancred fails to know her not because he mistakes her for someone else but rather because he does not even recognize this new body as human. Since this scene occurs soon after Clorinda's burial, the tree might also figure the immobility of the corpse, its exposure to blows against which it cannot defend itself. The moment of recognition, then, confronts Tancred with the repetition of his grave error. But, in addition, it leaves him with the unbearable (and perhaps unsymbolizable) responsibility for violence against an inanimate object. The horror that he experiences at his own act derives from the understanding that Clorinda was utterly defenseless at the moment he attacked her. Accordingly, this iteration of the conflict calls attention to the place of the inanimate in the first scene. Like the tree, Clorinda's armor is an inanimate shell. Like the shield against external stimuli, which Freud describes elsewhere in *Beyond the Pleasure Principle*, armor can only serve a protective function to the precise extent that it is dead.[19]

One might claim that the inanimate remains an external barrier that protects a living core; that it is dispensable precisely because it is lifeless; that it is there to be destroyed in place of the body just as the body is there to be destroyed in place of the soul.[20] But Tasso, much like Freud, emphasizes that such a barrier must also be exposed to violence in order to protect against it. Armor is not invulnerable, and it does not make its wearer invulnerable. On the contrary, it is a shell situated at the most vulnerable edge of the body and thus defiantly manifests the wearer's constitutive exposure to destruction. In much the same way, the corpse manifests the living body's exposure to destruction before and after death.

Another name for this most vulnerable edge of the body—exposed beyond the presence of the body proper itself—is simply the trace. As Derrida often insists, the trace can assume the complex form of an afterimage, ghost, or shell. Reading the death drive in terms of the metaphor of writing, then, has three consequences that become central to the concerns of *War after Death*: (1) it reveals that the object of the death drive is not necessarily "life" but the nonliving trace or shell of life;[21] (2) it suggests that the aim of the death drive is not "death" but rather destruction; and (3) it implies that life, even in the most rudimentary form, cannot cancel itself out without the projection—or the fundamental fantasy—of an agency of violence impinging from the outside. The event of life is uncontrollably metonymical; everything that comes into contact with it—even to kill it—bears witness to its passage. Even if it were possible to efface every trace of someone's existence, one would still have to identify and eliminate all the people who knew the victim or simply cared what happened to him and then everyone who cares what happens to those people.

In Sonnet 55, Shakespeare upholds the inviolate status of memory in the midst of war and destruction:

When wasteful war shall statues overturn,
And broils root out the work of masonry,

> Nor Mars his sword nor war's quick fire, shall burn
> The living record of your memory[22]

When it arises inside or outside war, however, the death drive wastes everything from statues and masonry to living record of memory; it bears unwitting witness to the uncontainable scope of intergenerational and intersubjective experience. Once life emerges, it cannot truly be canceled without destroying the entire world. The aim of the death drive—if it has one—is not merely to bring life to an end, but, more radically, to bring the entire world to an end. In his posthumously published memoir, *Prisoner of Love*, Genet recounts his visit to the Shatila refugee camp shortly after the notorious Phalangist massacre that took place there in 1982. Meditating on the eyes and faces of the victims still lying in the streets, he enters into a hyperbolic meditation on death:

> The dying saw and felt and knew their death was the death of the world. *Après moi le déluge* is a ridiculous claim, because the only *after me* is the death of all creation.
>   Understood in this sense, death is a phenomenon that destroys the world. To eyelids reluctant to close the world gradually loses its brightness, blurs, dissolves and finally disappears, dies in a pupil obstinately fixed on a vanishing world. So? The wide eye can still see the glint of the knife or the bayonet. The brightness that slowly approaches, pales, blurs, disappears. Then the knife, the hand, the sleeve, the uniform, the eyes, the laughter of the Phalangist have ceased to be.[23]

By virtue of its inherent hyperbolism, however, the death drive always gets lost in the labyrinth of the archive. Precisely because the death drive constitutes the living being's relation to its own life—to life as its own, the life it was born with—it goes beyond life "itself" (assuming there is such a thing) and brings into play all the metonymies that bear witness to its existence. Genet provides a fragment of this metonymical series as he imagines the world dying in the pupil of the victim's eye: "the knife, the hand, the sleeve, the uniform, the eyes, the laughter of the Phalangist have ceased to be." In order to retract the event of birth, it is not sufficient to extinguish life; it is necessary to gain access to subjective experience in order to write out of history (both public and secret) anything that might bear witness—however obliquely or figuratively—to this event.

In the preface to *Chaque fois unique, la fin du monde* (the French edition of *The Work of Mourning*, first edited in English by Michael

Naas and Pascale-Anne Brault), Jacques Derrida also asserts that
death is as large—or small—as the entire world:

> When anyone dies, though it happens in a more intensely irrefutable
> way when someone "close" or a friend dies, a certain beloved person,
> even when love is absent or terribly conflicted, bordering on con-
> tempt or detestation, I feel something that I do not have inclination
> or strength enough to uphold as a thesis: that the death of the other—
> not only but especially when one loves him—does not announce an
> absence, a disappearance, the end of *such and such* a life, which is
> to say, the possibility for an (always unique) world to appear to *such*
> a living being. Each time, death declares *the end of the world in its
> totality*, the end of all possible worlds; *each time the end of the world
> as a unique totality, thus irreplaceable and thus infinite.*[24]

Although Derrida does not explicitly mention Freud in this context—
to do so would be to enter into the game of developing a thesis—these
few sentences, to my mind, constitute the most extreme and therefore
the best possible articulation of the logic of the death drive. Key to
this articulation is precisely the claim that the object of the death drive
is not life or death—or even "survival" so long as this merely refers,
as in Martin Hägglund's work, to the successive temporality of a singular life—but what Derrida calls "the world as a unique totality."

This totality is unique because it is constitutively metonymical, and
the metonym that stands for the entire series, I would argue, is nothing other than what Derrida calls "the archive." The metonym for the
world in its totality, in other words, is the nonliving, material support of memory; the technical exteriority of memory that resists the
safeguarding—if not salvific—process of internalization. When Derrida explicitly evokes the death drive, then, it appears as the paradox
of what he calls *mal d'archive*—which means both "archive fever,"
as Eric Prenowitz translates the phrase, an archival desire or drive,
and the "evil" that inhabits or haunts the archive, destroying it from
within. He discovers the agency of the death drive not within the
proper body of the living being but rather on the level of the technical
prosthesis or the material support of archival memory:

> As the death drive is also, according to the striking words of Freud
> himself, an aggression and a destruction (*Destruktion*) drive, it not
> only incites forgetfulness, amnesia, the annihilation of memory, as
> *mneme* or to *anamnesis*, that is, the archive, consignation, the docu-
> mentary or monumental apparatus as *hyponema*, mnemotechnical
> supplement of representative, auxiliary or memorandum. Because the
> archive, if this word or this figure can be stabilized so as to take on a

signification, will never be either memory of anamnesis as spontaneous, alive, and internal experience. . . . The archive is hypomnesic.
And let us note in passing a decisive paradox to which we will not
have time to return, but which undoubtedly conditions the whole of
these remarks: if there is no archive without consignation in an external place, which assumes the possibility of memorization, of repetition, of reproduction, or of reimpression, when we must also remember that repetition itself, the logic of repetition compulsion, remains,
according to Freud, indissociable from the death drive. And thus from
destruction. Consequence: right on that which permits and conditions archivization, we will never find anything other than that which
exposes to destruction, and in truth menaces with destruction.[25]

The task of *War after Death* is to supplement this surprising construction of the death drive with a meditation on atrocity. Derrida
gestures toward the incidence of atrocity as a horizon when he specifies both that the conditions of archivization expose the archive to
destruction and, ultimately, that these conditions actively *menace*
it with destruction. The death drive itself, he suggests, is inseparable from the possibility of premeditated acts of violence committed against the archive. The agency of the death drive, in this sense,
vastly expands the category of violence. More important, it suggests
that destruction and atrocity are inseparable from what is called
"death"; and that "death" does not distinguish between the living
and the dead. From the perspective of the traditional narrative of
war-and-death, this displacement appears to diminish the gravity of
violence. The former dignity of war seems to become mired in a grow-
ing mass of collateral damage. When we take this displacement seriously, however, we see that this account of the death drive shows that
collateral damage is something other than a mere by-product of war.
All violence, structurally speaking, proves to be collateral damage—
including the death of the enemy on the battlefield. Despite appearances, the dignity of death—and perhaps, to an extent, that of war
itself—is thereby restored because it can no longer be used as an alibi
to justify and perpetuate the institution of war. At the same time, it
becomes all the more urgent to delimit the atrocities that take advantage of the traditional disregard for war after death.

CHAPTER ONE

Statues Also Die

When men die, they enter history.
When statues die they become art.
This botany of death is what we call culture.

—Chris Marker, *Les statues meurent aussi*

"A NEW KIND OF WAR"

In the immediate aftermath of September 11, there was as much discussion of rescue efforts at ground zero as of the ways in which this event revealed a change—perhaps long under way—in the nature of war. Only two weeks after the attacks, Secretary of Defense Donald H. Rumsfeld himself contributed to this discussion with a now-famous editorial in the *New York Times* titled "A New Kind of War," in which he analyzes how the coming war—later known as the "war on terror"—would no longer be recognizable as war in the traditional sense. In keeping with a long tradition of military leaders claiming to speak the hard truth, Rumsfeld begins, "President Bush is rallying the nation for a war against terrorism's attack on our way of life. Some believe that the first casualty of war is the truth. But in this war, the first victory must be to tell the truth."[1] Although such a preamble sets the stage for gritty realism, what Rumsfeld delivers is closer to a negative theology of war as a god who never shows his true face: "And the truth is, this will be a war like none other that our nation has faced. Indeed, it is easier to describe what lies ahead by talking about what it is not rather than what it is."[2]

The secretary of defense proceeds both as a military leader and as a philosopher of war, interrogating a series of binary oppositions that derive their meaning from the history and theory of modern war. The first such opposition differentiates territorial warfare focused on strategically valuable targets from a deterritorialized practice whose

18

primary goal is to gather intelligence, run interference, or disrupt imminent hostile initiatives. The coming war, Rumsfeld stipulates, *might or might not* involve the use of military force. The most important decision will not be whether to go to battle but whether armed conflict itself is still a relevant paradigm; or, more radically put, *whether the military itself is the best means to wage war.* Rumsfeld's schematic presentation of the war on terror offers an initial, chilling glimpse into the process—all too familiar since 9/11—of demilitarizing war and turning so-called civil society itself into a weapon.

> This war will not necessarily be one in which we pore over military targets and mass forces to seize those targets. Instead, military force will likely be one of many tools we use to stop individuals, groups and countries that engage in terrorism. Our response may include firing cruise missiles into military targets somewhere in the world; we are just as likely to engage in electronic combat to track and stop investments moving through offshore banking centers.[3]

Notably, in 1966, Martha Gellhorn published an article on the Vietnam War bearing exactly the same title as Rumsfeld's editorial. In the article, she reveals that her title is taken from a thirty-page "indoctrination lecture" that was distributed to all U.S. troops upon their arrival in South Vietnam. The relevant passage, in fact, pertains to the well-known injunction to go beyond fighting and killing in order to win the "hearts and minds" of the South Vietnamese people.

> From everything I've said, it should be plain to see that we're in a new kind of war. And the name of this new game is much, much more than just "Kill VC" (Vietcong). We've got to kill VC all right; but there's a lot more to it than that. To really and truly and finally win this war, we must help the Government of South Vietnam win the hearts and minds of the people of South Vietnam.[4]

During the Vietnam War, the claim that "we're in a new kind of war" appeared in an unpublished discourse ("mimeographed," Gellhorn specifies), circulated among and addressed particularly to soldiers at the moment they entered the war zone. On the eve of the "war on terror," however, the same phrase becomes the title of an editorial that the secretary of defense published in a national newspaper of record and thus addressed to the reading public. This shift in address would thus be inseparable from the very transformation of war that Rumsfeld seeks to adumbrate in his editorial.

War is not a time of promises. As Kant lucidly elaborated, the indispensable condition for any peace worthy of the name—nothing less than *eternal* peace (*ewige Freiden*)—is a true promise, a promise sealed without "secret reservation of material for a future war."[5] Men of war are by definition men of secrecy, not their word. Rumsfeld thus promises to tell the truth and at once breaks this promise. Rather than lay out clear strategies or state military and political goals, he does no more than adumbrate a number of equally possible actions that could, theoretically, be retracted at any moment. "Military force will *likely* be one of many tools we use to stop individuals, groups and countries that engage in terrorism. Our response *may* include firing cruise missiles into military targets somewhere in the world; we are *just as likely* to engage in electronic combat to track and stop investments moving through offshore banking centers." The hard truth, then, is that the secretary of defense makes no promises. And the first promise that he does not make is that the coming war will be fought by uniformed military personnel on a battlefield—which, traditionally, is the promise that establishes the very regularity of so-called regular war. What is new about this war is ultimately that it will be based on the possibility, if not the likelihood, that the U.S. government will break every promise that it makes. This is the fundamental policy for which this editorial primes its readership.

But Rumsfeld does venture one promise—a promise essential to the enterprise of war: that these possibilities, beginning with the possibility that all promises and conventions will be rendered moot, are not mere fiction. They are "likelihoods"—which is to say that they are *more than possible* because they are likely to be actualized. Before and after any targets are seized (or not), cruise missiles are fired (or not), terrorists and their supporters are stopped (or not), and electronic combat is joined (or not), "war" becomes the name for an ongoing process of calculating words and actions (and their intercourse) based on the principle of likelihood. The only guarantee that Rumsfeld offers in a discourse long on prospects and short on promises is that the United States is not playing games. On the eve of the "war on terrorism" and well before the advent of "homeland security," Rumsfeld's rhetorical strategy advertises the fact that the government never stops calculating threats and that it actually intends, in turn, to combat them, to enter into real combat with its enemies using all the weapons— new and old, military and civilian, conventional and unconventional—at its disposal. The public nature of this calculation itself would constitute a de facto declaration of war.[6]

Even if Rumsfeld doesn't traffic in fiction, this does not mean that his language is devoid of poetry. During his tenure as secretary of defense, in fact, he became notorious for the poetry of his statements to the press. Hart Seely published a humorous anthology of these (inadvertent?) "poems."[7] The best known among them is certainly the verses (which Seely titles "The Unknown") that articulate Rumsfeld's negative theology.[8] But such "poetry"—or any poetry for that matter—isn't necessarily the product of an artistic enterprise. It is not necessarily a joke to claim that Rumsfeld is a poet. Nor is it honorific. It is not a quality or a value but quite simply a matter of strategic calculation.[9] In *Targets of Opportunity*, Samuel Weber offers a series of essays whose "figural trajectory" traces many of the warlike metaphors whereby Western philosophy has "militarized" the life of the mind. Thinking, Weber concludes, is militarized through the metaphors whereby it situates its goals—for example, the metaphor of "targeting" that forms the central preoccupation of his book. "This link between what was originally a protective shield and an activity that seeks to 'hit' or 'seize' control of a more or less distant object acquires greater import when one considers the long-standing function of 'targeting' as a metaphor for thinking itself—that is, for what philosophers, from the scholastics to Husserlian phenomenology, have designated as 'intentionality,' which, in the modern period at least, has been employed to define the structure of consciousness."[10] The very relationship between thinking and its object, for Weber, is a poetic construction; and it is precisely this construction that—from Plato to Husserl—has militarized this relationship. The corollary of the militarization of thinking, then, would thus be a subtle and pervasive militarization of poetry. It is precisely because Rumsfeld's poetry is the unintended upshot of his strategic thinking that his discourse bears witness to the military "intentionality" of poetic language itself.

But Rumsfeld's poetics is less a matter of establishing a field of perception in which subjects and objects become targets than of measuring probability. In this respect, his discourse belongs to a tradition of poetics that begins with Aristotle. For Aristotle, poetry is precisely the discursive mode proper to the representation of probability or likelihood. After 9/11, a key passage from the *Poetics* seems to lay the groundwork for Rumsfeld's editorial:

> It is a further clear implication of what has been said that the poet's task is to speak not of events which have occurred, but of the kind of events which could occur, and are possible by the standards of

probability or necessity. For it is not the use or absence of meter
which distinguishes poet and historian. . . . [T]he difference lies in
the fact that one speaks of events which have occurred, the other of
the sort of events which could occur. It is for this reason that poetry
is both more philosophical and more serious than history, since
poetry speaks more of universals, history of particulars.[11]

Whereas history, for Aristotle, is the representation of what actually
happened in the past, poetic discourse is constitutively hypothetical:
it represents something that might have happened or might still happen in the future. Even within the terms of Aristotle's argument, however, poetry is not entirely foreign to history. Poetry's possibility, he
specifies, must be more than merely possible; it must also be necessary, probable, or likely. It may be fictional but not mendacious.
What Aristotle calls *mimesis* consists in the extremely complex task
of constructing *verisimilitude*. The French word *vraisemblable* is usually translated as "likely": true semblance. And the truth of this semblance inheres not in its correspondence to exterior or transcendental
reality but rather in its ability to stage probability—to model potential events and thereby to represent the formative principle whereby
their reality (or their likelihood) can be judged. The prime example of
"poetry" for Aristotle is tragedy, because the internal coherence (or
"dynamism") of tragic plot structure places limits upon what might
happen in the course of a single play. Form makes poetry "philosophical," as Aristotle writes, because it distinguishes universal (likely, cal-
culable) actions from particulars or anomalies. What happens once
or never, according to Aristotle's logic, cannot be universal. Before
poetry says or represents anything, then, it posits a virtual model that
responds to an implicit demand to determine (distinguish, select, calculate) which possibilities should be taken seriously.[12]

The militarization of poetry would thus be predicated upon a calculation that restricts the field of representation, that makes it possible to move beyond the sterile freedom of sheer possibility toward
history and life. Mimesis thereby proves to be the reality principle at
the basis of strategy and policy. No less than poetry, war demands
passage beyond history to poetry and back again; it demands that
we distinguish between the possible and the probable, to envisage or
to calculate likelihoods; it entails both the work of *poesis* and what
Aristotle, in *Nicomachean Ethics*, calls *phronesis*—the philosophical
discipline of prudence. Being threatened or under attack—"at war"—
produces a panic-inducing contraction of the usually distended

temporal horizon. There is literally no time. No time to lose on mere possibilities. In order to decide what action to take, we must know what situation or event is most likely to arise in the proximate future.

At the same time, it is important to remember that Rumsfeld's concern with verisimilitude is born of trauma. The attacks of September 11, 2001, opened a "new" horizon of likelihood. On this fateful day, things which had previously been discounted as merely possible turned out to be more than likely. The death drive foiled the reality principle.

Thanks to psychoanalysis (not only the work of Freud but also Pierre Janet and Abraham Kardiner) and to contemporary trauma studies, war is more or less automatically linked to the experience of trauma. Relevant as this linkage may be, however, it remains either too empirical or too much of an academic cliché unless it can be understood in terms of the epistemology of possibility. An event becomes traumatic not because it *did* happen but rather because it *could* happen. War constitutes a predicament in which, even after an event has happened, we do not cease to be shocked at its possibility. The pure possibility that adheres to the often horrible actuality of an event is ultimately what overwhelms our psychic defenses.[13] Indeed, this irreversible possibility is what continues to haunt the psyche long after the newsworthy actuality of the event has receded into the past. Even the historiography of past wars does not only recount the story of what *did* happen, but what *could* happen. Facts serve as examples, not of universal concepts, but of sheer possibility—even and especially the possibility of something that happens a single time. The questions raised by such facts are different. Not: what is it? Nor even: who did it? But rather: how is it possible? And can it happen again?

If, as Weber explains, the reality principle of war is founded upon a small number of key metaphors, it should not be surprising that war trauma has an impact on language. Whereas academic and psychiatric studies of trauma have emphasized its relationship to individual memory and repetition, Rumsfeld's discourse reminds us to consider its impact on the collective level of language. "Even the vocabulary of this war will be different," Rumsfeld pursues, noting how the coming war has already displaced the meanings of the words for war.[14] *Invasion, enemy, territory, victory, exit strategy,* even *battle,* no longer mean what they used to mean. Rather than refer to stable realities or institutions, these suddenly old concepts now name emergent possibilities. Indeed, Rumsfeld's reliance upon

old words—foremost among them, the word *war*—itself bears witness to the extreme urgency of the situation. There is no time to
invent new words, he implies. For the moment, we can only go on
using old words for new things. This moment might well last a long
time; it might already be as old as war itself. Perhaps *war* is the oldest of old words: perpetually urgent and obsolete, ever left behind
by the very thing it supposedly names. War gets old quickly, and
it always has. The word *war* would thus name nothing other—or
older—than the impossible history of its own untimeliness. "Continuation" describes the uninterrupted flow of time; but it can also
refer to the experience of time's onrush that besets a subject paralyzed by impending danger, a threat that leaves no time for change
or improvisation. Only defense. "War is the *continuation* of politics
by other means," Clausewitz writes. This dictum is usually understood to mean that war takes up where politics leaves off; but it also
evokes the way in which the time of war co-opts the subject's temporal and historical horizon, leaving him speechless and helpless.[15]
Rumsfeld's discourse is rife with quotation marks that declare: our
world has grown old overnight.

> When we "invade the enemy's territory," we may well be invading his
> cyberspace. There may not be as many beachheads stormed as oppor-
> tunities denied. Forget about "exit strategies"; we're looking at a sus-
> tained engagement that carries no deadlines. We have no fixed rules
> about how to deploy our troops; we'll instead establish guidelines to
> determine whether military force is the best way to achieve a given
> objective. The public may see some dramatic military engagements
> that produce no apparent victory, or may be unaware of other actions
> that lead to major victories. "Battles" will be fought by customs offi-
> cers stopping suspicious persons at our borders and diplomats secur-
> ing cooperation against money laundering.[16]

Even before the new war begins, it will have already changed war
itself. It will have changed the meaning of the word *war* or, more
troubling perhaps, its rhetorical status as a word. The coming war
will be "a new kind of war," it turns out, because it will "only"
be war in a metaphoric sense. But what is "war in a metaphoric
sense"? Is it less of a war—no more than a metaphoric war? Will
the fact that it only features so-called battles on so-called battle-
fields make it less destructive than previous wars? What is war
if not a military operation? What is war if not the invasion of
enemy territory? What is war without victory? What is a victory
that never appears as such?

Despite what one might expect, I would argue, the becoming-metaphor of "war" is nothing less than the becoming-war of "war." Metaphoric war, in fact, is the most warlike of all wars—in several related ways. 1) As Rumsfeld's metaphors show, the displacement of meaning lays the groundwork for a massive expansion of state violence. In the terms that Deleuze and Guattari elaborate in their "Treatise on Nomadology: The War Machine," this public declaration of war on language bears witness to the state's appropriation ("reterritorialization") of the nomadic war machine.[17] 2) Accordingly, such metaphors provide an example of the way in which every war—regardless of the humanitarian institutions that monitor its conduct—supposes the permanent possibility of displacing, if not expressly revoking, its own language, rituals, conventions, and institutions. 3) They ultimately point to the possibility that acts of violence are always both real and symbolic and that symbolic violence, far from being a lesser or token form of violence, is often the more horrific and bewildering.

The contemporary transformation of war is central to Saskia Sassen's reflection on what it could mean, today, to take a stand against war. Is opposition to war still viable, she wonders, if the meaning of war has changed beyond recognition? In order to move forward, it would be just as necessary for the antiwar movement to define this change as it is for the secretary of defense. Both Sassen's discourse and Rumsfeld's turn upon analogous attempts to measure the way in which war transforms language:

> "Anti-war" does not work any more as a word. Is it that war itself is a situated historical something and that we've moved beyond that historical period? Is it that we are no longer positioned in a clear way so that we can identify war?
>
> Can we say *anti-massacre*? We don't say that we are anti-massacre; we don't say that we are anti-bombing-of-sitting-ducks, those who can't bring your planes down when you bomb them with planes. Is it that war itself is really no longer what it used to be? . . . War is almost too good a name for what we are seeing and what we are against. What we are seeing is a form of cowardice. If war isn't quite war, then antiwar doesn't work either to designate the work that we are trying to do.[18]

Rumsfeld and Sassen may be speaking from opposite ends of the political spectrum, but their analyses are predicated upon a shared lament: *War is no longer war.* They both presuppose that "war" properly speaking is the name for an institution that possesses what Sassen calls a "tight architecture" and that the deconstruction of this architecture, which often occurs in the midst of war itself, forces us to change how we speak. They share, in brief, the presupposition that there is an essential relation between *war* and the *word* and that the word—perhaps more than (or through?) the body in pain—is the privileged object of war.

Beyond the mass destruction of helpless victims, for example, the act that Sassen calls "massacre" destroys language. She asks: "Can we say *anti-massacre*?" Confronted with massacre, we no longer know what words to say; or, more precisely, whether it is meaningful to say anything, whether we can do or learn anything about such violence by taking a position in language. In this sense, the experience of massacre (whether from the perspective of victim, survivor, bystander, or spectator) reveals something about the nature of words that is otherwise difficult to grasp: their meaning is inseparable from a social bond that consists in a complex set of conventions, institutional parameters, collective space and time, or frameworks of care, authority, and trust; and acts of violence that attack the infrastructure of the social bond also disrupt the validity of language. The language of "targeting," which Weber discusses, constitutes a collectively accepted epistemo-political presupposition that effectively founds war itself as a of social bond. It allows anyone who participates in armed conflict to situate himself within the sights of the other man and thereby to calculate his chances or his defenses. Operating within the parameters of this metaphor, as Weber suggests, one may suppose that violence, no less than thinking, is an intentional act; that it is performed by a conscious subject who can and should take responsibility for it; and, perhaps most important, that it is defined by its finality. Targeting is an act with an aim, and once this aim is achieved the act necessarily comes to an end. Killing is the exemplary act of targeting precisely because it comes to an end with the life that it extinguishes. In multiplying its victims, then, "massacre" openly attacks the conventions and expectations that structure the social bond that revolves around war as targeting. Perhaps even beyond the mass death wrought on the battlefield by modern technological warfare, "massacre" bears witness to a will to murder that does not recognize the finality of killing. Its wanton scope manifests the refusal ever to select victims on the basis of their strategic value or to accept any individual death as a symbolic limit upon its violence. Those slain in massacres become the corporeal support for unlimited violence.

What, then, is the relationship between war and the word? Why is the word *war* so important as a word in ethics, in politics, and in war itself? The answer to these questions, I believe, is both abstract and very concrete. Classical, Hobbesian political theory presupposes that war is the upsurge of human beings' natural aggressiveness. And the extreme violence of modern wars—whose protagonists often blatantly disregard all the "civilized" parameters of international humanitarian law—would appear to corroborate this theory. Against Hobbes, however, Étienne Balibar writes that contemporary violence is "post-institutional": rather than regress to a state that precedes the foundation of social and political institutions, "extreme violence arises from institutions as much as it arises against them, and it is not possible to escape this circle by 'absolute' decisions such as choosing between a violent or a nonviolent politics, or between force and law."[19] For Hobbes (and his inheritors: Kant, Hegel, Clausewitz, Schmitt, and perhaps even Benjamin and Derrida), war is defined by violent death; it revolves around the sovereign transgression of the biblical prohibition of murder. The act of murder itself thus manifests the prejuridical, preinstitutional status of war. For Balibar, however, the signal act of war would be *an attack upon the parameters of war itself.* Contemporary politics shows that war is—and perhaps always was—a complex game in which its frames, models, limits, and institutions are always at stake. War names a situation in which the individual and the collective horizon of expectation are themselves exposed to attack and thus liable to change at any moment. *The most warlike act is unilaterally to change the definition of war.* The word *war*, then, assumes an exorbitant value and importance to the extent to which it names an enterprise that aims—perhaps above all—to transform the meaning of the word itself. It is inherently unstable and expendable; but it is also the only word that functions to name the process whereby its own status is continually placed in jeopardy. It is a relic that, as such, retains all of its originary urgency. Consequently, the theory of war—no matter how academic or even pedantic—is always already inscribed within the space that it attempts to describe.[20]

In his essay, "What's in a War? (Politics as War, War as Politics)," Balibar arrives at this precise conclusion. Discussing the typologies of war that often appear in encyclopedias and treatises of so-called polemology, Balibar observes, first, that types of war are often classified "in the form of dichotomies which often involve value judgments, more precisely tending to distinguish between the normal and normative form of war and its excess, or its perversion, or its degenerate forms" and, second, that "new dichotomies are constantly invented, or suggested by history."[21] In support of this claim, Balibar provides an extensive if not exhaustive list of the dichotomies he has in mind: wars between states and civil wars; war and revolution; declared and undeclared wars; regular or conventional wars and guerrilla wars; war and crime; primitive, tribal, or ethnic wars and civilized wars; limited wars and total wars; open wars and secret wars. In Balibar's analysis, the constant invention of new dichotomies suggests that, despite appearances, their primary function is not normative.

> Although the dichotomies—as I said—are clearly value-based, and tend toward the identification of an ideal or regulative type of war, we perceive that their real use is to suggest that there is an element in war, lying precisely in its relationship with violence, that *remains uncontrollable*, or more precisely that associates the essence of warfare with an excess of the means over their hypothetic finality, making warfare exceed its own definitions and essence. *The deepest meaning of the dichotomies is not to set limits, but to approach the phenomenon of their transgression*, to indicate that the essential phenomenon, where we touch *the antinomy of this institution that cannot respect the rules of an institution*, only emerges when the oppositions are inverted and displaced.[22]

It is worth noting that Balibar's essay forms part of his long-standing series of reflections on violence and civility (now collected in the volume *Violence et civilité*)[23] that revolve around an explicit critique of political theory that depends upon the concept "state of exception." In spite of the fact that the state of exception is associated with the unfettered exercise of sovereign power, Balibar argues that this political concept is ultimately too limited to address and redress the "extreme violence" that appears at the far edge of what we call politics today. To the extent that war is understood in terms of the exception, the most important event in war is the suspension of the law. In the interest of self-determination or self-defense, the argument goes, the laws that bind citizens should not inhibit the action of sovereign power. For Balibar, however, the event that defines the war is a hyperbolic displacement whereby war transgresses both the norms or regulative ideals that structure the institution of war and the sacred manifestations of war's extremity. War is characterized not only by an escalating passage from bad to worse but also by a disjunctive leap from one worst to another worst.

"A SANDSTONE ENEMY UNABLE TO FIGHT BACK"

There is no question that the attacks of 9/11 were traumatic for the obvious reasons: they occurred literally out of the blue without advance warning; they constituted the first major incursion upon the territorial United States since Pearl Harbor; they leveled a major urban and architectural landmark. However, as I am arguing, the traumatic impact of these attacks was also due—perhaps in greater measure—to the fact that they caused lasting damage to the institution of war itself. Rumsfeld clearly registers both prongs of the attacks and, despite the obligatory patriotism of his discourse, distinctly privileges the problems posed by the transformation of war in general. Likewise, this is the aspect of 9/11 that has given rise to a multitude of philosophical reflections on war and terrorism. Attacks within war upon the prevailing paradigm of war invariably result in the greatest social and political disorientation; and, consequently, they demand a response on the level of thinking rather than action. The various actions that the United States has levied over the past decade in response to the attacks of 9/11 and their perpetrators have failed— precisely because they are actions—to address the urgent questions that this event imposed upon everyone who witnessed it from near and far.

Thanks to the haste with which the United States invaded Afghanistan and later Iraq, in fact, the opportunity was lost even to formulate and voice the appropriate questions. In order to approach these lingering questions today, I would like to suggest that it is necessary to turn the clock back only a few months in order to consider another set of attacks—less often memorialized but at least as important as 9/11.

Before the Taliban became forever associated with Osama bin Laden, they made world news six months earlier, in March 2001, for a campaign of religious purification that set out to destroy every last statue in Afghanistan and culminated, in defiance of an international outcry, in the destruction of the colossal pair of ancient Buddha statues located in the Bamiyan Valley. Andreas Huyssen has analyzed some of the formal parallels between the attacks on the World Trade Center and those on the Buddhas of Bamiyan:

> But as we know more about the extremely close relationship with, if not dependence of Mullah Omar on Al Qaeda and Osama bin Laden since the mid-1990s, it is difficult not to think about the relationship between the attack on the two sublime Bamiyan statues and

the subsequent attack on the differently sublime twin towers. It is
as if the dynamiting and collapse of the two statues last spring was
a carefully staged prologue to the attack on New York, symbolic
actions both, intended to whip up support in the Muslim world for
bin Laden's apocalyptic Islamism in the Muslim world. The parallels
are obvious. Two figures each, one taller than the other, like brothers, both invested in the aesthetic of the sublime; but not the terroriz-
ing sublime that makes the spectator feel small and overwhelmed, for
each allowed a view from the top, from the top of The World Trade
Center as from the top of the Buddha's cave. In both cases, in the
paranoid aggressive world of the Taliban and Al Qaeda, the aesthetics of the sublime represents only the demonic power of the other—
the other religion, the other way of life, the infidel. But we can now
surmise that the links go beyond symbolism.[24]

More than anything else, however, these two sets of attacks on twin
monuments have in common the fact that they were both immediately declared unmistakable acts of war. People who lived through the
morning of September 11, 2001, might remember the period of uncertainty that followed what turned out to be the first plane crash into
the North Tower. This long moment was filled with questions that
the silent image of the burning building could not answer: What is
happening? Was it an accident? Or was it somehow deliberate? If so,
how could it have happened? After the second plane crash, however,
such questions were put to rest. One crash might have been accidental
but not two. After number two, nobody doubted it was an act of war.
    The same inner logic governed the reception of the attacks on the
Buddhas of Bamiyan. Although the Taliban announced their intentions in advance and had already destroyed other museums and
monuments, the destruction of the Buddhas became the emblematic
moment within the larger iconoclastic purge. More than any other
act of violence, the twin destruction of the Buddhas set itself apart as
a distinct outrage. Whereas the destruction of a single statue would
have the status of a symbolic gesture, perhaps even functioning as a
sacrifice, the destruction of *both* functions to highlight the will of
the destroyer. The meaning of destroying a single object lies in the
contingency of the object itself. One asks: Why this object? What
did it represent? But the meaning of destroying both an object and
its twin goes beyond the objects themselves. It is now a question of
destroying things that go together; destroying both of them (which
is to say *all two* of them); destroying the entire series, line, race, generation, or genre. Huyssen suggests that these statues and towers

were *brothers*[25]—siblings from the same parents, generation, people, or nation. No family member is spared to represent the genealogical line; none is left to mourn the dead. The point is to kill without leaving survivors. These attacks, in fact, constitute nothing less than an instance of genocide—which turns upon political will as the will to completion.[26]

A wide range of commentators—journalists, UNESCO officials, and philosophers—seemed to agree that the word *war* was the only word to describe the destruction of the Buddha statues. In his reporting on the event for the *Guardian*, for example, Luke Harding emphasizes the Taliban's use of rocket launchers as demolition equipment. Rather than a religious act—the breaking of idols—he implies that the destruction of the Buddhas constitutes war against memory and history. Rather than wage war against living beings, he writes, the Taliban took up arms against what he dubbed "a sandstone enemy unable to fight back":[27]

> Deep in the heart of Afghanistan's once serene Bamiyan valley, the sound of gunfire and mortar explosions could be heard yesterday. Bearded men dressed in baggy salwar kameezes loaded and reloaded their rocket launchers under a clear azure sky. The Taliban fighters were busy—busy destroying two giant Buddhas carved into the hillside nearly 2,000 years ago, busy erasing all traces of a rich pre-Islamic past. Though no one knows for certain, it seems likely that the massive Buddhas, previously Afghanistan's most famous tourist attraction, have been pulverized. Taliban and opposition sources yesterday confirmed that troops spent all day demolishing them. . . .
>
> The isolated valley, deep in the Hindu Kush mountains, was the scene of heavy fighting last month, when it fell briefly to opposition forces. The Taliban retook it in massive numbers. Much of the hardware they used in that offensive litters the mountainside and is now being deployed against a sandstone enemy unable to fight back.[28]

In a similar vein, Isabel Hilton writes: "Already at war with the present and the future, the Taliban seem to have declared war on the past."[29] Barbara Crossette quotes Paula R. Newberg, an author and former adviser on Afghanistan to the United Nations: "The Taliban as a whole are a phenomenon of war, and I think even their attitude toward women is a phenomenon of war rather than a phenomenon of Islam."[30] Other commentators, however, avoid using the concept of war in such an attenuated sense. They prefer to evoke the helplessness of the statues themselves. As Harding suggests, this helplessness is inseparable from the material from which the statues were carved and that continues to support the resulting image—sandstone.

Despite this broad rhetorical consensus, however, the precise nature of the attacks on the Buddhas of Bamiyan remains uncertain to this day. Although Rumsfeld declares that the coming war on terror will be a "new kind of war," the force of his editorial lies in the presupposition—largely accepted by the public—that this war would still be war; that the word *war* remained the right word. In the case of the Buddhas, the relevance of this word choice is not so obvious. Although the word *war* was used and used often, no one dared to claim that the destruction of the statues announced a new kind of war. Each time the word appears, we are supposed to understand that war waged against statues is not war in the proper—which is to say, militarily or politically relevant—sense. But don't Rumsfeld and the events of 9/11 teach us precisely that this metaphoric extension of war actually brings us closer to the essence of war and that it might have catastrophic consequences? If so, it behooves us to consider more seriously how the destruction of two statues—nonliving victims—might help to formulate more precise questions about the transformation of war at the heart of contemporary social and political life.

In an editorial published in *Le Monde* on March 13, 2001, titled "Crimes against Culture Must Not Go Unpunished," Koichiro Matsuura—then secretary general of UNESCO—declares that the destruction of the Buddhas of Bamiyan was an "unprecedented act." The Taliban have arrogated the right to destroy something that properly belongs to the Afghan people and to the common heritage of mankind. "With their destructive actions, the Taliban have . . . murdered the memory of a people, the Afghan people, whose heritage provides the basis for their identity and values. By depriving Afghanistan of one of its jewels, they do a disservice to the very country they claim to lead."[31] Notwithstanding the long history of iconoclastic destruction, this was the first time that "a central authority—albeit unrecognized—has arrogated the right to destroy an asset that pertains to our common heritage."[32] In other words, this act represented the first time that a sovereign power had openly and provocatively flaunted the 1972 UNESCO *Convention Concerning the Protection of World Cultural and Natural Heritage*; and it was the first time that UNESCO confronted the formidable task of enforcing its own statutes (always problematic in cases of international law). "For the first time," Matsuura states, "UNESCO, enjoined by its constitutive act to preserve universal heritage, finds itself confronted with such a situation."[33] Unlike other commentators on this event, however, he prudently hesitates to claim that the destruction of the Buddhas was an act of war.

For the most part, Matsuura appears to accept the Taliban's claim that the destruction of the statues should be categorized as iconoclasm. The act was unprecedented because it offered the first real test of a recently framed statute. In another sense, however, it wasn't unprecedented at all. Iconoclastic violence might never before have become the object of an international juridico-political apparatus, but it is far from new. "Of course, we have seen such destruction in the past," Matsuura writes. "But it had seemed that we had entered a new era, an era of increased respect and admiration for cultural heritage, a heritage in which each person would learn to read the symbols that they have in common with everyone else."[34] In addition to providing legal protection for endangered cultural sites, then, the UNESCO world heritage convention aspires to embody a momentous historical transition: the progress of humanity beyond the era when religious leaders believed that idolatry threatened their personal authority and that of their religion. The very concept "world heritage" implies that—for "us," an "us" defined by this historical transition—certain religious artifacts, which would have been condemned as idols in a previous era, have become secular *symbols* and should be cherished as such. Whereas the idol is an object of worship, the symbol is an object of tradition. Indeed, the symbol is nothing other than an idol that has become an object of tradition, the idol transferred into the vast museum of mankind. Accordingly, Matsuura presumes that this historical transition from idol to symbol—which corresponds to the secularization of art and the institutionalization of modernity as a hegemonic paradigm—should, in turn, definitively render iconoclastic violence a thing of the past. The resurgence of such violence, then, bears witness to the fact that, in the words of Bruno Latour, "we have never been modern."[35]

In "Iconoclasm and the French Revolution," Stanley Idzerda shows very clearly that the modern institution of the public art museum was founded in response to the outbreak of iconoclastic violence during the French Revolution. The museum—with walls or without—constitutes a bulwark against iconoclasm in that it provides a protected space for political and religious art that might otherwise become objects of public hostility; but, as Idzerda lucidly analyzes, the museum is also an instrument of iconoclasm. The museum shelters cult objects by voiding them of the theological and political meaning whereby they provoke such fury: "Immure a political symbol in a museum and it becomes merely art—iconoclasm is thus achieved without destruction."[36] Statues also die. Chris Marker and Alain Resnais's documentary from the same year as Idzerda's study, *Les statues meurent aussi* (1953), turns upon an analogous argument. This film—banned in France from 1953 to 1963 for political reasons—highlights the way in which this iconoclastic function of the museum serves the project of French colonialism. African statues die (to Africans) at the moment they enter the French Musée de l'homme. "An object dies with the death of those who gaze upon it. When we have died, our objects will go where we send the Africans' objects: to the museum. African art: we gaze upon it as if its sole purpose were to give us pleasure."[37]

UNESCO is certainly not exempt from the structural imperialism of European museum culture. Matsuura makes perfectly clear, for example, that he considers the World Heritage List to represent the worldwide expansion of this iconoclastic project of the modern (post-revolutionary) museum. And yet, as it expands, this project becomes more ambiguous in certain respects. There are important distinctions between the category "world natural and cultural heritage" and the category "art," and thus between the World Heritage List and the institution of the museum. The world heritage conventions go to great lengths to underscore that the goal of the list is to protect precious objects of nature and culture in situ; to provide peoples—such as the Afghan people in the case of the Buddhas of Bamiyan—with a universally valid and accessible institutional mechanism whereby they or representatives of their interests can safeguard these objects for themselves. The preamble to the text of these conventions, for instance, emphasize that "the protection of this [world cultural and natural] heritage at the national level often remains incomplete because of the scale of the resources which it requires and the insufficient economic, scientific, and technological resources of the country where the property to be protected is situated."[38] On the one hand, then, this document insists that the world is not (and should not be) a museum; that heritage does not need to be killed—that is, exported from the life-worlds that give them meaning—in order to be protected. The World Heritage List would thus sublate the museum, negating its deathly mission. On the other hand, this sublation of the museum turns the world itself into a museum, underscoring the museal dimension of peoples' attachment to the life of their natural and cultural environment. Accordingly, despite Matsuura's explicit claims, his discourse does not rail against the uncanny resurgence of a historically superseded iconoclastic violence, a violence against which the museum is supposed to shelter its objects, but rather the repetition of a constitutively untimely violence to which the museum itself remains vulnerable; in fact, it is a violence to which objects are exposed *thanks to* their museal death, a violence from which this death offers no protection.

On the one hand, Matsuura implies that the destruction of the Buddhas constituted an unprecedented act because—regardless of the Taliban's claims to the contrary—it was not and could not be justified as iconoclasm. It was a political crime, an abuse of sovereign power, a premeditated defiance of accepted international statutes—and statues. On the other hand, Matsuura still concludes that the destruction of the statues was an act of iconoclasm; it represented the return of a supposedly outmoded form of violence. Matsuura might well suppose that violence as such is always regressive, that it always represents the return of something primitive or ancient, and, consequently, that the only possible novelty on earth lies in the advancement of civilization. In many ways, Matsuura's lament—"But it had seemed that we had entered a new era"—echoes the disappointed complaint that Freud ventriloquizes in the opening pages of his indelible "Thoughts for the Times on War and Death": "We have told ourselves, no doubt, that wars can never cease so long as nations live under such widely differing conditions, so long as the value of human life is so variously assessed among them, and so long as the animosities which divide them represent such powerful motive forces in the mind. . . . But we permitted ourselves to have other hopes."[39] Freud, too, considers war always to be a form of regression: "[War] strips us of the later accretions of civilization, and lays bare the primal man in each of us."[40] This set of presuppositions thus prevents Matsuura from considering the possibility that the destruction of the Buddhas constituted an unprecedented act, not only because it was the first test of a new law, but also because this law—in officially categorizing and protecting idols as symbols—implicitly categorized a new form of violence. Rather than merely allow an old form of violence (iconoclasm) to be arraigned under the sign of a new legal category (crime against culture), the law—perhaps unconsciously—recognizes a "new" type of violence: violence against the symbol.

THE OBJECT OF WAR

Although Matsuura does not take into account the possible emergence of new forms of violence, the text of the *Convention Concerning the Protection of World Cultural and Natural Heritage* does. The preamble begins by "noting" that "the cultural heritage and the natural heritage are increasingly threatened with destruction not only by the traditional causes of decay, but also by changing social and economic conditions which aggravate the situation with even more formidable phenomena of damage or destruction."[41] My entire discussion thus far is nothing but an attempt to frame the question of violence against the symbol as one of these "even more formidable phenomena of damage and destruction" that the convention envisages. In what sense is such violence new? What are its ethical, political, and historical consequences? Can it even legitimately be categorized as violence?

The stakes of such violence, I would argue, have only ever been measured in and through psychoanalysis; for, despite appearances, what is at stake in the agency of what Freud called the death drive, *das Todestrieb,* is not the extinction of life but precisely the destruction of the symbol.

To say that the destruction of the Buddhas of Bamiyan manifests a new type of violence is to make two related claims. First, this violence is not simply the resurgence of an ancient form of violence in a modern context. Thanks to the invention of new juridico-political instruments, this context is defined by the formalization of a new object—world heritage—and the violence in question is manifest and measured in terms of damage to this object. Second, the fact that this violence is manifest and measured in terms of a specific object does not mean that its relevance is limited to the sphere of cultural and natural preservation or even, more generally, to the spheres of cultural or environmental studies. As soon as the attacks on the Buddhas became public knowledge, commentators presumed—no matter the rhetorical contortions that it cost them—that they were a phenomenon of war. It was immediately clear that this violence against statues was a form of political violence. However, this is not merely an example of the politicization of art and culture. What the commentators acknowledged on the level of their rhetoric, if not in their explicit statements, was that the manifestation of violence against world heritage, or "heritage terrorism," effectively transforms the concept of violence in general and thus demands a new critique of violence. In brief, these attacks reveal that violence needs to be reconceived starting from violence against the symbol. The *Convention Concerning the Protection of World Cultural and Natural Heritage* might well usher in a new era, but rather than a new era of respect and admiration for cultural heritage, it is a new era of war.

The war and revolutions of the twentieth century resulted in what Martin van Crevald has called the "transformation of war." The century abounds in reflections on the movement of war beyond war. In addition to van Creveld's work, *The Transformation of War* (1991), there is Carl Schmitt's *The Nomos of the Earth* (1950); Deleuze and Guattari's "Treatise of Nomadology: The War Machine," from *A Thousand Plateaus* (1980); and Mary Kaldor's *New and Old Wars: Organized Violence in a Global Era* (1999). Alain Badiou's *The Century* (2005) might be considered a late addition to this list that punctuates the general trend. This is not the place to enter into detailed discussion of these works. For my purposes, I limit myself to the observation that they all elaborate the transformation of war in terms of the relationship between sovereign power and the distribution of space, between *polis* and *nomos*. But another approach to the transformation of war is possible and necessary. The great novelty of Giorgio Agamben's *Homo Sacer* (1995) is that it theorized the transformation of war and therefore of politics starting from the *object* of war. Although Agamben himself hardly ever mentions Freud, his work has been especially productive in the field of psychoanalytic theory precisely because of its emphasis upon the object of politics. Such an emphasis is specific to the application of psychoanalysis to nonclinical fields. As the title of Freud's "Thoughts for the Times on War and Death" suggests, this text approaches war starting from what Freud considers its primary event: killing. But the principle of such an analysis of the object is stated most clearly in Freud's first discussion of Sophocles in *The Interpretation of Dreams*. Framing his interpretation of *Oedipus Rex*, Freud briefly considers the tradition of Aristotelian readings of the play that account for the "tragic effect" of the play in terms of great oppositions that structure its plot. He ultimately decides that the force of the drama can lie only in the "particular nature of the material" to which the plot lends form.

> If *Oedipus Rex* moves a modern audience no less than it did the contemporary Greek one, the explanation can only be that its effect does not lie in the contrast between destiny and human will, but is to be looked for in the particular nature of the material on which

that contrast is exemplified. There must be something that makes a
voice within us ready to recognize the compelling force of destiny
in the Oedipus. . . . His destiny moves us only because it might have
been ours—because the oracle laid the same curse upon us before our
birth as upon him. It is the fate of all of us, perhaps, to direct our first
sexual impulse towards our mother and our first hatred and our first
murderous wish against our father.[42]

It has often been objected that psychoanalysis has very little to teach
us about literary form. And it is true: psychoanalysis not only teaches
us little about form; it teaches us almost nothing. Freud often pretends that he does not deal with questions of aesthetics and form for
lack of expertise. An attentive reading shows, however, that he considers such questions a distraction from the burning questions raised
by the logic—the logic of fantasy—inherent in the content. We can
learn *something* about *Oedipus Rex* by studying the structure of its
plot, its characters, or even the mythical heritage of which the material is woven. But we can understand what is most *essential* to the
play, what makes it a unique and particularly unforgettable experience, only if we have some knowledge about what a mother and a
father are within the logic of infantile fantasy.

The cultural and political meaning of the destruction of the Buddhas of Bamiyan lies in what this event reveals about the object of
war. By all traditional accounts, it is utterly meaningless to wage war
against an enemy who, although he has a body, is not and has never
been alive. War is by definition waged between living beings against
each other. As Carl von Clausewitz insists, war at its most extreme—
which is to say, at its most warlike, at the limit where it comes closest to itself—is a game of reciprocal bloodshed: "Kind-hearted people might of course think there was some ingenious way to disarm
or defeat the enemy without too much bloodshed, and might imagine that this is the true goal of the art of war. Pleasant as it sounds,
it is a fallacy that must be exposed. . . . If one side uses force without compunction, undeterred by the bloodshed it involves, while the
other side refrains, the first will gain the upper hand. That side will
force the other to follow suit; each will drive its opponent toward
extremes. . . . This is how the matter must be seen."[43] Where blood
flows, life is at stake. Carl Schmitt is even more explicit about the
role of life in war. In *The Concept of the Political*, he defines the
concept of the political in terms of the possibility of war and war in
terms of what—using an oddly tautological phrase—he calls the "real

possibility of physical killing."[44] Schmitt's treatise is famous for its distinctions between friend and enemy and between the enemy as the object of private animosity and the enemy as occasion for public hostility. To these distinctions, it would be necessary to add the distinction between "real physical killing" and killing that is less than real and less than physical because it would only be killing in an extended or metaphoric sense, such as emotional or spiritual death, killing in effigy or in absentia, or the "killing" involved in what Orlando Patterson has called "social death."[45]

One might claim, then, that the public discourse surrounding the destruction of the Buddhas of Bamiyan turns upon a forced trope or catachresis—an attempt to name the unnameable. The rhetorical displacement of the name of war, in fact, bears witness to the transformation of war "itself" or, more specifically, a transformation in the object of war. The refusal to abandon the rhetoric of war may appear to result from a kind of discursive sclerosis, but it would also be possible to claim the opposite: that this insistence manifests an immediate collective certainty that this illegible act of violence *is* war and that war in general, despite the long history of political and theoretical attempts to formalize its rules, should be defined by its metamorphoses rather than its parameters. If the Taliban as a whole are a phenomenon of war, what they exemplify is the tendency of war, not only to go to extremes—as Clausewitz famously posited—but also to overstep, or perhaps to sidestep, the culturally sanctioned manifestations of war's extremity. The Taliban's violation of the Buddha statues is more extreme than killing. But this is where the rhetoric of hyperbole becomes potentially misleading. The point is not that this violence "goes further" than killing. Clearly, it does not. Not a single living being was so much as touched. With a paradoxical restraint, then, this violence reveals the existence of a liminal zone—which perhaps haunts every theater of war, if not every place in general—in which the finitude of life no longer provides the measure of extremity or natural limits that define human rights. In this zone, attacking a stone might be worse than attacking a life, not because some animism or anthropomorphism secretly endows the stone with life, but precisely because it is an inert dead thing and deserves absolute respect as such. The institution of the museum gives us access to this zone because—as Izquerda and Marker reveal—it "kills" things in order to justify protecting them from unsuspected or underestimated forms of violence. Rather than bringing a life to an end, however, this constitutively ineffectual "killing" reveals that its objects are already dead—which does not mean that they were once alive (in fact, they never were) but rather that they have always been exposed to a violence that does not, and never has, recognized death as a limit. The force of death as a limit—the cult and culture of death in both war and peace—derives from the horror provoked by the illegible violence that always haunts it. The sandstone enemy is helpless, we might conclude, both because of the deathlike immobility of its colossal body and because none of the existing customs and conventions of warfare could have helped it or anyone else anticipate the displacement of war that was necessary for the attacks to take place. In this sense, it would be both possible and necessary to conclude that these attacks should not be categorized as war after all; that, in attacking the parameters of war, the Taliban passed beyond war to crime—war crime or even crime against humanity.

Indeed, one of the possible consequences of these reflections on war and violence against the nonliving is that there is an essential relationship between war and political crimes that have been classified as war crimes or crimes against humanity. If we continue to hold that there is an essential relationship between politics and war, it would then be necessary to conclude that crime is a constitutive dimension of politics. The adjudication of war would no longer be a matter of distinguishing between the legitimate uses of force and extreme or criminal uses of force but rather of a complex political and cultural calculation that seeks to determine which crimes are acceptable, which may be used for political purposes, and which must be censured.

The destruction of the Buddhas of Bamiyan lays bare the crime that never fails to occur at the very heart of war. There is no such thing as sheer killing. On the one hand, this means quite simply that the "state of exception" is powerless to suspend the law and thereby powerless to reduce murder to killing. When all is said and done, war will have been murder—albeit the murder of statues. On the other hand, it also means that the crime of war goes far beyond killing or murder; that war ultimately revolves around violence that, beyond disrespect for the distinction between combatants and noncombatants, exposes the fragility of the differences between the living and the dead, the idol and the symbol, the symbol and the person. In a short essay on the destruction of the Buddhas of Bamiyan published in the French daily *Libération*, Jean-Luc Nancy does not hesitate to categorize this "massacre of symbols" as a crime against humanity:

> Why is the projected massacre of the Buddhas of Bamiyan particu-
> larly odious? . . . The first reason is that the destruction of symbols is
> an attack upon what does not only form the possibility of the human
> in man (sense), but also the impossibility of exhausting the "nature"
> or the "truth" of the human and the possibility in man of "going
> infinitely beyond man" (Pascal) and thereby going, precisely, to the
> bottom of things, himself, or the world. It is embarrassing to assume
> such a solemn tone: but, finally, what's at stake is nothing less than
> the essential.
>   In this sense, the massacre of symbols, which are not only large
> in size but above all in culture, is a form of crime against human-
> ity (against the essence of man). Indeed, real individuals have been
> exterminated as symbols each time that genocide or crime against
> humanity has taken place. Such crime is symbolic in its structure and
> aim. In a sense, the destruction of inert symbols, works of art and
> religion, lays utterly bare what is at stake: when killing persons, it is
> possible up to a certain point (very quickly attained) to seem to play
> the game of defending oneself against an enemy [*jouer le jeu de la
> défense contre un ennemi*]. But the symbol cannot be an enemy; and
> it only becomes a weapon if one makes it into one, which is foreign to
> its being (imagine an insurgent throwing part of a statue instead of a
> paving stone).[46]

Killing, Nancy suggests, is essential to the game of defending oneself
against an enemy. It is telos and limit of the game; the moment in the
game that brings an end to the game. "Up to a point," Nancy writes,
it is possible "to seem to play the game"; but this point is rapidly
attained. The game is mere semblance—verisimilitude; and, despite
attempts to regulate war through law and discipline, the veracity of
this semblance doesn't hold. The role of killing in the game of war
guarantees that it will be more than mere play, that it will always be
a game with real stakes. Nonetheless, this reality itself pertains to the
semblance of war. The destruction of the Buddhas, then, suggests that
the game of war tends not only to open beyond play (toward reality),
but also beyond the game itself; it brings violence into play that is no
longer part of the game; or, in other terms, it brings into play an unfettered play—which Nancy calls "symbolic crime"—that is both more
horrible and less real than any game. There is no such thing as killing because the death blow always does more than kill; it both extinguishes a life and maims a body; it both strikes living being and the
"inert symbol," the statue that each human being is even before being
petrified in death. On the surface, war revolves around the rhythms of
attack and defense, risk and self-preservation. But this extreme enterprise involves its participants in an unconscious process of defense

against the uncanny emergence of even more extreme violence. The entire Clausewitzian theater of the duel, of force and counterforce, of strategy, of killing and being killed, is merely a game to the extent to which it functions to conjure away the specter of symbolic crime, violence that goes beyond self-defense, beyond killing, and beyond death. War might well be the continuation of politics by other means; but it is precisely the repression of the symbolic dimension of war itself that makes it possible to distinguish between war and crime and thereby to make war into a reliable political instrument.

WAR BEFORE DEATH

The object of war is life. But the aim of war is death. In other words, the function of life in war is to set the stage for the event of death, to make it possible for death to intervene itself within political space. Death—"physical" death—is central to the reality principle of war; it is the event that makes it possible to distinguish between real and unreal killing, between literal death and metaphoric or metaphysical deaths of various kinds. Clausewitz's treatise, for instance, begins with a phenomenological reduction of war to its elementary particle—the duel—which provides a stage for the instant of death. Despite a long history of literary duels, Clausewitz insists that it is never a matter of fiction or even of discourse. It is the very heart of the matter—or, precisely, the element (*das Element*) of war, the small war of which every large war is constituted. The whole of war as such—war considered in terms of its own immediate aim (*Zweck*) rather than the eventual political goal (*Ziel*) that it serves to achieve—is contained in each duel. "I shall not begin by expounding a pedantic, literary definition of war, but go straight to its element, to the duel. War is nothing but a duel on a larger scale. Countless duels go to make up a war, but a picture of it as whole can be formed by imagining a pair of wrestlers [*zwei Rigende*]. Each tries through physical force [*physische Gewalt*] to compel the other to do his will; his *immediate* aim [*nächster Zweck*] is to *throw* his opponent in order to make him incapable of further resistance."[47] Clausewitz turns to the image of the wrestlers because the object of a wrestling match, unlike the object of swordplay but very much like that of war, is not to *touch*, *impale*, or *hit* the opponent but to *throw* him (*den Gegner niederzuwerfen*). Moreover, wrestlers embody force itself in its magnitude and physicality. The goal of the wrestling is properly hyper-bolic (*hyper* + *ballein*: literally, "to throw out or beyond"): each combatant seeks less to prove himself the stronger or the faster than simply to do whatever it takes to expel the other from the combat, to overcome his resistance, to neutralize his force, to render him a nonthreat. Wrestlers exchange hyperboles; each tries his best to do his worst—which makes the duel less a face-to-face contest than an impersonal (or transpersonal) passage to the extreme. This passage to extremes is, in its turn, the proper object of the theory of war. Death—as the passage to the most extreme limit of the extreme—is never a mere accident in war; it is inseparable from the logic of the duel-form itself. Responsibility for passage to the extreme, therefore, cannot be ascribed to any single combatant; nor can any person involved in war as a participant or spectator simply choose to wage war without death. The hyperbolic escalation that defines war is a function of the duel-form itself and thus appears as a third term: the hyperbole of hyperboles, a fury or folie à deux that implacably seizes both combatants as soon as they enter into the space of the duel.

The object of war is life. The aim of war is death. But the role of this aim, in turn, its function within the logic of the duel, is to force a decision (victory or defeat) where there is no authoritative third party to intervene. On the stage of international politics, war is the only form of judicial decision that a sovereign power can recognize while remaining absolutely sovereign—even if, paradoxically, this judgment results in one power ceding its territory and its power to another. War is a trial—albeit a trial by fire. In his essay on perpetual peace, Kant provides the concise definition of war from which none of his inheritors (which include Clausewitz, Schmitt, and Freud) radically departs:

> For war is only the regrettable expedient in the state of nature (where there exists no court that could adjudicate the matter with legal authority) to assert one's right by means of violence. In war neither of the two parties can be declared an unjust enemy (since such an assessment presupposes a judicial decision). It is rather the outcome of the war (or 'divine judgment', as it were) which decides whose side is in the right.[48]

On the one hand, this decision takes the form of simple domination; it is the superiority of force that subjugates and divides the enemies from one another. On the other hand, the decision has the status of a *victory* that, although it can only go to one side, comes about through the intervention of a postulated third party (in the form of a quote-unquote "divine judgment" or "declaration"). Though the decision bears witness to the sovereignty of one side (deciding who is "in the right"), it is at the same time imposed (as if from the outside) upon all sides. "The only enemy is the victor, always already victorious. It isn't one side or another that wins the war but war itself."[49] It is both the sanction of a superior force and a restriction upon this force: it gives military force the force of law but only at the price of its further exercise. The outcome of the conflict that was achieved through violence ends up dividing violence from itself. Moreover, as Kant explicitly states, this division of violence—as the assertion of "right" by "might"—is itself the *goal* of war. War bears the promise of an exit from the state of nature rather than its expression and its perpetuation. It is the "natural" exit from the state of nature and thus manifests what in nature already pertains to history.

Although Kant does not explicitly conceive of this "divine judgment" in terms of death, in the context of war death alone is sufficiently neutral and immanent to function both as intervention of a hypothetical third party and to manifest the definitive withdrawal of any such instance. Only "death's decision"[50] (to use Kierkegaard's phrase) is sufficiently judgmentlike and Godlike (Hegel will identify death with the Master) to justify calling it "divine." The status that the structure and practice of war grant to death establishes the "autonomy" of war itself as an institution—albeit an autonomy without or before the law, an autonomy founded upon *limits* rather than *laws*. What political philosophy calls "natural law" could thus be understood as an attempt to codify this paradoxical autonomy of war. Thanks to the intervention of death, war is self-limiting rather than self-legislating.

The proof of this claim in Kant's own text can be found in his discussion of what he calls "war of extermination." Such a war, in Kant's analysis, would be the inevitable outcome if either party to a conflict fails to honor the rights of sovereignty accorded by victory in war. The use of "dishonorable stratagems" (spies, assassins, poisoners) during wartime and afterward, in order to continue war by other means even after open hostilities have ceased—after death—can only lead to a "war of extermination," "in which both parties and, moreover, all right can be eradicated simultaneously, [can] bring about perpetual peace only over the great graveyard of humanity."[51] Rather than a war without limits, a war of extermination is the hyperbolic outcome of an attempt to impose death as a limit upon subjects or nations who do not recognize its authority. In other words, a war

of extermination would not be a war fought between political enemies that would be "adjudicated" by death; it would be a war fought
against the enemies of war itself—a war to end all wars fought in the
name of war and death as limit and end.

War is frequently understood as the paradigmatic form of legitimate violence. During wartime, the legal provision for states of exception temporarily suspends the prohibition on murder. Carl Schmitt's
use of the word *killing* rather than *murder,* for example, reflects the
suspension of customary law that exempts acts of war from legal and
moral censure. If the concept of the exception—both in the traditional sense and the expanded "biopolitical" sense that Agamben
tries to elaborate—is inseparable from the sovereign right to declare
war, I would argue that this concept is itself justified by an unspoken
understanding of death. The sovereign right to declare war and the
violence that it authorizes can only be legitimized if this violence ends
in death. Whether it achieves this end is another matter. It is justifi-
able only to the extent that it is defined in terms of death as its ultimate aim (its *Zweck,* to return to Clausewitz's distinction between
Zweck and *Ziel*). As an event that takes place within the framework
of a duel, death isn't simply the end of life; it also has the juridico-
political status of a decision. Even in a war in which nobody is killed,
death still represents the possibility that the conflict could end in
decision—a decision that would retroactively justify the original decision to wage war. Killing is the point at which the aim or tendency
(*Zweck*) of war in itself and its political goal or telos (*Ziel*) coincide; it
is the point at which what Freud in "Why War?" called the "drive of
destruction" would be "soldered" to a socially and culturally predetermined object—the life of the soldier—and pursue the correspond-
ing aim—killing. Analogously, in *Three Essays on the Theory of Sexuality,* Freud analyzed the way in which the sexual drive is only ever
soldered—tenuously at best—to the genitalia of the opposite sex and
thereby bound up with heterosexual intercourse and the project of
human reproduction.[52]

Let us look more closely at the status of killing and death in
Schmitt's work. In the *Concept of the Political,* after Schmitt
determines that the essence of the political lies in the distinction
between friend and enemy, he goes on to define the enemy itself in
terms of war. And war, for Schmitt, at least in this text, is always
defined according to the most classical, dictionary definition: war
is combat, and combat is armed conflict. The passage in which

Schmitt draws this series of conclusions is one of the most chilling in his treatise.

> The distinction of friend and enemy denotes the utmost degree of intensity of a union or separation, of an association or dissociation. It can exist theoretically and practically, without having simultaneously to draw upon all those moral, aesthetic, economic, or other distinctions. The political enemy need not be morally evil or aesthetically ugly; he need not appear as an economic competitor, and it may even be advantageous to engage with him in business transactions. But he is, nevertheless, the other, the stranger; and it is sufficient for his nature [es genügt zu seinem Wesen] that he is, in a specifically intense way, existentially something different and alien, so that in the extreme case conflicts with him are possible [so daß im extremen Fall Konflikte mit ihm möglich sind].[53]

To my reading of these sentences, the chilling part is the final turn of phrase. For an initial moment, Schmitt seems to be saying that the enemy is an a priori category, that what we call the enemy is simply the political face of the stranger as such. The emergence of the enemy would thus be inseparable from the political organization of human coexistence. Closer reading, however, shows that this is not a political ontology. Schmitt is not just saying that *there are* enemies, but rather, more enigmatically, that there *must be* enemies *so that* there can be war. If the enemy did not exist, we would have to create him. For Schmitt, in other words, war is more than a mere "expedient" for reaching a political decision (as Kant writes); it is the essential and irreplaceable instrument for achieving any such an outcome. Even more troubling, the very existence of the enemy itself would be an instrumental component of this instrument: the other *must be* a stranger *so that* there may be war.

At the same time, for Schmitt, the goal of war is not the destruction of the enemy. The goal of war for Schmitt—no less than for Kant— is decision. After making the alterity of the enemy into the condition future conflict, Schmitt adds: "[Such conflicts] can neither be decided by a previously determined general norm nor by the judgment of a disinterested and therefore neutral third party."[54] The enemy must be a stranger—rather than a criminal—so that conflicts with him do not become the execution of a judgment about him, so that, in other words, the decision or verdict can be left to conflict itself. This implies the counterintuitive notion that the decision on the enemy is not a judgment but rather, on the contrary, the temporary suspension of judgment. The decision that divides friend from enemy is the decision to defer the ultimate decision to the impersonal agency of war. Only the outcome of the conflict, which results from the escalating interplay of force and counterforce, may decide who is in the right.

Even though it entails the real possibility of armed conflict, the sovereign decision authorizes itself as a kind of humility. I am convinced, in this regard, that the turn of phrase that structures Schmitt's definition of the enemy—"it is sufficient for his nature that he is, in a specifically intense way, existentially something different and alien, *so that* in the extreme case conflicts with him are possible"—points to the kerygmatic inflection of his political thinking. Schmitt's various discussions of the book of Daniel (in *The Nomos of the Earth*), the Gospel of Matthew, and the book of Genesis, are more or less well known. In the present instance, I would argue, Schmitt's turn of phrase echoes the passages in the Gospel of John when Jesus foretells the resurrection of Lazarus:

> Mary was the one who anointed the Lord with perfume and wiped his feet with her hair; her brother Lazarus was ill. So the sisters sent a message to Jesus. 'Lord, he whom you love is ill.' But when Jesus heard it, he said, "This illness does not lead to death; rather it is for God's glory, so that the Son of God may be glorified through it." (John 11:3–4)

Later, the narrative culminates in the same turn of phrase:

> "Our friend Lazarus has fallen asleep, but I am going there to awaken him." The disciples said to him, "Lord, if he has fallen asleep, he will be all right." Jesus, however, was speaking about his death, but they thought he was referring merely to sleep. Then Jesus told them plainly, "Lazarus is dead. For your sake I am glad I was not there, so that you may believe." (John 11:11–15)

Exactly as Jesus allows Lazarus to die *so that* divine agency may be revealed through his resurrection, Schmitt's enemy must be radically other so that war with him is possible. War, for Schmitt, is implicitly the field where divine providence manifests itself. Accordingly, in *The Concept of the Political*, the enemy par excellence is what he calls the "providential enemy"; and, in *The Nomos of the Earth,* he speaks of the nomos of the earth as a "primal drama" divided into three acts: appropriation, distribution, and production.

> I speak of a new nomos of the earth. That means that I consider the earth, the planet on which we live, as a whole, as a globe, and seek to understand its global division and order. The Greek word nomos, which I use for this division and order, stems from the Greek verb

nemein. Nemein is the same word as the German *nehmen*. First
nomos means *Nahme*; second, it also means division and distribution
of what is taken; and third, utilization, management, and usage of
what has been obtained as a result of the division, i.e. production and
consumption. Appropriation, distribution, and production are the
primal processes of human history, three acts of the primal drama.[55]

Of these three processes, Schmitt accords the second, division (*Teilen*),
a special privilege, always associating it with the prophetic writing on
the wall from the book of Daniel—widely considered the only apocalyptic book in the Hebrew Bible. Although he does not emphasize the
point, it is clear that Schmitt associates division with the prophetic
interpretation of the writing on the wall. There are three ciphers
that the disembodied hand writes on the wall of Belshazzar's palace:
MENE, TEKEL, UPHARSIN. When summoned by the king, Daniel
interprets them as a sentence that condemns the king and then numbers, weighs, and divides the kingdom.

> This is the interpretation of the matter: MENE, God has numbered
> the days of your kingdom and brought it to an end; TEKEL, you
> have been weighed on the scales and found wanting; PERES, your
> kingdom is divided and given to the Medes and the Persians. (Daniel
> 5:26–28)

This second act of the three-act drama is the moment in which the
word alone holds center stage. *Nomos* takes the form of *logos*, or perhaps *dik*. Each of the words inscribed on the wall refers to weighing
and measuring, judgment based on careful deliberation. The decision
that results from the process, in principle, imposes itself upon God
himself as much as upon the one whom it punishes. The inscription
is thus essential to the character of the word as judgment; it imposes
God's word without his voice, just as the hand writes without a
body—emphasizing the singularity of the decision itself rather than
the presence of the one who decides. The authority of the word, its
lawfulness, lies in its separation; its force lies in the eventual act of
understanding rather than in the theater of its utterance. In another
commentary on the same passage, Schmitt remarks that this judgment
is accomplished providentially through the contest of war: "When
the numbering and weighing of what has been appropriated is com-
pleted, the process of distribution raises new and further questions.
At all times, at the origin and foundation of a legal and economic
order, this process has been decided by lot, i.e. by divine providence,
such as war and conquest."[56] The outcome of war and conquest bears

witness to the just word—the juris-diction—of a God who remains withdrawn from the conflict, who has himself structurally renounced violent means.

The *nomos* of the earth itself is thus structurally providential, taking the form of an impersonal sentence determined according to epochal configurations of power and technology. Schmitt, in turn, puts himself in the position of the anointed interpreter of these ciphers. To the extent that it depends on divine agency, therefore, war is an act of humility: precisely to the extent that it entails a decision, a decision on the exception, it also implies the renunciation of any human perspective from which the course of history could be predicted or legislated. In *Political Theology*, Schmitt claims that the decision is a secular miracle.[57] The decision on the exception is a miracle in the sense that it is an event that breaks with the chain of natural causation. The sovereign makes his decision based upon the variables that immediately impinge upon him in the present situation rather than being grounded in a deliberation that seeks to measure its wisdom based on the science of history or concern for the long-term preservation of peacetime institutions.

Schmitt is an apologist for war: he defends war as transcendental, as a limit upon human agency and human knowledge. Politics, for Schmitt, is the practice of this limit. It is also always potentially the practice of killing. This is perhaps the aspect of Schmitt's concept of war that is easiest to misunderstand. For Schmitt, killing, which he always calls "physical killing," or the "existential negation of the other," also implies a kind of humility, the acceptance of human limitation. This is a fundamental limitation—more fundamental, presumably, than the limitation of the law that forbids murder.

The insistence that war is defined by killing manifests a respect for the victim that does not exclude the possibility of his consecration. Killing as such, to the extent that it stops at the death of the victim, is an inherently limited form of violence that opens a space for the afterlife. The final lines of the *Aeneid* are exemplary in this respect: "Relentless,/ he sinks his sword into the chest of Turnus./ His limbs fell slack with chill; and with a moan/ his life, resentful, fled to the Shades below." War thus manifests the boundary between this world and the next, between human knowledge and divine providence.

The drama of war thus revolves around the distinction between the physical and the metaphysical, the human and the divine. Physical death is decisive because of its constitutive limitation. It can function as a definitive end precisely because it is *no more* than the death of the body; it occurs as a fleeing instant, a bright line, that clears a path into the beyond. But what if death, in practice, is always somewhat less than decisive? What if death never quite possesses the self-evidence or the physicality of physical death? And further—glancing back and ahead to the Buddhas of Bamiyan—what if the object of war isn't life or the "body in pain" but something nonliving—whether it be a part of, inside of, identical with, or entirely separate from the human body?

CHAPTER TWO

Open Letter to the Enemy

Jean Genet, War, and the Exact Measure of Man

J.G. seeks, is searching for, or would like to find—or never to find—the delicious disarmed enemy, whose balance is off, whose profile is uncertain, whose face is unacceptable, the enemy broken by a breath of air, the already humiliated slave, ready to throw himself out a window on the least sign, the defeated enemy: blind, deaf, mute. With no arms, no legs, no stomach, no heart, no sex, no head: in sum, a complete enemy, already bearing the marks of my bestiality that—being too lazy—need not make any effort. I want the total enemy, with immeasurable and spontaneous hatred for me, but also the subjugated enemy, defeated by me before ever knowing me. Not reconcilable with me in any case. No friends. Especially no friends: a declared enemy but not divided. Clean edges, no cracks. What colors? A tender green like a cherry with effervescent purple. His size? Between the two of us, he presents himself to me man to man. No friends. I seek an inadequate enemy, one who comes to capitulate. I'll give him all I've got: whacks, slaps, kicks, I will have him gnawed by starving foxes, make him eat English food, attend the House of Lords, be received at Buckingham Palace, fuck Prince Phillip, get fucked by him, live for a month in London, dress like me, sleep where I sleep, live my stead: I seek the declared enemy.[1]

This brief text was not actually published until 1991. It was, however, almost published in 1975 in a book of homages to William Burroughs and Brion Gysin. It was to have been preceded by the following explanation of its origins, written by Gysin:

In Tangiers in 1970 Genet asked me what had happened to the underground English newspaper *The International Times*. When I told him that the editors were having trouble with the English authorities because of the personal ads run by people searching for "special friendships" [*amitiés particulières*], he exclaimed: "Why friends? Personally, I am looking for a suitable enemy [*un ennemi à ma taille*]." And he then wrote the following text . . . [2]

Hence the empirical reason for the form of the personal ad. In 1991, the text was published—according to Genet's wishes—as the first page of his posthumous collection of political writings and interviews, *The Declared Enemy*. But as the editors note, "This collection opens with a text that does not strictly belong to the rest of the writings included here."[3] The other texts from the collection consist in Genet's occasional interventions in the public sphere. Each bears upon his involvement in specific political events (the 1968 Chicago Democratic National Convention, the Chatila massacre) or with named political figures and groups (the Palestinians, the Black Panthers, the Baader-Meinhof group, George Jackson, Angela Davis), whereas the form of the text that he wrote for Gysin seems to number it among his literary works.

The different status of the ad is marked by the liminal place that it occupies in the book itself. It presents itself as a traditional paratext, situated on the threshold between book and its public. The final line of the text becomes the title of the book in which it appears. However, there is evidence that Genet might have considered this text even more liminal than a paratext. During the process of selecting texts for *The Declared Enemy*, which began before his death, he called it the "page from Tangiers." More page than text, this loose leaf would be inserted between the pages rather than bound among them—a *prière d'insérer* archived where it is bound to get lost.[4]

This chapter sets out to argue that the reading of these ambiguities that interfere with the attempt to understand how Genet's personal open letter to the enemy fits in the collection of his political writings is essential for a precise measurement of what remains politically open in his later work. Both the placement of the text and the discreet "genre" of the personal advertisement itself suggest that Genet here seeks, in his book, to displace the "openness" of its publication, to manifest that the very publication of this text does not necessarily pertain to the "public sphere." The form of the personal ad suggests that the openness of the public sphere is itself open, that it is constitutively folded into a space that it cannot dominate. The ad would have been published in the *International Times*, an "underground" paper that is also "international," which suggests that it pertains to an "international" political space that would not simply be an extension of the rational public sphere, but would have the dimensions of this other elusive openness, both more secret and more unbounded.

Consideration of these material ambiguities will also be essential to understanding the address of this letter to "the declared enemy." Just as the public sphere enfolds an openness that it cannot dominate, it necessarily includes those "enemies" to whom the law does not apply. Public space opens beyond the space of the republic that defines the application of the laws (even and especially when this beyond is situated within the territory of the republic itself). Does this mean that, contrary to the hopes that animate Enlightenment political philosophy, the public sphere is inseparable from the space of war?[5]

I

The direct address of the text suggests that it might be given the status of a traditional theatrical prologue: it takes the form of a dilatory metatheatrical parabasis in which the actor introduces himself in character to the spectators and frames the upcoming play as a fiction intended for their delectation. Genet himself has Archibald Absalom Wellington resort to such a prologue in the opening minutes of his play *The Blacks*.

> (*to the audience*): This evening we shall perform for you. But, in order that you may remain comfortably settled in your seats in the presence of the drama that is already unfolding here, in order that you may be assured that there is no danger of such a drama's worming its way into your precious lives, we shall even have the decency—a decency learned from you—to make communication impossible. We shall increase the distance that separates us—a distance that is basic—by our pomp, our manners, our insolence—for we are also actors. When my speech is over, everything here—(*he stamps his foot in a gesture of rage*) here!—will take place in the delicate world of reprobation.[6]

Much as Archibald addresses himself to the audience, Genet's personal advertisement seems directly to address its intended reader, the "declared enemy." The ad is different, however, in that it secretly inverts the function of the prologue: instead of pretending to transmit a fiction to a real live audience, "comfortably settled in their seats," its address claims to expose a real addresser ("J.G." addresses "himself") to a fictional addressee (*un ennemi à ma taille*, "the declared enemy").

The example of *The Blacks* is also important because it clearly manifests the structure of this inversion. Genet dubs this play *une clownerie*, "a clown show," perhaps because it only pretends to address its audience. Through the manifest self-consciousness of one player, "Archibald," the play "shows" itself addressing the assembled audience while it in fact always addresses someone other—not other than the audience but one among them, who will always be there without ever being present. A token white man. A blank. A dead man. *Un mort.* A dummy. A brief note (signed "J.G.") that prefaces both play and prologue discreetly indexes this other address.

> This play, written, I repeat, by a white man, is intended for a white audience, but if, which is unlikely, it is ever performed before a black audience, then a white person, male or female, should be invited every evening. The organizer of the show should welcome him formally, dress him in ceremonial costume and lead him to his seat, preferably in the front row of the orchestra. The actors will play for him. A spotlight should be focused upon this symbolic white throughout the performance.
>
> But what if no white person accepted? Then let white masks be distributed to the black spectators as they enter the theater. And if the blacks refuse the masks, then let a mannequin be used.
> J.G.[7]

The ironic projection of the "unlikely" possibility that the play would be performed before a black audience allows Genet to reveal that the play was written, not so much for an actual white audience, but for an audience who would "symbolize" a white audience; or, further, for one "white person" (*un Blanc*)—even if the "blank" person of one white mannequin—who would symbolize an audience (in the absence of any actual audience). Even when performed for a white audience, the play will always be addressed to someone other than the number of audience members assembled in the theater. On the one hand, any of those present can occupy the place of the addressee: everyone can wear his mask. On the other hand, none of the actual ones present can ever be this addressee; no one can occupy the place of the mask "itself."

Genet advises: if his play were ever performed before a black audience, "then a white person, male or female, should be *invited* every evening." What would this invitation look like? How would it be phrased? It could well read like the personal ad that opens *The Declared Enemy*, which is also a kind of exorbitant invitation. The treatment that Genet prescribes for the play's guest white person is at least formally analogous to the welcome that J.G. claims to have in store for the enemy who responds to his advertisement. With thinly veiled malice, acknowledged only in the suggestion that no one would accept the invitation, Genet directs the organizer of the play to dignify his invited guest: "welcome him formally, dress him in ceremonial costume and lead him to his seat, preferably in the front row of the orchestra." Likewise, J.G. advertises an array of dignities and indignities for the one who responds to his ad: he offers all the whacks, slaps, and kicks that he can summon, on top of "feeding him to starving foxes, making him eat English food, attend the House of Lords, be received at Buckingham Palace, fuck Prince Phillip, and be fucked by him, live for a month in London . . . " Moreover, in each case, the invitation is addressed to one who will substitute for the author himself. The stage direction specifies that *The Blacks* was written *by* and *for* a white man; by a white man for "himself"—or for another white man (or mannequin) who will take his place. J.G. ends the personal ad with the promise to make the enemy "dress like me, sleep in place of me, live in place of me."

But the most important aspect of each invitation is that it reserves this particular "personalized" treatment for a discrete presence without identity. Each invitation exclusively asks for the mere ("symbolic") presence of the person without the person himself or herself. "A spotlight should be focused on this symbolic white throughout the performance." Genet insists on the spotlight to index (to both dignify and abject) this discrete but unidentified presence; it obliges the larger audience to notice the white man in their midst—among their number but not of their group. Rather than invite the enemy "himself" to respond, the "personal" ad seeks the one—anyone or no one—who would lend the presence of his person to the name, the one who would "accept" to symbolize the Enemy, and, ultimately, the one who would accept to symbolize the reader both of the ad and the volume for which it serves as a prologue.

On any given night, the audience of *The Blacks* is liable to see the play performed for a mannequin (or for a person invited so that the organizers of the play will not have to use a mannequin). The reader of the ad, or of *The Declared Enemy*, reads a text that is addressed to an anonymous other. Rather than simply published or performed for the public, these texts are addressed to one particular person who is not there—or only there in effigy. Addressed to no one, therefore—if no one does not mean none but marks the negation of the singular, the irreplaceable one and only. No one is always "no one here," none among the many who remain, those who have in common that no one among them is the one, the addressee of the address.

The presence of a mask amid the audience of *The Blacks* turns the theater into a space of hearsay. This figure shows the public that it attends a spectacle addressed to someone absent in their midst. The personal ad projects this address into the sphere of political discourse. Perhaps more than another book, a collection of political writings posits a straightforward address to its reading public. But Genet advertises that the addressee of his ad lies beyond the public of assembled citizens. The ad designates no lesser person than the public enemy as its reader—a gesture that, at a minimum, distinguishes the potential reader from the citizen. The ad suggests to the book's public that in order to read its text, they can only overhear a discourse destined for a single reader among them. The open space of this hearsay, where the public must intercept a discourse in order to become its readers, can no longer be called the public sphere without further discussion. Genet thus requires that each reader of his ad and *The Declared Enemy* situate himself in a political space beyond the space governed by public speech.

II

The demand for such a conception of political space does not imply that the fundamental aspirations of the Enlightenment public sphere must be abandoned. The function of the rational public sphere is to secure a place for truth beyond all political authority, a place from which it becomes possible to demand that authority justify its decisions with reference to verifiable truths; and thus to provide a basis on which the citizen may contest the legitimacy of any authority that fails to justify itself in such terms. Truth is also at stake in the political space of hearsay, perhaps more radically than in the procedures whereby the institutions of the public sphere uphold the sovereignty of the truth claim.

The public sphere secures truth through infinite conversation, understanding, and procedures of verification, in the form of the grammatical proposition around which these forms of discourse revolve. The place of the proposition, in its turn, is secured through the free speech whereby it opens toward the other. In order for any given proposition to remain open to discussion, it must circulate (and continue to circulate) as an open letter addressed to all those who can understand and thus test its claims. This model of public discourse, however, reduces the address to a condition for rational discussion. The address of the proposition is only ever understood as the demand to understand what the proposition says in logico-grammatical terms. What never enters into this model of discourse, or the politics of truth that corresponds to it, is the demand that the address be considered in its own right, that it be received as something other than the demand to understand the meaning of the proposition that it transmits.

When a proposition is circulated in public, it not only asks us to consider what it says, but also what its saying itself means. When one person addresses another, the other may always (and perhaps always does) ask: Why do you say that? What do you mean by saying that? Or further: What do you mean by saying that *to* me or indeed *to* anyone? What do you have to gain or to lose? Am I the one you are really speaking to? Through the address, in other words, questions of context, of addressee, and of "object" beyond the grammatical object of the proposition enter into the interpretation of the proposition itself. These factors enter into its interpretation with such urgency, in fact, that they tend to push the problem of verifying its grammatical statement into the background. The address of the proposition—rather than the transmission of a statement—is what offers access to the truth.

The politics of truth that opens with the reading of addresses cannot be entirely other than the politics of open discussion that constitutes the Enlightenment public sphere. Even as the address makes discussion possible, it opens a political horizon that is not defined by such discussion. For Genet, therefore, the personal ad functions to manifest one of the points at which the public sphere explicitly bears witness to the truth that the production of its legitimacy necessarily excludes.

III

The personal ad presents itself as a kind of small roman à clef— except that, rather than a novel, it would be an *adresse à clef*. The personal ad does not tell the story of an unnamed person to whose identity the author openly holds the key. The personal ad withholds the identity of the *addressee* of the letter. And this secret is open to such an extent that even the author of the ad does not have the key to it. This seems the point of a personal ad: when you take one out, you do not know whom you are addressing. (Or perhaps you take one out precisely in order not to know whom you are addressing). It is the addressee himself who has the key. Only he knows who he is. When he responds to the ad, however, it will not be to give away the secret. He responds because he wants the other to tell him who he is. So the key is nowhere.

In this respect, it is useful to compare the personal ad to the institution of the open letter. The one is in fact the inverse of the other. The open letter and the personal ad have in common that they address a readership over the head of their addressee. But whereas the open letter uses its address to a particular addressee as an occasion to address a reading public, the personal ad uses an address to a reading public as a way of finding its addressee. Accordingly, whereas the publication of the open letter shows its actual addressee to be its readers in the absence of the person it names, the publication of a personal ad is the only way in which it can name an unnamed person as its addressee. Instead of being written to "one and all," it is open to "all and none."

Perhaps it will never have been addressed to anyone. To the extent that every reader, as part of the reading public, remains anonymous, every reader becomes the absence of the person to whom the ad would have been addressed. No matter how many people respond to the personal ad, its text will never have been addressed to anyone. The fascination with reading the personals has to do with this absence of address, with reading as the experience of a constitutive anonymity (reading absolved of the responsibility of reading).

But why does anyone respond if no one is addressed? How does one pass from being a reader to being an addressee? And why? The addressee is the one who must decide to name himself. If reading is constitutively anonymous, and without address, to become an addressee, the reader must interrupt his reading—naming himself an addressee and retroactively asserting the letter to have been an address. And he does so because his access to the truth, and perhaps access to truth as such, is at stake.

This passage from anonymous fraction of a reading public to addressee is perhaps the very activity of reading as such—insofar as it involves a truth claim. Beyond interpretation, which shows a text to have hidden folds or dimensions beneath its literal surface, the act of reading shows that the surface of the text, the very openness of the letter, is itself hidden, constitutively effaced. But this does not mean that the letter is closed, just that it has another, discreet, openness. The named reader retroactively ascribes this discreet openness—the erasure of the open letter of the text—to his own reading. And the future anterior of this ascriptive claim is called the address. Therefore, the address does not inhere in the letter but is an emergent claim about the letter: the claim that the very openness of the letter becomes accessible only with the incursion of the proper name.

The simple form of the personal ad deconstitutes this claim, exposes the decision that it involves, the decision in the proper name. In this respect, Genet's ad is a cynical one, the type that addresses the other by calling attention to the logic of the address. It calls attention to this claim upon the letter, calling it "defeat," "capitulation." The text thus incorporates the absence of address into its address. Since the personal ad addresses *no one*, those who respond defeat themselves. This defeat occurs where truth opens.

Rather than present an image of the desired object, it presents the dismantling of that image, of the image of the body in particular— "no arms, no legs, no stomach, no heart, no sex, no head"—in the hope of addressing the desired subject, "the complete enemy."

Early in *Prisoner of Love,* Genet's posthumously published memoir of the years he spent alongside the Palestinians and the Black Panthers, he considers the larger political stakes of such an address. The capitulation of the enemy, evoked in the personal ad, appears in this context as a God-willed victory; the letter is less the opening of a discussion than a victorious struggle; the address, rather than circulate as an advertisement, pertains to the opening verse of the Qur'an. Genet solicits these motifs in a digressive meditation on the letters in the signifier FATAH—the reverse acronym for *harakat al-tahrir al-watani al-filastini* (Yassir Arafat's Palestine Liberation Army):

> The consonants F, T, and H, in that order, form a triliteral root
> meaning fissure, chink, opening [*fissure, fente, ouverture*]; also a
> breakthrough before a victory [*ouverture proche d'une victoire*], a
> victory willed by God. Fatah also means lock, and is connected with
> the word for key, which in Arabic is *meftah*—where the three basic
> letters recur, preceded by *me*. The same triliteral root gives *Fatiha*,
> meaning "the one that opens" [*celle qui ouvre*]: that is, the first sura,
> the one that opens the Qur'an [*celle qui ouvre le Coran*].[8]

I see three hidden meanings in the three words *Fatah, meftah,* and *fatiha. Fatah*—chink, fissure, opening—suggests the expectation, the

almost passive expectation, of a God-willed victory. *Mefta*—key—
suggests almost visibly a key in an opening or lock. *Fatiha* also means
an opening but a religious one, the first chapter of the Qur'an. So
behind the three words derived from the same root as *Fatah* lurk the
ideas of struggle (for victory), sexual violence (the key in the lock),
and a battle won through the grace of God.

  Struggle, sexual violence, a battle won through the grace of God:
like the ad, this exercise in paranomasia makes these signifiers inter-
sect at points where the act of war, the opening toward victory, turns
into withdrawal in the face of divine intervention. Both texts stage
this withdrawal as a function of the letter—the letter as "the one
that opens," the *incipit*, the first verse or turn, or simply the *initials*
("J.G.") that collapse a proper name. In the Qur'an, Genet remarks,
the opening sura constitutes a "religious" event. The letter situates the
point where an actor takes initiative by ceding it to the Other; where
he begins without beginning because the Other is the one who begins
in his stead; where the Other takes over before the first leaves off, or
even before he has a chance to begin. In the personal ad that opens
Genet's political book, too, the letter becomes the form in which the
one can act without doing anything (except perhaps making the "least
sign"—the occasion for the enemy to cease deferring his self-destruc-
tion: "the already humiliated slave, ready to throw himself out the
window on the least sign"). The letter is the form in which one can
project a struggle without action and victory without commitment—
either on the part of one enemy or the other. In this war, victory and
defeat occur in the nonencounter between two passivities; the divine
appears on the horizon of the letter.

IV

In an important interview at the end of his life with Rüdiger Wisch-
enbart and Layla Shadid, Genet makes a distinction between his early
works, written in prison, and the late works that emerge from the
time that he spent "among" the Black Panthers and the Palestinians.
(I will come back later to Genet's way of situating himself *among*
these groups rather than *with* them). He refers to two "disciplines":
the discipline of "grammar" and the discipline of "the real." I would
like to argue that these disciplines pertain to two different versions
of political space, and two different politics of truth. The discipline
of grammar that Genet exercised in prison would refer—ironically

enough—to the Enlightenment politics of the rational public sphere; the discipline of the real would entail a political space beyond the national public sphere, and perhaps the international public sphere, defined by the horizon without horizon of divine violence.

When asked about the difference between his early books and his current work, Genet responds: "In those books, and in prison, I was master of my imagination. I was master over the element on which I was working. Because it was entirely my own daydream."[9] On the other hand, he continues, "I am no longer the master of what I saw, I am obliged to say: I saw men tied up and bound. I saw a woman with her fingers cut off! I am obliged to submit myself to a real world."[10] And earlier in the same interview, he explained: "[You] can act upon dreams in a way that is almost unlimited. One cannot act on the real to an unlimited extent. You cannot act upon the real in an unlimited way. A different discipline is necessary, one that is no longer a grammatical discipline."[11]

By virtue of the logical subordination of predicates to the subject of the statement that characterizes grammatical construction, grammar bears witness to the presence of a master—not only the self, but the master to which the self should have submitted in order to attain self-mastery, to become an autonomous subject. This master—and not the individual or the self—is the subject of public communication, the ground for the politics of truth. According to an expression that Kant cites in "What Is Enlightenment": *Caesar non est supra Grammaticos.*[12] Grammar, in other words, is the permanent institution of the right to speak truth to power. This right to insubordination, however, is founded upon the higher form of subordination to a symbolic order—embodied in the syntactical order of grammatical predication.

Grammar, for Kant, would hold the position of the subject ("the empty I") in public, constituting the public use of reason as the public use of one's *own* reason. The problem of mastery is a problem at all because grammar is more than a formality of communication, more than a set of discursive rules to be "mastered." Grammar is inseparable from autonomy of the Subject—both ethico-political autonomy and, indissociably, the autonomy that situates the human as a break in the chain of natural causality.

As Hegel analyzed in the preface to the *Phenomenology of Spirit,* both forms of autonomy are actualized in the infinite replaceability of the predicate that grammar makes possible. Because no object requires specific predicates, one learns language by mastering grammar as a system rather than memorizing a whole archive of singular propositions. (The responsibility for such an archive comes into play only when speaking goes beyond making one's own voice heard, when it becomes a matter of transmitting an opaque message or tradition—perhaps coded, perhaps in an idiom foreign to the messenger—to an other who is supposed to understand.) The presupposition that the object is liable to receive any number of predicates would also be the presupposition of the (free) subject of knowledge. Grammatical predication is the activity of a subject who, by virtue of his constitutive independence from the reality that he expresses in language, is defined by an inexhaustible ability to know. Grammar makes knowing into the expression of a free will—the same free will that is both the subject of ethics and the subject of the Enlightenment public sphere. The public sphere is said to be *open* to the precise extent that, grammatically speaking, the object of any proposition can be understood through an open series of predicates. "Freedom of speech" is the freedom to which this activity of predication bears witness. It is no accident, therefore, that the term that Hegel uses to designate the activity of predication, or the formulation of empirical propositions, is *Räsonieren*, usually translated into English as "argumentation," the same word that Kant uses (in the article on enlightenment) to designate the free public use of reason.[13]

Genet writes: "I was master of the element upon which I was working. Because it was my dream and mine alone." Mastery, in this sense, constitutes a negative freedom, and its goal is the subordination of the object to the infinite forms of its communication. The "discipline of grammar" would be the agent of this subordination and would thereby confirm that imagination submits only to the internal limit of the infinite combinations and recombinations of grammatical formulas. Grammar, it would seem, does not just impose logical form upon imaginary material. In acting upon such material, grammar comes into its own as mastery. Grammatical predication renders every object, as object, indistinguishable from a product of the imagination. Further, the effect of mastery that arises at the intersection of grammar and imagination does not just involve the numerical limitlessness of formulas but also actualizes a more impressive epistemological limitlessness.

The "discipline of the real," therefore, would limit grammatical action. "I am no longer the master of what I have seen . . . " "[You] can act upon dreams in a way that is almost unlimited. One cannot act on the real to an unlimited extent. You cannot act upon the real in an unlimited way. A different discipline is necessary, one that is no longer a grammatical discipline." However, this discipline would not simply oppose the resistance of empirical reality to the freedom of the imagination. The principles of empirical verification always function within the parameters of grammatical predication, and thus also within the terms of the imagination.

For Hegel, the predicative judgment that founds the search for knowledge leaves no place for truth. "Truth haunts [predicative] judgment, but judgment alone cannot ground it."[14] No scrutiny of the logic of a sentence will ever determine whether it is true or untrue. In order to verify or refute the claim of a sentence, it is always necessary to establish its correspondence or noncorrespondence to an empirical state of affairs. But any corroborative claim or counterclaim derived from such research will necessarily suffer from the same problem as the original claim. As long as one understands the proposition as a logical construction, its truth will always reside elsewhere than in the proposition itself; it resides either in the knowing subject or the empirical reality that this subject represents to itself.

The mutual exclusion of knowledge and truth is both the possibility and the impossibility of enlightenment. On the one hand, because predication and truth are structurally incompatible, no single proposition can ever become the basis for an authority. It must always be subjected to a trial of verification. On the other hand, because predication cannot ever found a truth claim, the epistemological field is left open to illegitimate claims to know without recourse to any verification procedure.

Alfred Tarski gave a rigorous form to the tautological back and forth between proposition and verification—giving truth itself the status of a predicate: "'The snow is white' *is true* if and only if the snow is white." The point (or one of them) is that the truth of a predication claim can only ever be established by abandoning the proposition that articulates it for an empirical state of affairs, so that the proposition itself will never be true on its own terms. The irony is that the "empirical state of affairs" has the exact same form (minus the quotation marks) as the proposition itself. [15]

Given these problems, truth can only be established through unrestricted public debate. Because truth doesn't inhere in any given proposition, it can only be constituted in the form of consensus *between* propositions. A truth claim becomes valid only if can be independently verified by a community of researchers. But research is hardly immune from the problems of predication in general. The work of any group of researchers can only ever result in one further predicative claim, so that the process of argumentation must ultimately contradict its avowed goal: rather than become the object of universal consensus, truth ultimately inheres in the authority of a subject supposed to know.

The contradictions that beset the project of enlightenment also trouble the politics of truth based on it. The danger that lurks in these contradictions is that, rather than consensus being generated through the process of verification that puts every supposedly authoritative claim into question, consensus can always—and perhaps always does—become the means through which supposed authority acquires the status of truth without recourse to any verification procedure whatsoever. The inability of predication to found truth gives a potentially unlimited scope to ungrounded assertions and the will to lie.

Public speech implies modesty: it sacrifices the claim to represent an incontestable truth in order to become the exercise of freedom. Each proposition constitutively limits itself to the claim that it is *truthful*. The question of its actual truth remains open to potentially infinite challenge and discussion. Such modesty is necessary, however, and must be vigilantly upheld, because the language of predication *inherently* exceeds the limits of its form—and thus it tends arrogantly to put an end to the discussion that such limits keep open. Even speaking "truthfully" does not only entail a demand that the other believe that I am speaking without the intent to deceive. It is always inseparably—if not primarily—the demand that the other believe that what I say is in fact true. By the fact of its communication in predicative form, every public claim anticipates the eventual recognition of *its* objective validity. In Tarski's example, the verified fact that the snow is white simply confirms what the assertion, "the snow is white," already said to be true. Seeking the fact of the matter serves ultimately to show that the assertion itself already confirms its own claims—has always already lifted its own quotation marks. Challenge and discussion will thus never be vigilant enough to prevent the modest claims of the public speaker from sooner or later becoming the illegitimate claims to a self-appointed authority.

V

When, in the interview from 1983, Genet speaks of a discipline of the real, it is in the midst of a discussion of "Four Hours in Shatila,"[16] an essay that he wrote soon before he began *Prisoner of Love*.[17] On the one hand, this text is a work of straightforward reporting, an account of what Genet saw during his visit to the Shatila refugee camp after the Phalangist massacre in 1982. On the other hand, a key moment in the account involves what Genet calls an "invisible vision" that impinges upon his mind. There are few places where the extremity of Genet's politics of truth becomes clearer. His discipline of the real interrupts the infinity of discussion, not through recourse to empirical reporting, but rather through the insistence of something *incontestable*. When Genet asserts, "I am no longer master of what I have seen," it means that no one can contest the truth of this vision. He cannot contest it either. This vision is "invisible" to the extent that it doesn't belong to him; it isn't something that he saw with his own eyes. It is an experience that he bears within himself as an insurgent memory—perhaps a *souvenir*, the deceptively ironic name that he gives the clusters of digressions that make up *Prisoner of Love*.

Genet describes himself walking over the corpses that litter the streets of the ravaged Shatila encampment. Rather than simply detail what he sees, he describes the turn of his mind toward what cannot be seen. "Amidst them or rather alongside them—all the tortured victims—I cannot get this *'invisible vision'* out of my mind: the torturer, what was he like? Who was he? I see him and I do not see him. He is everywhere I look and the form he will ever have is the one outlined by the grotesque poses, positions, and gestures of the dead, attended by clouds of flies in the sun."[18] He returns to this same vision in altered terms toward the end of his souvenirs:

> Dying with their eyes wide open, they knew the terror of seeing every created thing—man, chairs, stars, suns, Phalangists—tremble, convulse and blur, knowing they were going to vanish because those who would be their victims were driving them to nothingness. The dying saw and felt and knew their death was the death of the world. *Après moi le déluge* is a ridiculous claim, because the only *after me* is the death of all creation.
>
>   Understood in this sense, death is a phenomenon that destroys the world. To eyelids reluctant to close the world gradually loses its brightness, blurs, dissolves and finally disappears, dies in a pupil obstinately fixed on a vanishing world. So? The wide eye can still see the glint of the knife or the bayonet. The brightness that slowly

approaches, pales, blurs, disappears. Then the knife, the hand, the
sleeve, the uniform, the eyes, the laughter of the Phalangist have
ceased to be.[19]

The invisible imposes itself without recourse. Accessible only to the
other's eye, such a vision can never be forgotten by the one to whom
it remains invisible but only hidden or destroyed. Because this vision
has been destroyed along with the other and along with the universe,
it can never be rendered visible—for example, reconstructed according to more or less plausible hypotheses, criminal investigations, and
eyewitness testimony. If the destruction of the other is the destruction
of the world, nothing would remain on the basis of which such recon-
struction could be based. The "vision" is therefore "real"—absolute,
incontestable; and it is as such that it works upon the mind. Genet
makes this work into the principle of a discipline. This "vision" is
itself all that would remain of the abolished world. And it does not
remain either. What does remain is the body of the victim, the tortured corpse. The body remains after the end of the world. Is this
not the basis for the belief in the resurrection of the flesh? The resurrection would manifest that the body itself is not part of the world
but opens onto it, in much the same way that the gaze opens onto it.
Indeed, Genet's texts suggest that the invisible imposes itself in yet
another way. Especially in the passage from the earlier text, he does
speak of vision but not of sense perception: the torturer that he sees
effectively blinds him (*il me crève les yeux*), so the only possible vision
opens in the wounds, the postures, and the grotesque bodily gestures
of his victims. When Genet returns to the episode in the memoir, the
contorted bodies have become the eye of the world or, even less, a
single pupil, the hole in the eye.

VI

For Hannah Arendt, in an essay on politics and truth, the truth is
by definition incontestable. No truth worthy of the name can be or
should be open for discussion. In accord with a philosophical tradition
that runs from Hegel and Heidegger to Lacan, Arendt holds that truth
is something other than *adequatio* or objectivity, other than the con-
formity of logical judgments to their object. Truths are distinguished,
she writes, "in their mode of asserting their validity." Over and over
again, she insists that the specific "mode" in which truth asserts its
validity is coercive, or even tyrannical. The truth undeniably imposes

itself upon me. No one can persuade me of the truth—or, for that matter, of the untruth.

> For those who accept [these truths], they are not changed by the numbers or lack of numbers who entertain the same proposition; persuasion or dissuasion is useless, for the content of the statement is not of a persuasive nature but of a coercive one. . . . Truth carries within itself an element of coercion, and the frequently tyrannical tendencies among professional truthtellers may be caused less by a failing of character than by the strain of habitually living under a kind of compulsion.[20]

The truth is coercive or compulsive in that it imposes itself upon the truthteller herself as an address that resists understanding as a proposition. If "the content of the statement is not of a persuasive nature but a coercive one," this implies that the content cannot be rephrased, analyzed grammatically, open to debate. Of particular interest, then, is the way in which Arendt articulates the relation between the truthteller's tyrannical tendencies and the politics of open discussion. According to her analysis, the coerciveness of truth does not offer an empirical certainty that puts an arbitrary end to public discussion but rather, quite to the contrary, safeguards the possibility of legitimate discussion.

> Facts and opinions, though they must be kept apart, are not antagonistic to each other; they belong to the same realm. Facts inform opinions, and opinions, inspired by different interests and passions, can differ widely and still be legitimate as long as they respect factual truth. Freedom of opinion is a farce unless factual information is guaranteed and the facts themselves are not in dispute. In other words, factual truth informs political thought just as rational truth informs philosophical speculation.[21]

Facts in politics serve a function analogous to mathematics in philosophy. They provide light and enlightenment, Arendt writes, but without transparency. In this sense, she openly contests the notion that "transparency" is the necessary condition of democratic politics.

> No opinion is self-evident. In matters of opinion, but not in matters of truth, our thinking is truly discursive running, as it were, from place to place, from one part of the world to another, through all kinds of conflicting views, until it finally ascends from these particularities to some impartial generality. Compared to this process, in which a particular issue is forced into the open that it may show itself from all sides, in every possible perspective until it is flooded and made transparent by the full light of human comprehension,

a statement of truth possesses a peculiar opaqueness. Rational truth enlightens human understanding, and factual truth must inform opinions, but these truths, though they are never obscure, are not transparent either, and it is in their very nature to withstand further elucidation, as it is in the nature of light to withstand enlightenment.[22]

Much as the real occurs to Genet in the form of an "invisible vision," Arendt upholds the truth as both opaque and luminous. Facts are opaque because they impinge upon the mind as a fragment of an other's experience—that of a witness or chain of witnesses. They are luminous because they are always addressed to the other; they are open secrets. Indeed, the etymological root of the word *coercion* is the Latin *arcere*, which means "to shut in" or "to enclose." The word is thus related both to the words *ark* (as in the ark of the covenant) and *exercise* (as in the subtitle of the book in which Arendt's text appears: *Eight Exercises in Political Thought*)—an etymologically determined series that shows coercion to entail precisely those elements of the truthteller's ethos: withdrawal, invisibility, and secrecy, if not also holiness and divinity. That the truth "carries within itself an element of coercion" means that the truth carries within itself an element of invisibility; that it is at least partially withdrawn and that it cannot be subjected to grammatical analysis or public discussion without falsification.

This conception of truth leads Arendt—remarkably—to conceive a politics of truth beyond self-legislation or democratic process.

The question is whether power could and should be checked not only by a constitution, a bill of rights, and a multiplicity of powers, as in a system of checks and balances, in which, in Montesquieu's words, *le pouvoir arrête le pouvoir*—that is by factors that arise out of and belong to the political realm proper—but by something that arises from without, has its source outside the political realm, and is as independent of the wishes and desires of the citizens as is the will of the worst tyrant.[23]

Arendt concludes that the openness of a democratic political system can only be maintained if such a system allows for the incursion of a truth that resists the process of discussion and deliberation whereby the system establishes its legitimacy.

To sharpen the paradox, the openness of the system can only be upheld if it allows for the contestation of its openness as such. This is a radical position in that it does not only advocate allowing uncomfortable facts into the open air of public discussion, the vigilant denunciation of lies, and so on. It is a contestation of the public sphere as such, or of the identification of the political with the public sphere. For Arendt, the only truly "open" politics is one that allows for both the phenomenality of the public sphere and that which "arises from without" and thus constitutively withdraws from this sphere. Both the visible and the invisible.

VII

Would Arendt accept that the "mode" in which the truth asserts its validity is the end of the world? Even if not, her work makes it possible to measure the political ramifications of such an assertion. That which has its source outside the political realm is nothing less (or more?) than the world itself. Which means that what arises from without is not something that makes its appearance in what Arendt calls "the world of appearances" (more or less synonymous with the political realm as such). What arises is another openness than the one that is synonymous with the world of appearances. An invisible or a virtual openness, or an openness that is so slight as to be almost closed—more an opening, a chink, a fissure. The entire sphere of the open society would thus function as the disavowal of this deterritorialized (abolished, discrete, virtual) openness.

Nonetheless, it remains important to Arendt that the truthteller address herself to the scene of the shared world of appearances. Much of Arendt's work after the controversy over *Eichmann in Jerusalem* is preoccupied with the politics of the invisible. *The Life of the Mind*, for example, might be read, not simply as a foray into the consolations of philosophy, but as a more ambitious attempt to elaborate a new concept of the political. "The life of the mind" is precisely the dimension of thought that remains constitutively invisible or withdrawn from a political point of view.[24] But the phrase also connotes the ethos or habitus of the thinker who leads the life of the mind, a life withdrawn from the interests of the political realm. She gives various examples of the truthteller, and the institutions that attend upon him, all of which have in common that they are social permutations of a fundamental *solitude*. Arendt continues:

> The standpoint outside the political realm—outside the community to which we belong and the company of our peers—is clearly characterized as one of the various modes of being alone. Outstanding

among the modes of truthtelling are the solitude of the philosopher,
the isolation of the scientist and the artist, the impartiality of the historian and the judge, and the independence of the fact-finder, the witness, and the reporter. . . . These modes of being alone differ in many
respects, but they have in common that as long as any one of them
lasts, no political commitment, no adherence to a cause is possible.[25]

It would be tempting to claim that Genet himself occupies the position of Arendt's solitary truthteller, and that, among the Palestinians,
or among the Black Panthers, he played the role of the fact-finder, witness, or reporter in the strong sense that she outlines. However, the
personal advertisement, or "announcement," that opens his political
writings—and was written near the beginning of his time with the
Palestinians—is already an indication that what he means by solitude
does not correspond to Arendt's conception; and that he also conceives differently the withdrawal whereby the politics of truth opens
beyond public sphere.

The discreet address of the personal ad entails a space that
Arendt's truthteller opens but does not inhabit. Solitude, for Genet,
becomes the solitude of decision, adherence to a cause, acceptance
of the invitation. After speaking of his inability to lie to himself,
Genet pursues the point in these terms: "And it's in solitude that I
accept being with the Palestinians. It's not when I say yes to Layla
[Shadid], yes, I'll go with you . . . it's not at moments like that. It's
when I'm alone and I decide on my own. And there I believe that I'm
not lying."[26]

Genet's position is impartial only to the extent that he claims to
have his eyes in the front of someone else's head. As often occurs in
dreams, he sees himself from behind. "Is it a privilege of my present age or the misfortune of my whole life that I always see myself
from behind, when in fact I've always had my back to the wall?"[27]
Political commitment is a matter of deciding to become part of the
world in the other's gaze, a decision that necessarily takes place in
solitude because that world is invisible, if not always already abolished. Thus, on the very first page of *Prisoner of Love,* Genet insists
that his period with the Palestinians was "time spent among [*auprès
de*]—not with [*avec*] the Palestinians"[28]—just as he speaks of himself
walking among (*auprès de*) the tortured dead of Shatila. Later in the
memoir, he will describe how he only ever finds his own gestures—
or, more precisely, as he writes, his own *size*—in the interstices of the
gestures of the fedayeen, in much the same way that he described the

dimensions of the enemy vanishing into the gestures of those dead among which he walked.

> As I am not an archivist or a historian or anything like it, I'll only have recounted my life in order to recite a story of the Palestinians. The strangeness of my situation now appears to me either in three-quarter, or in profile, or from the back, for I never see myself, with my age and my size [*ma taille*] apparent, from the front, but from the back or in profile, my dimensions marked by the direction of my gestures or those of the fedayeen, the raised cigarette going down, the lighter lifted upward, and the direction of each of these gestures write lines restoring my size [*ma taille*] and my position within the group.[29]

VIII

Much like the solitary white person seated in the front row before the spectacle of *The Blacks,* Genet presents himself telling the truth with his back turned to the public sphere. Rather than face those whom he addresses, he faces those who address him. Even if he sees himself from behind, his back is to the wall. This averted stance is the posture in which he becomes responsible for transmitting an address that no amount of frontal dialogue will allow him to dominate.

The personal ad reiterates this posture, emphasized by its recourse to the motif of size that runs throughout Genet's political writings. In the midst of addressing the enemy, the ad turns to the question of what size the enemy is or should be. "Sa taille? Entre nous, il se présente à moi d'homme à homme." "His size? Between the two of us, he presents himself to me man to man." In the brief conversation that Gysin reports, too, he emphasizes size: "Je cherche un ennemi à ma taille." "I am looking for a suitable enemy (an enemy my own size, an enemy who measures up to me)." But Genet also represents his size (*ma taille*) in a less belligerent fashion when he represents himself from the back or in profile as he circulates among (*auprès de*) the Palestinians and—not as explicitly—when he recounts how he walked among (*auprès de*) the corpses in Shatila. Perhaps most remarkably, Genet's entire politics of truth, to the extent that it is inseparable from "going with" or "walking among" stateless peoples, might only be understood through a reading of this discreet motif. Further, as we'll soon see, this motif links the politics of truth to the logic of divine warfare.

The irony of the answer that the ad gives to the question of the enemy's size has to do with the difficulty of determining the size of a

man as a man between men. "From man to man" suggests a peaceful exchange between subjects, citizens, or equals—an exchange that
should render differences in size irrelevant. The only measure that
matters in such an exchange is the measure of man himself, which, as
the measure of all things, is itself properly measureless.

The conventions of the personal ad often prescribe inclusion of
physical description, either of the addresser or of the desired addressee.
Such descriptions almost invariably include specifications of size or
measurements (height, weight, clothing size, shoe size), usually with
some mention of color (hair, eyes, skin, etc.). In Genet's ad, however,
the addresser offers nothing of himself but the address to the other.
About the addressee, in turn, it specifies only that he should have a
size—the size of a man—and a strange color ("A very tender green
like a cherry with effervescent purple") but nothing about features
or traits. Genet has thereby subtracted from this minor genre all that
might connect it to the art of resemblance—such as the landscape or
the portrait.

The landscape and the portrait are the primary artistic presenta-
tions of the measure of man. In certain landscapes, the figure of a
human being will be included to give a sense of scale—not size but
scale, that is, the size of things determined only with respect to the
measureless measure of man.[30] And the function of the portrait is to
make the size of the picture irrelevant. There is a profusion of minia-
tures and fewer huge portraits (e.g., Chuck Close). But there is no portrait that claims to resemble the "actual size" of its subject. Is it even
possible to *resemble* a size? Portraiture is the painting of the absolute;
it is the resemblance of *the subject*. Resemblance is produced even if
the picture is huge or miniature and even if a huge portrait is reproduced in miniature or vice versa.[31] What Genet offers, then, is not
a description that gives an image of a person but the description of
a person without an image. Or, paradoxically, the description of an
image. A minimal *ekphrasis*. Without an image, there is no way to
distinguish between the description of a person and the description of
an image. In either case, one can only describe what the image itself
should render superfluous—such as size.

Size turns out to be the exact measure of the absolute. A measure
that inheres, not in the image, but in the circulation of the copy of the
image and the copy of the copy. The simulacrum.[32] Although a portrait resembles its subject no matter its size, a copy of the same portrait will always be generated as a copy of a certain size. It is because

the original itself has a specific size that one can claim it to be a virtual copy—not of its subject, whose resemblance it will always preserve, but of itself. Moreover, the same could be said of anyone or anything that has a size. But, in the case of Genet's ad, the importance of the simulacrum has less to do with the epistemological vertigo that it introduces into the world picture than with the material separation and the finitude of the image. Each copy has its own size, its own exact measurement. Even if this size can be infinitely duplicated it can never be imitated. Even if one copy is the same size as another, this sameness is not that of imitation. It is literally the same size, reproduced without analogy. The reproduction of *different* copies—different in their separation, not in their appearance. Such reproduction is what allows for the circulation of the image, for its archivization, but also for its disappearance—for instance, through its destruction or its theft.[33] Simulation is the mortality of the image. A simulacrum is a mortal image. While resemblance cannot be destroyed, copies of the image that resembles can be destroyed as rapidly and as long as they are reproduced.

The ad thus figures the declared enemy as a person without an image, or as the copy of an image. In this respect, the text adheres to a specific political logic. One might, for example, read Carl Schmitt's attempt to separate the political enemy from moral and aesthetic categories as the reduction of the image to the dimensions of the simulacrum. There is no portrait of the enemy. The enemy will never resemble "the enemy." This reduction is not a phenomenological operation but occurs through the *intensity* of antagonism that Schmitt identifies with the political as such.

> The enemy need not be morally evil or aesthetically ugly; he need not appear as an economic competitor, and it may even be advantageous to engage with him in business transactions. But he is, nevertheless, the other, the stranger; and it is sufficient for his nature that he is, in a specially intense way, existentially something different and alien, so that in the extreme case combat with him is possible.[34]

It is as an image of a certain size, as a simulacrum, that an image—or a person—becomes an enemy vulnerable to its enemy. When Genet makes a man's presentation of himself "man to man" into the measure of his size, this gesture implicitly strips man of his stature as the measure of all things and makes him into the measure of the size of the other man—as Schmitt says, his "existential difference." And he thus reduces man to the dimensions of his finitude, to a copy of a man. "Man to man" comes to mean between one copy and another. Between men who have measure in common but not humanity. The one and the other man can no longer confidently dispense with measure in the name of an equality established with reference to a measureless standard. Strictly speaking, the *inadequate* enemy: not just the enemy who is not equal to combat but also the enemy of a size beyond the measure of equality.[35] Each man is now a quantum to the other—which is to say an *other* to the other, of measurable force but unknown intentions.

A man of certain size is what man becomes in the light of an invisible world. The relation between men thus turns into an occasion for literally sizing the other up (and for sizing oneself up in relation to the other): for attempting to divine what remains unknown about him and, failing that, to measure his size and strength. In other words, the relation between subjects becomes a relation between enemies. Genet's "humanism of the other man" (to borrow a phrase—perhaps ironically—from Emmanuel Lévinas) would be a humanism of the enemy to the extent that relation is a measurement of size rather than the welcoming of the face.[36]

The reference to humanism is not entirely amiss in this conflictual space. Genet's ad does not only reduce the measure of man to the size of an other marked for defeat; it asks that this defeat be internal to the other as such. Again, the enemy that the ad seeks is the inadequate enemy. Not only the enemy who is unequal to combat but also the enemy who inadequacy elides combat altogether, "comes to capitulate," "defeated by me before he even knows me." On the one hand, then, the inadequacy of the enemy would refer to his size, which is constitutively inadequate with respect to the measureless measure of human equality. On the other hand, this inadequacy would refer to the a priori capitulation—subjugation without combat—of the enemy to the enemy whose violence precedes him. Precedes both the one and the other: a subjugation that precedes the ability of the one to know who it is that violates him and that precedes any actual violation on the part of the other. The aggressor in this strange scenario is not the declared enemy who comes to capitulate, because, as the ad stipulates, he should not directly defeat himself but rather should offer himself to be defeated. Nor, however, is the aggressor the "I" who demands that the enemy be defeated by "me"; for this "I" contributes nothing to the defeat—except the

violence or the "bestiality" whereby it is accomplished (thus a violence without action). Moreover—and very important—the aggressor is not the hypothetical sovereign who declared the enemy in
the first place. This declaration only has a shadow presence in the
text of the ad, invoked only in the past tense; an act already performed elsewhere than in the space of the ad's address. The declaration corresponds to the space of official hostilities, while the ad
addresses a hostility without declaration and without combat (and
without space other than the address itself). Indeed, it seems that
the ad *seeks* the declared enemy in particular—the public enemy—
in order to uphold this other hostility *against* the openly declared
hostility that pertains to the political realm. It seeks this hostility
in the enemy in much the same way that, according to a traditional
narrative turn, the defeated adversary himself seeks to capitulate
to his own weapon before he falls into the hands of the victors.[37]
The addresser of the ad claims to separate his "bestiality" from his
action, and from his will, in order to offer himself, not as the victor,
but as a weapon that the enemy would turn against himself in order
to access a glory beyond the conquest of any victor.

That the publicly declared enemy must be *sought* at all, that he
must be addressed, is already an indication that he is sought as
something other than what he is called. What the addresser seeks
in the "declared enemy" is the other enemy who has been defeated
without declaration, and who thus withdraws no less from open
combat than from competition between private adversaries; both
from the status of public enemy (*hostis*) and that of private enemy
(*inimicus*).[38]

But one would also have to say that Genet's search for the
declared enemy implies that such an enemy is scarce. Ultimately, it
isn't another enemy than the public enemy himself who withdraws
from combat: the capitulation of the enemy described in the ad is
nothing other than the withdrawal of the declared enemy as such.
Without the presence of such an enemy, the extreme situation of war
also becomes impossible to determine; and without the possibility
of war, in Schmitt's terms, the political as such must be lacking.
Playing with the discreet address of the *petite annonce*, Genet thus
stages what Schmitt calls "depoliticization."[39] It is as if the process
of depoliticization culminated in the personal ad itself—without
putting an end to the enemy. Seriously and unseriously, he declares
war on (and in) war.

IX

It is through the address itself that the addresser reduces himself to a weapon. The subjugation of the enemy is no more the action of the weapon than the response of the addressee to the address is the action of the addresser. Genet's personal ad dramatizes the mechanism of the personal ad itself—exposing the mechanism of the thing, stripping it of that which makes this form of address seductive and reassuring—the image. Genet's claim that he seeks only a suitable enemy amounts to the demand for someone who does not make the delivery of an image into the condition of his response to the letter. Someone who responds unconditionally to the letter itself. Someone whose response is strictly to the letter, to the letter of the letter. One might paraphrase Genet's text in terms of what is ultimately the stark message of every personal ad: I am seeking anyone who responds to this letter. Anyone who accepts being the one who responds no matter what, regardless of who he believes he is and who he believes that the one who addresses him wants him to be.

What the addresser of the ad seeks, therefore, is the unconditional, even the measureless—not the measurelessness of the measure of man, but *a movement beyond measure immanent to the exact measurement of the size of a man*. Inadequation: on the one hand, it is the reduction of the enemy to the size of a man "so that" (as Schmitt says) combat with him is possible and the a priori capitulation that precedes any possible victory, whereby the enemy opens hostilities by withdrawing himself from them; on the other hand, it is the worthlessness of the copy that permits its distribution, and exchange, or confers it to unchecked destruction.

The more one speaks of such spontaneous defeat, the more one begins to wonder to whom the victory must redound. If neither enemy acts upon the other, could it not be imputed to God? The more the inadequacy of the enemy is absolute, the more glorious becomes divine victory. The more the key to his own existence is lacking, the more the enemy is penetrated by the mystery of God.

The weapon manifests divine presence. In biblical passages that describe the fall of the enemy before the army of the Israelites, it is precisely the "sword" or, more specifically, the "edge of the sword" that figures the dominance of unopposed sovereign violence. Among many passages, one might cite one from the book of Joshua (6:20): "So the people shouted and the trumpets were blown. As soon as the people heard the sound of the trumpets, they raised a great shout, and the wall fell down flat; so the people charged straight ahead into the city and captured it. Then they devoted to destruction by the edge of the sword all in the city, both men and women, young and old, oxen, sheep, and donkeys."

The question now is whether absolute capitulation of the enemy is in fact an opening, as I have been arguing, or the exact contrary—the abdication of any opening whatsoever. For the horizon of divine victory tends to reterritorialize the enemy under a public declaration. When the addresser separates himself from his own brutality, and when God becomes the agent of defeat, the enemy then becomes the openly declared enemy of God. It is precisely such combat without combat, in which neither side actually fights the other, that distinguishes the "institution" of holy war. In *Holy War in Ancient Israel,* the biblical scholar Gerhard von Rad extracts the constituents of this institution from the Hebrew Bible: (1) the Israelite army constitutes the people of Yahweh; (2) the wars that they fight are declared to be Yahweh's wars against Yahweh's enemies; and, finally, (3) Yahweh is the one who "gives" the enemy into the hands of the battalions. Holy war is thus a strange institution in which, despite a clash of enemies that consigns whole cities to destruction, God himself emerges as the only agent. According to von Rad, the oracle that Moses delivers to the people at the Red Sea is the clearest articulation of the holy war tradition. When the Israelites fearfully complain that it would be better to serve the Egyptians than to die in the desert, Moses replies:

> Do no be afraid, stand firm, and see the deliverance that Yahweh will accomplish for you today; for the Egyptians whom you see today you shall never see again. Yahweh will fight for you, and you have only to keep still. (Exodus 14:13–14)

This is, at least, how the coming war will appear to the eventual victor. On the side of the enemy—much as in Genet's ad—the mere representation of the event induces panic or total loss of courage. For example, after harboring Joshua's spies in Jericho, Rahab comes and speaks to them of the legend of what Yahweh did for the Israelites at the Red Sea.

> I know that Yahweh has given you the land, and that dread of you has fallen on us, and that all the inhabitants of the land melt in fear before you. For we have heard how Yahweh dried up the water of the Red Sea. . . . As soon as we heard it our hearts melted, and there was no courage left in us because of you. (Joshua 2:8–12)

Another example in the same vein from Leviticus is especially relevant to the present discussion because it describes the torment that Yahweh plans for the Israelites themselves—but also because it projects the loss of courage as a defeat without struggle that will come from within.

> As for those of you who survive, I will send faintness into their hearts in the lands of their enemies; the sound of the driven leaf shall put them to flight, and they shall flee as one flees from the sword, and they shall fall though no one pursues. They shall stumble over one another, as if to escape a sword, though no one pursues; and you shall have no power against your enemies. You shall perish among the nations and the land of your enemies shall devour you. (Leviticus 26:36–38)

The one whom Genet calls the "declared enemy," therefore, is the enemy of God. The open letter itself would be the form in which the "person" (rather than the people) of God "stands firm" or "keeps still" and opens the way for God to do battle. Alternately, it would be the form in which God "in person" keeps still—literally does nothing but wait for the enemy to defeat himself. In this sense, Genet's ad appears faithfully to disguise the lines from Leviticus as a person-to-person communication cut to the measure of the modern public sphere. "I seek the one with faintness in his heart in the lands of his enemy; the one whom the sound of the driven leaf puts to flight; the one who flees as one flees from a sword, who falls though no one pursues him; the one who comes only to stumble over himself, who is powerless against his enemy. He shall perish in exile and be devoured by animals in the land of his enemies." The difference between the personal ad and a holy war, however, is not that it takes place between man and man but rather that its address takes the form of a search. Although the Hebrew Bible abounds in instances where God addresses one particular man or engages in a struggle with him (e.g., Moses on Sinai, Jacob wrestling with the Angel, the ordeals of Job), there are fewer, if any, places where God seeks a man but cannot find him.

Abraham Joshua Heschel has proposed a reading of the Bible that inverts the traditional relation between man and God: man does not seek God; God goes in search of man. More remarkably, this search is articulated as a manhunt. "The Bible speaks not only of man's seach for God but also of God's search for man. 'Thou dost hunt me like a lion,' exclaimed Job (10:16). . . . 'From the very start Thou didst single out man and consider him worthy to stand in Thy presence.' This

is the mysterious paradox of biblical faith: God is pursuing man."[40]
Hunting or pursuing, however, is different from searching. Though
the prey may not yet have been killed or caught, hunting presupposes
that he has been found. As the saying goes, he can run, but he cannot
hide. The enemy is the form in which man is never lost to God. Holy
war would then be the form in which human history bears witness
that man has (always already) been found. Were God truly to be in
search of man, such a search would imply the loss of man, loss that
would precede and remain irreducible to the Fall; and such a man
would have to remain unfound, if not unfindable. He would be the
last man to come before the first man. The open letter of the personal
ad implies such a search. The address to the declared enemy does not
only advertise the lack of the other man. More radically, it declares
the lack of the enemy—the lack of the form in which man has always
been accessible to God's pursuit. In this sense, the letter supposes the
death of God—if the death of God is inseparable from the death of
man before he became the object of God's desire. The ad does not
seek the enemy so that he will be defeated at the hands of God; it
seeks the enemy who will literally find himself and defeat himself. The
open letter is there to prevent this defeat from being ascribed to any
instance of divine terror; it stands in the way of mistaking the enemy's
capitulation for a hyperbolic act of self-immolation in which he identifies himself with the sovereign power that destroys him.

The advertisement subordinates the entire scene of holy war to the
dimension of the letter. In order to capitulate, the enemy must first
come; he must respond to the letter. This response is of an order different from the scene of capitulation that it promises to open. Whereas
this effortless capitulation upholds the threat of divine violence, the
mere response to the letter presupposes the death of God; or rather,
what perhaps amounts to the same thing, it presupposes the restriction of God's action to what remains within the uncreated horizon
(without horizon) of the letter.

Holy war resolves the predicament wherein the addressee must
respond to the naked invitation to respond, to respond without
answers to someone without answers. The one who comes to capitulate, in the absence of any one who could give him access to his truth,
yields to the other, not as the one who promises him his truth, but
as the final abdication of his truth. In return, the other, rather than
promise access, consecrates God's declaration of the enemy with the
laziness of his own aggression. Indeed, the function of the declaration

is to render truth permanently inaccessible: the enemy is the "total enemy," eventually a mere casualty of war.

Truth becomes eminently inaccessible when the declaration of the enemy is rendered with the complicity of God. In a short documentary on Abbas Kiarostami, the Iranian filmmaker is asked whether he believes in God. He responds angrily that this question is the most intimate question that one can ask another person. He says that he would never answer, adding that it is not a question that one should ever ask. The capitulation of the enemy named in Genet's text is the opposite of this position. Rather than uphold an intimate truth that lies with God, it asserts that God is precisely the absolute obstacle to the truth. He is the warrior God to whom the subject is anathema.

The final torture that J.G. promises to lavish upon the enemy ("sleep in place of me, live in place of me") also pertains to the logic of the declaration, in that this torture consists in the radical annihilation of the distance from which the promise of the letter emerges (and the distance in which an absolute hostility might detach itself from all declared hostility—even that of God). The promise of this torture obeys a strange logic, almost the opposite of Saint Paul's famous lines on the opportunism of sin from his letter to the Romans (chap. 7). Sin—the enemy—seizes the opportunity of the flesh to divide the self from itself, and thus shows itself as the opening of the horizon upon which the messiah will appear. But the ad promises that the self will forcibly substitute itself for the enemy in order definitively to separate him from the horizon of truth.

What happens to the politics of truth in the face of a hostile God? The most powerful answer to this question is the Christian answer, elaborated by Saint Paul. This answer could be briefly formulated in the following way: God destroys his enemies in the name of the law. In this respect, Paul's displacement of the Judaic tradition is clear; in his theology, the defeat of the enemy is no longer a victory for God himself but for the law.

This displacement entails the reinvention of the people of God. After the death and resurrection of the messiah, the people of God are no longer those who belong to the tradition of the law but those who follow the law whether or not they are inheritors of the tradition. Accordingly, the enemies of God are no longer the enemies of the historically constituted people of Israel but the enemies of the law itself—that is, not the enemies of the law as the sacred extension of a people but the enemies of the praxis of the law and the goals of this praxis. Paul calls such enemies "sinners." As a result of this shift, however, the enemy is no longer simply defined in terms of political conflicts (ethnic, national, territorial disputes), but is now defined in terms of ethical praxis. For example, Paul would never recognize the possibility that a people or a nation as such would be constitutively incapable of adhering to the commandments enumerated in the Torah or would refuse to adhere to them. Sin is not an attribute; it is a defect, or a failing, and it is always to be distinguished from an attribute. This distinction is what is at stake in Paul's demonstration that sin proliferates through a failing in the logic of the law itself. The point of this demonstration—and the reason that Paul absolutely cannot do without reference to the law and the Jewish tradition—is not to denounce the law, once again to uphold the spirit over the letter, and so on; it is rather to prevent sin from ever being understood as a determinate attribute (for the positing of universal sinfulness is the basis for the reconstitution of the people of God). The culmination of this argument is Romans 7:13, where Paul comes to the defense of the law as itself the measurelessness of sin: "It was sin, working death in me through what is good, in order that sin might be shown to be sin, and through the commandment might become sinful without measure."

This reinvention of the people entails a new concept of holy war. No longer the armed struggle for the victory of the people of God over the enemies of God, holy war becomes the unarmed struggle against the power of sin (sometimes figured as the ultimate Enemy). "Indeed, we live as human beings, but we do not wage war according to human standards; for the weapons of our warfare are not merely human, but they have the divine power to destroy strongholds. We destroy arguments and every proud obstacle raised up against the knowledge of God, and we take every thought captive to obey Christ. We are ready to punish every disobedience when your obedience is complete" (2 Corinthians 10:2–6).[41] No longer the struggle of the people of God, that is, the people to whom God gave the law, against *its* enemies, it is now a struggle that takes place within the measureless horizon opened by the law itself (or even by the reading of the law). Accordingly, the goal of such a war is not merely military victory, but a measureless obedience. What this means, however—and this is the crux of Paul's transformation of the tradition—is that God's own belligerence takes place within the horizon of the law; God himself is submitted to the law. The sacrifice of Christ is the form in which God

folds himself into a horizon that he created. Salvation, as the victory
of God over sin and death, does not only mean the redemption of the
human condition but is also the sign of God's own obedience. "For
God has done what the law, weakened by the flesh, could not do: by
sending his own Son in the likeness of sinful flesh, and to deal with
sin, he condemned sin in the flesh, so that the just requirement of the
law might be fulfilled in us" (Romans 8:3–4). This restricted belligerence—restricted but thereby measureless—is what Paul calls *the fulfillment of the law.*[42]

To an extent, Genet's ad opens within the horizon of this belligerence. Just as Paul upholds an infinite holy warfare against all temporal powers, so Genet upholds the hostilities that seem to happen
of their own accord in the relation between addresser and addressee
against the sovereign declaration of the enemy. Further, in each case,
the agency of this differend is the letter. For Paul, the letter of the
law. For Genet, the open letter of the advertisement. The same logic
is legible in an article from 1968 on the Vietnam War, "A Salute to
100,000 Stars," that Genet wrote for *Esquire*.[43] The article opens
with the interrogation, "Americans, have you fallen asleep?" And it
finishes with this "afterthought":

> You can take comfort in the thought that it was not the Americans,
> who for the most part invented everything, who invented death. And
> in any case the Vietcong, like the Americans, and like all men every-
> where, must die. If there has been a great deal of talk since Nietzsche
> about the death of God, one must bear in mind the thought that it
> was God who started it all by decreeing the death of man. Yes. But if
> that is true, and this seems to me vitally important, every man who
> kills makes himself the accomplice of God, or, what comes to the
> same thing, his instrument, as the Inquisitors were wont to say. On
> this point, the Bibles on your night tables, to which you turn for guid-
> ance, will give you the latest word. But what if God were really dead?
> Personally I have no knowledge of the matter, but it appears indeed as
> if he were hiding for the moment. And what if God were really dead?

Genet upholds the measurelessness of divine violence—the universality of death—against the limited violence—militarily inflicted
death—of specific authorities and powers (i.e., the American government). Even such powers must ally themselves with God in order to
kill their enemies—which means that, in the very act of asserting their
power, they cede the ultimate victory to God himself; no matter their
intentions, they end up participating in the salvation of the enemy
rather than his destruction. As in Paul, the paradoxical confirmation

of this structural victory would be God's own submission to the horizon that he opens. This submission Genet seems to call "the death
of God." In order for the saving violence to be truly measureless,
God too must die. When he reaches this paradox, Genet breaks off,
because the consequences of his thought become numerous and con-
tradictory. On the one hand, the death of God would mean the withdrawal of the safeguard against the sovereignty of temporal powers: it
turns out that one's life actually does belong to those with the monopoly of force. On the other hand, the death of God would give to death
itself a transcendence that no longer needs divine protection. But the
question then is whether such transcendence is still divine, whether
its invulnerability is a correlate of divine victory; in other words,
whether it is just a refined nihilism or whether it is has the dimensions
of a hostility without victory, a measurelessness closer to the size of
man (i.e., the death drive).

CHAPTER THREE

Mayhem

Symbolic Violence and the Culture of the Death Drive

'What are you bringing me,' she cried,
'riding so fast?' 'War and death,' he replied.

—Torquato Tasso, *Jerusalem Delivered*

The fact that slaughter is a horrifying spectacle must make us take war
more seriously, but not provide an excuse for gradually blunting our swords
in the name of humanity. Sooner or later someone will come along with a
sharp sword and hack our arms off.

—Carl von Clausewitz, *On War*

The attempt to theorize or master war, to subordinate it to absolute knowledge, becomes a way of perpetuating or repeating war itself. But to suggest
that war is in some sense the repressed of its own conceptualization—that
is, of any attempt to think it—might be a way of explaining why we are
never prepared for the full horror of war.

—Jacqueline Rose, *Why War?*

WAR AND DEATH

It is axiomatic that war entails killing and death. Even if we have
never had firsthand experience of war and even if no one in our
families or communities has ever died in war, we know this to be
the case. Lenin famously presaged that twentieth-century imperialism would yield an era of wars and revolutions. The ensuing
wars and revolutions did not fail to reconfigure the entire world—
"globalizing" it in the process. But these conflicts also brought to
light an even more encompassing history: the history of war and
death.

The Cold War, Hannah Arendt suggests in the opening pages
of *On Revolution*, constitutes the historical moment at which

war-and-death emerges as the ultimate horizon of human history and politics; for it "poses the threat of total annihilation through war against the hope for the emancipation of all mankind through revolution."[1] At least in the twentieth and twenty-first centuries, war-and-death is one of the most frequently told stories. Or rather, it is a story we know without knowing who told it, as if it were transmitted without ever being properly recounted. To the extent that it has no determinable origin, this story is analogous to myth. But this story, so we are told, is not a myth; it is a true story, and there might be none truer. It is an undeniable fact. Through knowledge of this fact, we—citizens of the world—are expected to recognize our embeddedness in world history. To accept this fact, then, amounts to nothing less than owning the historicity of our own existence. At the same time, precisely because the fact of war and death is undeniable, we don't often remember that we know it; we don't often grasp that we have already accepted it as fact until we are confronted with an attempt to erase it. "We don't do body counts," General Tommy Franks famously declared in the first moments of the Iraq war.[2] It might turn out, however, that the dissemination of this story is so pervasive and omnipresent—as if the channels of intersubjective transmission were opened for the sole purpose of rehashing it—because it can never be presumed that "we" have accepted it once and for all and, consequently, that we never share an adequate sense of historical fact. There is always something within us that denies the undeniable. "In the unconscious," Sigmund Freud wrote just after the outbreak of World War I, "each of us is convinced of his own immortality."[3]

In response to a primordial disavowal of mortality, then, the story of war and death restores our sense of finitude and history. But this same story has another, related function: it establishes what Adi Ophir has called an "order of evils."[4] Beyond imposing death as the utmost fact, the history of war also entails the premise that killing is the most extreme or the worst form of political violence. War teaches us that the real corresponds to the extreme. For those who already uphold the validity of this premise (and we all do, to a certain extent) it does no more than restore killing to its rightful position and thereby make it possible—for political and military leaders, soldiers, and civilians—to calculate the (political *and* human) toll of war. To consider killing as anything less than the worst would be to take it and war—in which it plays a central role—too lightly. Not to predicate killing as the worst would be to pretend that it's something other than killing.

In direct opposition to General Franks's declaration, for instance, the Iraq Body Count Project (IBC) keeps an ongoing record, compiled in accordance with the most rigorous standards of modern information gathering, of "the violent civilian deaths that have resulted from the 2003 military intervention in Iraq," the function of which is to establish death as an incontestable reality and thereby to restore this reality to its proper place in contemporary war; or, more brutally put, to show that contemporary war remains *war* in the strong sense (i.e., Hell).[5] IBC presents itself as an antiwar initiative; it proceeds as though restoring the severed connection between war and death is tantamount to denouncing war as such, and, further, as though denouncing war were the same thing as opposing it. In actuality, its project is more basic and more ambivalent. The victims of war and those who speak against war on their behalf do not have the monopoly on antiwar discourse. Many of the most resounding maledictions of war come from political and military leaders, the same individuals who are responsible for launching attacks that result in vast death and destruction. In his September 12, 1864, letter to Atlanta mayor James M. Calhoun, for example, William Tecumseh Sherman wrote: "You cannot qualify war in harsher terms than I will. War is cruelty, and you cannot refine it; and those who brought war into our country deserve all the curses and maledictions that a people can pour out."[6] Has anyone who has ever been directly involved in the project of war not denounced war? Isn't there an element of resistance to war that is inseparable from the pursuit of war? Even and especially for the most hawkish hawks, would it be possible to wage war without hating it properly—that is, without refusing to underestimate the true cost of war (even if this refusal takes the form of attempting to foist this cost and its calculation entirely upon the enemy)?[7]

With and against this profoundly compelling story, however, I would like to explore the ways in which it might be necessary, in order to understand the phenomenon of war in general but especially the wars of the twentieth and twenty-first centuries, to unlink war from the act of killing and death. This is not to disavow that people die in wars. On the contrary, I would like to suggest that, even when the death toll is massive, killing is the least that happens and that the traditional, if not ideological, connection between war and death functions to disavow the range of violence that stops short of killing

Figure 3.1. Francisco Jose de Goya y Lucientes (1746–1828), *Esto es peor*
[This is worse], plate 37 of *Los desastres de la guerra* [The Disasters of
War], 1810–14, pub. 1863, etching 15.7 x 20.8 cm. (Private Collection)

the enemy, that deprives him of a proper death, or that does not cease
to violate his body, his home, or his culture after his death.

There is perhaps no better place to begin thinking about violence
than two analogous plates from Francisco de Goya's series of etchings
Los desastres de la guerra (The Disasters of War). The first of these
(no. 37), bearing the hyperbolic caption, *Esto est peor* (This is worse),
and the other (no. 39), bearing the difficult caption, *¡Grande hazaña!
¡Con muertos!* (A heroic feat! With dead men!), both represent postmortem violence committed by Napoleon's soldiers against the dead
bodies of Spanish partisans (see figures 3.1 and 3.2).

The foreground of the first image shows an armless body impaled
through the anus by the broken trunk of a dead tree; in the background, uniformed soldiers toil with dead bodies and sabers. The
second image shows at least three male corpses—all castrated—also
strung up on a broken tree. One man hangs from the tree's trunk
upside down, feet high, his neck and shoulders uncomfortably drag-
ging along the ground near the feet of another corpse tied upright to
the same trunk. The latter man's dead head sinks down toward the
open wound where his penis used to be. Following the rhythm of inver-
sions established by the first two figures, then, the third—decapitated

Figure 3.2. Francisco Jose de Goya y Lucientes (1746–1828), *Grande hazaña! Con muertos!* [Great deeds! With the Dead!], plate 39 of *Los desastres de la guerra* [The Disasters of War], 1810–14, pub. 1863, etching. 15.6 x 20.8 cm. (Private Collection).

and armless in addition to being castrated—hangs upside down from a branch with his *own* head at his feet. Next to the clenched face, two arms hang from the fingertips, bound together.

Although the Spanish caption that accompanies the latter picture clearly reads, *"con muertos,"* "with dead men," the vast majority of English translations evidence confusion about how best to translate these words. The Dover edition of the etchings, originally published in 1967, translates the caption to plate 39 in this way: "Great deeds—against the dead!"; and reproductions of the image in Anglophone contexts mostly conform to this translation.[8] In particular, Jake and Dinos Chapman produced several infamous appropriations of the image—such as the 1994 sculpture, *"Great Deeds! Against the Dead!"*—which adopt the same translation of this caption. *Con*— "with"—is thus consistently mistranslated as "against" (which in Spanish would be *contra*). Like most mistranslations, this one makes all too much sense; and its hubris bears witness not so much to the limits of the English language (since there is no linguistic reason why *con* should not be translated as "with" in this context) as to the limits of traditional concepts of violence. We possess no language for articulating violence whose object is the nonliving. It would seem that, precisely because such violence—which is, structurally speaking, violence committed both before and after death—can no longer be understood in terms of a contest between opposite living forces, it puts the observer into the grammatically uncomfortable position of conceiving deeds committed *with* the dead. This position would also be politically uncomfortable. The illogical logic of grammar suggests that the space of conflict has been disordered or dismembered along with the bodies whose fate it predicates: this is an act of war that disregards the identity of opposing "sides" and therefore appears to be driven by an objective that goes beyond the search for strategically valuable targets and ultimately beyond military victory.

Mayhem would be the right word to designate the political chaos produced by the irruption of violence that does not appear to have any predetermined aim or object, violence that it would be impossible to anticipate, calculate, intercept, or inhibit. But the word is doubly appropriate in the case of Goya's image because it also refers to a specific act: to commit mayhem simply means to maim or to dismember; to ruin the bodily integrity of the enemy in order to compromise his ability to defend himself. It would only be necessary to add to these dictionary definitions that the specificity of this act lies in the fact that it does not suppose any distinction between living and dead bodies; and, therefore, that it is not merely a matter of depriving the enemy of his defenses but also, more radically, of confronting him with a primordial defenselessness that necessarily preceded his (or her) ability to mount a defense.

The irony of Goya's exclamation—"Great deeds! With the dead!"—is no doubt meant to display the point at which acts of potential courage turn into a kind of barbaric cowardliness. But it also suggests that the "great deeds" in question, because they cannot oppose the dead, aim *with* and *through* the bodies of the dead *at* some other target. The theatricality of the way in which the bodies are arranged for display suggests that these deeds can only reach their intended target via an aesthetic address—or, at least, an address that co-opts an aesthetic space. Susan Sontag has cited Goya as the exemplary witness to the "pain of others," to the human suffering that results from war: "With Goya, a new standard for responsiveness to suffering enters art."[9] In Sontag's analysis, the *Disasters* stage a confrontation with (and within) their ostensible viewer, inviting her to look at atrocities from which she (or something in her) would naturally avert her gaze. Goya's famous captions—such as "One can't look" (*No se puede mirar*)—thus acknowledge the inner struggle that the images are bound to produce, the better to urge (or seduce) the viewer to overcome her spontaneous inclinations in the name of the greater good. "While the image, like every image, is an invitation to look," Sontag writes, "the caption, more often than not, insists on the difficulty of doing just that. A voice, presumably the artist's, badgers the viewer: can you bear to look at this?"[10] Sontag's analysis of looking at war images is prudent and subtle. But Goya's captions do more than demand that we *look*. They demand that we *read*—especially in the case of grammatically and performatively unstable captions like the one that is my focus. "Great deeds! With the dead!" is not about responsiveness to suffering. Accordingly, this image and its caption are not merely about war, but rather the *transformation* of war. Great deeds, Goya tells us, are no longer great. Rather than a response to the pain of others, then, the artist's excoriating irony marks an excess in the use of force, a suffering beyond pain, beyond pleasure, and, indeed, very precisely, beyond the pleasure principle. It marks the specific passage from killing to overkill, from sacrifice to desecration, and from war to theater—or rather, from war to a theater that is no longer the theater of war.

From Tragic Irony to Political Irony

To a certain extent, Goya's irony evokes the tradition of tragic irony. However, in order to grasp the specific psychic and political meaning of his image, it is important to distinguish the scene of war after death from a scene of tragic misrecognition. Were it not for Goya's caption to the one image, there would be no way of knowing, or we might not even think to conclude, that these corpses were violated after death—violated *as* corpses. And the standard (mis)translation of the double exclamation proceeds to repress this knowledge. What Goya explicitly represents as a premeditated atrocity, the translation renders as a misguided act of valor. If the great deeds were *against* the dead, this construction suggests a battlefield scene in which combatants—misguided by hallucination or the so-called fog of war—would fail to perceive the moment of the others' (or even their own)[11] death and thus continue to fight even after the conflict should have ended.

In the Sophocles tragedy named after him, Ajax awakens from a hallucinatory battle against his former compatriots to discover that he has, in fact, slaughtered a host of cattle. Goya's image, too, might well represent such a moment of discovery, its irony giving voice to the horrified self-consciousness that arises within the soldier himself—or perhaps the witness who must now share the legacy of this violence—upon perceiving that all his heroic efforts ("great deeds") amount to nothing but atrocity, that they were expended upon utterly defenseless—beyond defenseless—victims rather than equals in war.

The narrative of hallucination and its aftermath reduces "Great deeds! With the dead!" to a traditional antiwar statement. War justifies violence by staging it in the form of conflict, struggle, resistance, distinction, and opposition. Without real opposition, violence cannot be justified. This statement thus contends that violence is never justified precisely because there is no such thing as *real* opposition. Opposition is always an illusion that ineluctably gets dispelled at war's end or perhaps even at battle's end, at which point we must confront the senselessness of our actions. Understood in terms of this statement, then, Goya's etching becomes an allegory of war in which "the dead" stand for the common humanity that must be forgotten in order for human beings to justify war to themselves. But a closer reading of the image and its caption reveal both to be less allegorical. It does not stage, nor does it participate in, any illusion. The atrocity that it depicts is sober, calculated, and instrumental; it is not the tragic outcome of *fighting* against the dead *as if* they were alive but rather the spectacle produced by *doing things with* the dead *as* the dead.

The claim that war is illusion is ultimately predicated upon the myth of war as a frenzy that regularly but temporarily seizes hold of human beings and leads them to destroy one another. The denunciation of war limits itself to discrediting war as such while implicitly justifying the acts of individuals who participate in wars. War itself—everywhere and nowhere—would thus be guilty of the atrocities that individuals commit in its thrall. This myth thus underlies the distinction between killing and murder. Goya, however, imagines the unimaginable: war is not War; ultimately—at the hyperbolic limit in play at every instant ("the worst")—it consists in a series of individual deeds for which individuals themselves could and should be held responsible. In his late récit, *The Instant of My Death*, Maurice Blanchot also suggests as much: "This was war: life for some, for others the cruelty of assassination."[12] War is not a matter of valor and struggle, killing and being killed, but the cruelty of individual violence (and, as Blanchot suggests, cruelty is always a singular act), albeit on a mass scale. Rather than a mythic agency that folds individual will into its implacable movement, providing an iron-clad alibi to all who participate in it, war would thus be never more than a pretext that implicitly gives individuals permission to commit crime. The cruelty that emerges when war ceases to function as an alibi is precisely what Goya calls *disaster*. Rather than tragedy, war is nothing but a string of disasters.

Goya's art is less a matter of *recognition* (what Aristotle called *anagnorisis*) than of *vision*.[13] If the gaze and the voice that inhabit these images could be ascribed to anyone, it would be to the unidentified "seer" who appears in the opening plate, which bears the caption, "Sad presentiments of what has to come" (*Tristes presentimientos de lo que ha de acontecer*). Each image stages the difficulty of looking (à la Sontag) only in order to evoke the unblinking vision of a gaze that cannot look away, helplessly transfixed by the worst. In an important discussion of Goya's political realism, Ian Baucom offers an analysis of the enigmatic image that opens the *Disasters*: "The bleak, foreboding message of Goya's opening plate is that, in the disasters that imperial war visits upon the world[,] . . . time-present and time-future become time-past: what-is and what-is-to-be find themselves brutally replaying what-has-been."[14] Baucom reads Goya's etchings, as I do, as an essential contribution to political theory. The seer's prophetic vision is less a matter of second sight than of political knowledge; these disasters "have to happen" not because they are fated but rather because they are the work of an immanent, sovereign power that is defined by its absolute freedom from any constraint. In other words, the seer's clairvoyance does not come from God or some supernatural instance but rather from the "vision" of man's inescapable self-knowledge (see figure 3.3).

The *Disasters* close with a series of haunting, allegorical etchings, one of which is the necessary counterpart to the opening image and, indeed, to the images of human dismemberment that I have been discussing. The caption that identifies this plate (no. 74) reads: *¡Esto es lo peor!*—"That is the worst of it!" (see figure 3.4).

But this image—unique, in this respect, among all the *Disasters*— also contains a further inscription embedded in the scene it represents. It depicts a snarling wolf of human stature, seated among indistinct huddled masses, with a scroll open in his lap. He is writing. A

Figure. 3.3. Francisco Jose de Goya y Lucientes (1746–1828), *Tristes presentimientos de lo que ha de acontecer* [Sad forebodings of what is to come], plate 1 of *Los desastres de la guerra* [The Disasters of War], 1810–14, pub. 1863, etching 17.8 x 22 cm. (Private Collection)

friar kneels before him (positioned to be the first reader of the writing), seemingly distraught, as he inscribes what appears to be a verdict: *Misera humanidad, la culpa es tuya*—"Miserable humanity, the fault is yours." The downcast eyes of the wolf thus provide the dialectical counterpoint to the upturned gaze of the seer in the opening image. The latter is directed, we presume, not *outward* at an unseen interlocutor but rather *inward* at a series of mental images much like those reproduced in the subsequent pages. Goya shows us the disasters of war from the perspective of a seer who knows what will happen before it actually happens. Each of the images thus represents something that has *already* been seen—seen *inside* a person as opposed to *by* a person; it records both something that *did* happen and something that *must* happen. Thus it becomes impossible to determine whether the declaration, "I saw it" (*Yo lo vi*)—one of the most famous captions—refers to the seeing or the foreseeing of the events. Goya's history is both visionary and documentary. An apocalypse of the past.

Figure 3.4. Francisco Jose de Goya y Lucientes (1746–1828), *Esto es lo peor!* [This is the worst!], plate 74 of *Los desastres de la guerra* [The Disasters of War], 1810-14, pub. 1863, etching. 17.9 x 22 cm. (Private Collection).

The vision of this seer consists of "sad presentiments"; but it is impossible to tell whether what he sees in the future makes him sad or whether sorrow itself is prophetic, whether the one who mourns is the only one who truly sees—without recoiling from—the disasters of war. In keeping with the structure of this vision, however, this "sadness" is provoked, not by the suffering of those whose fate he glimpses, but rather by the irreversibility of this fate. Goya's images confront us less with the pain of others than with their helplessness—and with the helplessness of vision itself to change what it sees. The seer is perpetually exiled from his own field of vision. His power of sight is infinite, but his power of intervention is nil. He can never change what he has seen and is condemned to live with the knowledge of his own powerlessness.

The visual index of this powerlessness, within the etchings themselves, is the heap of bodies—which figures centrally in *Tanto y mas* (All This and More; no. 22); *No hay quien los socorra* (There is no

Figure 3.5. Francisco Jose de Goya y Lucientes (1746–1828), *Muertos recogidos* [Harvest of the dead], plate 63 of *Los desastres de la guerra* [The Disasters of War], 1810–14, pub. 1863, etching 15.5 x 20.8 cm. (Private Collection)

one to help them; no. 60); *Muertos recogidos* (Harvest of the dead; no. 63). Most often, these morbid aggregations appear alone in featureless landscapes without a living being in sight (see figures 3.5 and 3.6).

Other images—such as *Serà lo mismo* (It will be the same; no. 21)—depict soldiers stripping the dead of their valuables, and in so doing they appear to mix with their victims. Their own bodies, although living, are already stocky and moundlike so that, visually, when they bend toward the supine corpses, they collapse into the mass from which they would extract some object of fleeting value.

The so-called Black Paintings—such as *El gran cabrón* (Witches Sabbath), *Atropos* (The Fates), and *Cabezas en un pasaje* (Heads in a Landscape)—feature analogous mounds of hunched figures. The usual horizontality of landscape has been reduced to ground without horizon, ground and background without sky. André Malraux writes that there is no light in Goya but only lighting.[15] Here and there, Goya will insert a half-dead tree or a vague ruin; but it would be more accurate to say that these outcroppings, much like the minimal

Figure 3.6. Francisco Jose de Goya y Lucientes (1746–1828), *No hay quien los socorra* [There is no one to help them], plate 60 of *Los desastres de la guerra* [The Disasters of War], 1810–14, pub. 1863, etching 15.4 x 20.7 cm. (Private Collection)

landscape elements on Beckett's stage, struggle to keep upright rather than strain toward the heavens. Likewise, the ground is nothing but the ground: not earth, terrain, territory, terra firma, land, soil, or even the dust to which all dust returns, but the ground as the placeless place where falling bodies fall, the zero degree of elevation. Ground zero. Behind the body impaled upon the tree in *Esto es peor*, indistinct soldiers appear to toil along or even under the horizon line—as if the horizon corresponded to the edge of a ditch. Another of the Black Paintings, *Duelo a garrotazos* (Duel with Clubs), represents a duel between two immobile men; neither can run or hide because their legs have been buried up to their knees in the hard ground. Even *El perro* (The Dog) follows this same pattern: it is unclear whether the line beneath which the animal seems to sink is sea or land, surge or hole. Perhaps it wasn't the spectacle of bodies in pain that attracted so many people to these images after 9/11 but rather because they transmit something about the essence of ground zero.[16] Each "disaster" would be a *disaster area*—a former place reduced to a zone marked for destruction. What precisely does Goya's seer know? For what fault

Figure 3.7. Francisco Jose de Goya y Lucientes (1746–1828), *Serà lo mismo* [It will be the same], plate 21 of *Los desastres de la guerra* [The Disasters of War], 1810–14, pub. 1863, etching. 14.8 x 21.8 cm. (Private Collection)

precisely must "miserable humanity" bear the blame? The most obvious answer, of course, is that humanity is responsible for its own misery or suffering. There is no transcendental evil or mythical Fall to blame for the disasters that people now endure. A closer reading of plate 39 ("A heroic feat! With dead men!"), however, opens toward a more specific and revealing answer.

As I have suggested, the odd use of the preposition *with* in the etching's caption suggests a form of violence that cannot be narrated as conflict, war, and death. To commit deeds *with* the dead, rather than against them, suggests an intimacy—perhaps what Arjun Appadurai called "intimacy gone berserk"[17]—that cannot be translated into opposition. On the most basic lexical and grammatical level, however, such intimacy might be unrepresentable if not unthinkable. Remarkably, the first and oldest definitions of *with* in the *Oxford English Dictionary* associate the preposition with terms—opposition, resistance, or discord—that make it synonymous with its apparent contrary.[18] *With*, it turns out, means nothing other than *against*. The translation of the one into the other takes place on the level of the word itself, such that the published translations of the *Disasters* would merely repeat and thereby render explicit this primal translation (without translation).

Like *unheimlich* (uncanny), it is what Freud called a "primal word" (*Urwort*) with an "antithetical meaning" (*Gegensinn*)—an antithetical word for antithesis itself.[19] In Goya's language—Spanish—there is an obvious etymological relation between *con* (with) and *contra* (against). In French, one can speak of *separation d'avec soi* or *différence d'avec soi* to indicate an internal scission that separates or opposes me to myself. In English, too, "with" always implies opposition, struggle, and division. One can speak interchangeably of fighting *with* an enemy and of fighting *against* him. But what's at stake in Goya's etching goes beyond the ambivalence of any violent struggle between self and other, whether bellicose or amorous, and even beyond the intimacy of killing.

Violence committed after death ("with dead men") would not be able to achieve separation—assuming that separation is even its goal. Rather than strike out against their object as if from elsewhere, deeds *with* the dead would operate in and through the dead, on their side, which is now our side, as if, through such atrocities, we internalize them and—even more uncannily—they internalize us. To a certain extent, perhaps, these acts do strike against the enemy; but they necessarily do so without reason, result, or benefit—or, at least, without a reason, result, or benefit that can be measured in terms of the traditional logic of war, structured, as Carl Schmitt theorized, by the distinction between friend and enemy. From a strategic or political perspective—and perhaps even from the perspective of the war machine itself—such acts are utterly pointless, nothing more than a waste of valuable time, energy, and resources. And yet I would argue that they seem pointless only because they are incompatible with the avowed goals of war. If such apparently senseless acts are sufficiently disorienting to provoke systematic mistranslation, it is because, like a symptom or acting out, they bear witness to the agency of an "other scene" within the theater of war, a logic of fantasy that both overdetermines and undermines the undeniable reality of war, that constitutes the truth of this reality—thereby demonstrating that the truth of war and its reality do not coincide.

A Third Besides

Like Goya's *Disasters of War*, Heinrich von Kleist's theater took up the challenge of representing the unlimited hostility unleashed in the partisan wars against Napoleon. Schmitt writes in *Theory of the Partisan* that Kleist's *Die Hermannsschlacht* is "the greatest partisan work of all time."[20] But Kleist's *Penthesilea* could also be read as a partisan work, the staging of the "irregular" movement of war beyond war. Upon his return from the scene of the furious battle between Achilles and Penthesilea, Odysseus claims to have witnessed the agency of a "third power" beyond force and counterforce:

> And now begins
> A struggle, friend, such as has not been fought
> Since Gaia loosed the Furies on this world.
> I thought till now that Nature knows but force
> And counterforce, and no third power besides.
> Whatever quenches fire will not bring water
> Seething to a boil, nor vice versa.
> Yet here appears a deadly foe of each,
> Upon whose coming, fire no longer knows
> Whether to trickle with the floods, nor water
> Whether to leap with heaven-licking flame.[21]

These lines present another problem of translation—again, less linguistic than poetic and political. Staying closer to the German, it would be more appropriate simply to write that Odysseus witnessed a "third" (full stop) beyond sheer force and its resistance: "So viel ich weiß, gibt es in der Natur/ Kraft bloß und ihren Widerstand, nichts Drittes" (As far as I know, there is in nature/ . . . no third). The economy of Kleist's verse and the logic of the scene don't clarify whether we should add what the ellipsis leaves suspended, whether the "third" constitutes a power at all. Odysseus claims that his own knowledge is based on nature's instinctual self-knowledge (i.e., "force," *Kraft*): water knows that it quenches fire and always behaves according to this knowledge. But this "third" estranges nature from itself, renders its self-knowledge inoperative: "fire no longer *knows*/ Whether to trickle with the floods, nor water/ Whether to leap with heaven-licking flame." Accordingly, this third thing is a "deadly enemy" (*ein grimmter Feind*) of both force and counterforce. Not simply an enemy force, but the *enemy of force*; an enemy whose advent upsets the invariants that make force a knowable quantity, cannot be fought with force, and thus demands another knowledge than the ("physical") knowledge of nature.

Carl von Clausewitz defined war as a duel, an interaction of forces, whose inner logic results in a transpersonal passage to extremes: "The thesis then must be repeated: war is an act of force, and there is no logical limit to the application of that force. Each side, therefore, compels its opponent to follow suit; a reciprocal action is started which must lead, in theory, to extremes."[22] Each side does his best to do the worst—or, to use an English idiom, "to worst" the other. War is inherently hyperbolic—perhaps even hyper-hyperbolic, the hyperbole of hyperboles. Nonetheless, Kleist ups the ante. As unlimited as war may be, for Clausewitz, it remains bound within the limits of force. War is essentially physical or even psychophysical (although perhaps not psychosomatic). The passage to extremes entails no more than the application of ever more force. Kleist, then, bears witness to the emergence in war of a passage beyond force—and thus beyond the limits that the use of force imposes upon any violent conflict. Kleistian war is anti-Hobbesian. Rather than hearken back to a presocial state of nature, this war is postnatural; and it thereby reveals that, perhaps even in Hobbes, the physical laws of nature already constitute a primordial social institution.

Like Goya's art, Kleist's vision of war continues to resonate in twentieth-century accounts of the worst. Using language that appears to echo Kleist's *Penthesilea*, for example, W. G. Sebald writes the "natural history of destruction" in terms that explicitly underscore the transgression of natural law. His attempt to envision the area bombing of Hamburg in World War II turns upon rhetoric that exchanges the attributes of fire and water. Fire surges like water, and water blazes. Neither "knows" what, according to the laws of nature, it is supposed to do:

> The fire . . . snatched oxygen to itself so violently that the air currents reached hurricane force, resonating like mighty organs with all their stops pulled out at once. The fire burned like this for three hours. At its height, the storm lifted gables and roofs from buildings, flung rafters and entire advertising billboards through the air, tore trees from the ground, and drove human beings before it like living torches. Behind collapsing façades, the flames shot up as high as houses, rolled like a tidal wave through the streets at a speed of over a hundred and fifty miles per hour, spun across open squares in strange rhythms like rolling cylinders of fire. The water in some canals was ablaze. The glass in the tramcar windows melted; stocks of sugar boiled in bakery cellars. . . . Residential districts so large that their total street length amounted to two hundred kilometers were utterly destroyed. Horribly disfigured corpses lay everywhere. Bluish little phosphorous flames still flickered around many of them; others had been roasted brown or purple and reduced to a third of their normal size. They lay doubled up in pools of their own melted fat, which had sometimes

already congealed. . . . Elsewhere, clumps of flesh and bone or whole
heaps of bodies had cooked in water gushing from bursting boilers.
Other victims had been so badly charred and reduced to ashes by the
heat, which had risen to a thousand degrees or more, that the remains
of families consisting of several people could be carried away in a
single laundry basket.[23]

Goya. Kleist. Sebald. These texts all bear witness to the emergence
of another reality—both more and less real—amid the reality of
war or to the passage of force beyond force. Each represents this
other reality in radically different terms, but it remains clear that
they are all evoking the same thing. In *Politics and the Other Scene*,
Étienne Balibar also underscores the role of such a "third term"
in politics. "Power," Balibar writes, deliberately echoing Lacan,
"cannot be all: in fact in essence it is 'not-all,' that is, lacking—
even if we include in it its opposite and adversary, counter-power,
that is, revolution and rebellion, 'anti-systemic' movements, and
so on."[24] Balibar provides yet another name—"with some arbi-
trariness"—for this agency beyond the power principle: cruelty.
Cruelty, he underscores, is something heterogeneous to war insofar as the latter is defined as a conflict between sovereign powers
or violence as an exercise of might or force. The "other scene" of
politics would open at the point where war and violence end and
cruelty begins.

> [A] phenomenology of violence has to deal, at the same time, with
> the intrinsic relationship between violence and power (expressed
> in the term *Gewalt*) and the intrinsic relationship between violence
> and cruelty, which is something else. . . . The phenomenology of
> power implies a spiritual dialectic of power and counter-power,
> state and revolution, orthodoxy and heresy, which, throughout its
> development is composed of violent deeds and relations of violence.
> But it also includes—not beyond or apart from this development—a
> demonstration of cruelty, which is another reality, like the emer-
> gence or glimpse of another scene. Although an essential part of
> the question is to understand why power itself, be it state power,
> colonial domination, or male domination, and so on, has to be not
> only violent or powerful or brutal, but also cruel—why it has to
> derive from itself, and obtain from those who wield it, *jouissance*—
> it seems to me that the key issue is that, contrary to what happens in
> the dialectics of the Spirit, there is nothing like a center, not even a
> centered center, in cruelty.[25]

Goya's "A heroic feat! With dead men!" provides an excellent example of what Balibar calls a "demonstration of cruelty." On the one

hand, the violence depicted in this image takes place in the course of a dialectical conflict between power and counterpower—more specifically, the partisan war between Spanish insurgents and Napoleon's imperial army. On the other hand, it clearly represents a "demonstration of cruelty" that goes beyond the development of this dialectic (the history of struggle, victory, defeat, and the "conversion" of violence into legitimate political order).[26] To the extent that the irony of Goya's caption marks the passage from the great deeds of war to the "great deeds" of cruelty, we could even say that this image seeks to capture the very opening of this scene. It represents acts whose cruelty lies in the attempt to appropriate the space of representation itself, to *enact* the transition between one scene and the other.

But what does it mean to claim that violence with the dead is cruel? Can violence be cruel if its object is not alive? Is cruelty possible without pain or bloodshed? In fact, Balibar's argument helps us to see that violence with the dead is a form of cruelty—perhaps even the exemplary form. And Goya, in turn, helps us to grasp more concretely the specific difference between power and cruelty.

The violence in Goya's image is cruel precisely to the extent to which it is committed *with* the victims after their death. It is utterly gratuitous or redundant, supporting no development, indulged for its own sake. The *jouissance* of which Balibar speaks, which characterizes the act of cruelty, would thus be perfectly embodied in the spectacle of this redundant show of force—assuming that the violence demonstrated in this case can still be grasped in terms of force. The passage from violence against the living (or even against the dead) to violence with the dead, therefore, also signals the passage from the dialectic of power and counterpower to the demonstration of cruelty.

The demonstration of cruelty does not just perform cruel acts out in the open; it consists in an act that is carefully calculated to operate the transition between the reality of war and the other scene. The act of violating the dead demonstrates, quite simply, that the victor cannot be trusted to care for them. In so doing, however, it also flaunts *death itself*—insofar as death functions as a conventional limit to potential hostility in the traditional practice of warfare. The great deeds that Goya depicts, therefore, do not more or less accidentally happen within the framework of war; they represent a concerted attack upon the institution of war itself. If, as I suggested above, these deeds were aimed *with* the dead *at* targets other than dead themselves, this target would be the institution of war itself.

SUBLIMATION AND THE CULTURE OF THE DEATH DRIVE

Balibar's turn to psychoanalysis in order to supplement the phenomenology of violence suggests that a digression on the death drive
would be relevant at this moment. Let us begin, once again, with a
problem of translation. The problem of the death drive *is* the problem of its translation into language and social space. For many years,
the standard English translation of the Freudian concept *Trieb* was
"instinct." The same was true in French translations of Freud. Thus,
der Todestrieb—to take an example that is indispensable to the
present discussion—would be translated as "the death instinct" (or,
in French, "l'instinct de mort"). But, as Jacques Lacan was the first
to insist, a close reading of Freud's texts reveals that *Trieb* has little to do with the traditional concept of instinct. This concept—
which Kleist articulates perfectly—refers to a kind of knowledge
within nature, nature's knowledge of its own laws and its spontaneous adherence to them. The translation of *Trieb* into English as
"drive" or into French as "pulsion" thus emphasizes the fact, which
Freud elaborates in the opening pages of *Three Essays on the Theory of Sexuality,* that it cannot be defined in terms of any inborn
aim or object: "Experience of the cases that are considered abnor-
mal has shown us that in them the sexual drive and the sexual object
are merely soldered together. . . . We are thus warned to loosen the
bond that exists in our thoughts between drive and object." Unlike
instinct, in other words, the drive doesn't know its own laws. As
Freud testifies most famously in the opening paragraphs of *Triebe
und Triebschicksale* (Instincts [*sic*] and Their Vicissitudes, or,
alternately, Drives and Their Destinies), the drive remains among
the most enigmatic objects of psychoanalysis.[27] Since it does not
embody any preexisting knowledge, the knowledge of the drive can
only be constructed through psychoanalytic work. Paradoxically, it
can only be presupposed as a future acquisition. In other words, the
knowledge of the drive—if there is such a thing—lies not in nature
but in the unconscious.

When Goya represents violence after death, when Kleist evokes the
"third" and the "enemy of force and counterforce," or when Sebald
speaks of a tidal wave of fire and rivers ablaze, what's at stake is
the emergence of "the drive" into the psycho-socio-physical space of
war. The *death drive*? Yes and no. Before committing to an unequiv-
ocal affirmation, it is important to avoid—something that often

happens—exploiting the "death drive" as an occasion to fold the drive into the state of nature from which it breaks or to translate drive back into instinctual knowledge. The death *drive* does not suppose— as a death *instinct* would—that death is the ultimate aim of the drive, the aim from which the drive can never divorce itself, the natural aim of the drive, the aim that bears witness to the essence of the drive as a "primitive" or "savage" force of nature. On the contrary, the "death" part of the "death drive" names the constitutive opening of the drive beyond any predetermined object or aim—even death. This is why Freud has so much difficulty separating Thanatos from Eros, death from life. Because many of Freud's readers naturalize death, they tend to endow Thanatos with the power to darken all erotic striving.[28] Rather than veer toward death, however, the death drive, as Freud actually theorized it, turns away from its putative aim—and thus from its "own" name or any name. What we call "life," in this sense, refers to the constitutive illegibility of death and thus of any so-called death drive.

Truer to Freud, no doubt, Joan Copjec writes of the constitutive *inhibition* of the death drive rather than its illegibility. Ultimately, however, the one implies the other.

> The paradoxical Freudian claim that the death drive is a speculative concept designed to help explain why life aims at death, in fact, tells only half the story: the other half is revealed by a second paradox: the death drive achieves its satisfaction by *not* achieving its aim. Moreover, the inhibition that prevents the drive from achieving its aim is not understood within Freudian theory to be due to an extrinsic or exterior *obstacle*, but rather as part of the very *activity* of the drive itself. The full paradox of the death drive, then, is this: while the aim (*Ziel*) of the drive is death, *the proper and positive activity* of the drive is to inhibit the attainment of its aim: the drive, *as such*, is *zielgehemnt*, that is, it is inhibited as to its aim, or sublimated, "the satisfaction of the drive through the inhibition of its aim" being the very definition of sublimation. Contrary to the vulgar understanding of it, then, sublimation is not something that happens to the drive under special circumstances; it is the proper destiny of the drive.[29]

The death drive is an unsolvable enigma. For the most part, Freud theorizes the drives in terms of their "vicissitudes" (*Shicksale*)— that is, their inherent capacity to change aim and object, to displace and invert libidinal investments in a manner that bewilders the ego. When he creates the concept of the death drive, then, this represents the only instance when he designates the unwavering aim of a drive and names it after this aim. In fact, the "death drive" is a coinage not unlike the nicknames that he gives to the analysands in his case histories—naming them after their orginary fantasies. The "death drive":: the "Rat Man":: the "Wolf Man." In this sense, the death drive would constitute the drive of drives, the drive "in person." The drive that manifests the aim of the drives in general, beyond their irreducibly plural vicissitudes. No matter the contingent aim or the object that shatters the drive, lending it each time a singular destiny, it always also leads the subject to death. Death, once again, proves to be the absolute master, the predictable terminus that flattens all contingency, the sad truth. In *Beyond the Pleasure Principle,* Freud writes in no uncertain terms: "the aim of all life is death."[30] In *Three Essays on the Theory of Sexuality*, he explicitly rejects any interpretation that would assign the drive a natural aim or object (human reproduction, heterosexual copulation). The theory of the drive that elaborates its opening beyond the pleasure principle, then, would return it to nature. It is difficult not to recognize the grip of natural law in the ultimate predictability of the drive's long and winding road to death.

Copjec reminds us, however, that the death drive is the exemplary drive because it is constitutively ill named. It is both the best and the worst word for its object. Death cannot become an object or an aim—least of all for the drive. Rather than the ultimately sad truth of the drive, and of life, the death drive names the point at which such truth proves definitively inaccessible. Accordingly, this concept also articulates the rupture of the drive and of life itself with the predictability of natural law. The death drive opens onto a death beyond natural death—and, indeed, beyond violent death to the extent to which the eventuality of such violent death belongs to the Hobbesian projection of a preinstitutional state of nature. If, as Copjec writes, "the proper and positive activity of the drive is to inhibit the attainment of its aim," then "inhibition" (coterminous with "life" itself) names the drive's primordial break with any natural law. Sublimation, in turn, would be antiphysis and even antilogos.

In both Freud and Lacan, the theory of sublimation goes hand in hand with the application of psychoanalysis to art and literature. Without question, the psychoanalytic theory of sublimation is essential to understanding the unique status of art and literature, especially in their relationship to language and the social bond. The reverse is also true: it is impossible to grasp the stakes either of psychoanalysis or of its theory of sublimation without studying art and literature. Nonetheless, such an emphasis upon art and literature can also reinforce the erroneous supposition that psychoanalytic theory upholds a moral distinction between nature and culture, *physis* and *technē*, that sublimation and art are somehow cultural alternatives to violence and death as forces of nature.[31] Despite many passages in his works that suggest the contrary,[32] however, Freud's theory of the drive is not Hobbesian. He does not hold that death is the natural aim of life or of violence or that culture is defined by a break with a supposed state of nature. More than any other theorist, perhaps, Freud attends to the ways in which violence emerges from cultural formations and is often exercised against them. This dimension of his thinking comes most explicitly to the fore in *The Ego and the Id* where he speaks of a "pure culture of the death drive."[33] This phrase occurs in a complex discussion of the way in which melancholia may trigger a dangerous transformation (which often leads to suicide) of the relationship between the ego and the superego. To reconstruct this intricate argument would lead too far afield. I would simply emphasize that the very existence of this phrase bears witness that the Freudian theory of the death drive necessarily opens the critique of violence beyond its traditional parameters and that, in the course of his argument, Freud makes clear that sublimation, far from breaking away from violence and death, produces new forms of violence that traditional political theory is helpless to understand or even to describe.[34]

It is not surprising that works of art and literature focus on such violence. In the culture of the death drive—or, one might even say, *the vicissitudes of sublimation*—the artwork encounters its own project in distorted form. What Kleist's Odysseus calls "the third" would be predicated upon a "sublimation" that opens war beyond the "physical" conflict between force and counterforce, struggle limited by the natural properties of bodies. Rather than simply call this violence metaphysical, it would be more precise to note that—much like the "new kind of war" that Donald Rumsfeld evoked in his notorious *New York Times* editorial—it disrupts the relationship between war and the word and, further, the relationship between names and attributes. Thanks to the emergence of this third enemy "fire no longer knows/ whether to trickle with the floods," which means, in turn, that we no longer know how to speak about fire, which attributes are appropriate to its nature (and thus "literal") and which are forced upon it (and thus "figurative"). This unstable oscillation between literal and figurative, proper and improper, knowledge and rhetoric, is precisely what characterizes literary language in general.

Goya's "A heroic feat! With dead men!" is even more explicit in this respect. The scene that it depicts is already a scene—a scene staged by absent "doers." It entails both the documentary record of real events and the "mechanical reproduction" of something akin to an artwork. Indeed, Goya's caption explicitly underscores the "artistic" dimension of this violence. The irony of the exclamation suggests that the great deeds of war have become another kind of deed: the act of an artist or *metteur-en-scène* who configures bodies for public view. The public display of these bodies is what clearly differentiates this act from an act committed under the influence of a fever dream or a hallucination. The point is not only to lament the dismembered state of these corpses or to rage against their abuse; it is, more precisely, to demonstrate as unmistakably as possible that someone has done something with these bodies *after death*. Only on the basis of this display is it possible to see that the dismemberment was inflicted upon these bodies after death rather than in the course of regular combat; or, ultimately, that the act of dismemberment alone does not suppose the victim to be either alive or dead.

This technique of mise-en-scène is what "inhibits" violence from attaining its supposedly natural ("negative") aim of death and thereby endows it with a horrible positivity. Rather than stop short of death, this violence continues beyond it. At the same time, it suggests that violence which stops short of death ("violence inhibited from attaining its aim") is something other than violence that has not *yet* attained its aim; it should *also* be characterized as violence that aims at something other than death. The meaning of this display is enigmatic because it literally leaves this "something" open to question. In addition, since Goya's caption does not refer to violence *against* the dead, as I have argued, the *object* of this violence is no less enigmatic. The image raises the possibility that violence can be inflicted upon a body that is not its "proper" object; that one body—whether living or dead—might (and perhaps always does) function as a substitute for another body—or perhaps something other than a body; that this violence reaches its object through a symbolic display or demonstration rather than by direct attack.

DEATH AND VULNERABILITY

I would like now to consider the potential objection that I have been
reading Goya's image of postmortem atrocity *too literally*. The depiction of dismembered bodies arranged for public display, one might
argue, is an allegory of human vulnerability. "The dead" represent
the embodiment of human beings and constitutive exposure of the
human body to violation and abuse. The dead, in other words, are
other than the dead; they stand for the vulnerability of the living.

A heroic feat! With dead men! The unusual formulation of this
exclamation, as I have discussed, suggests an intimacy that is incompatible with the traditional narrative logic of warfare; it evokes a violent act that does not oppose its object. In her 2004 review of two
books on suicide bombing, Jacqueline Rose speculates that the special
horror and revulsion that people experience when confronted with
such attacks is due to the unbearable intimacy—which she calls a
"deadly embrace"—between the bomber and his or her victims.

> The horror would appear to be associated with the fact that the
> attacker also dies. Dropping cluster bombs from the air is not only
> less repugnant: it is somehow deemed, by Western leaders at least, to
> be morally superior. Why dying with your victim should be seen as a
> greater sin than saving yourself is unclear. Perhaps, then, the revul-
> sion stems partly from the unbearable intimacy shared in their final
> moments by the suicide bomber and her or his victims. Suicide bomb-
> ing is an act of passionate identification—you take the enemy with
> you in a deadly embrace. As Israel becomes a fortress state and the
> Palestinians are shut into their enclaves, and there is less and less pos-
> sibility of contact between the two sides, suicide bombing might be
> the closest they can get.[35]

Like the violence that Goya articulates, Rose's description of the relationship between the suicide bomber and his victims turns repeatedly upon the preposition *with*. "Why dying *with* your victim should
be seen as a greater sin than saving yourself is unclear . . . Suicide
bombing is an act of passionate identification—you take the enemy
with you in a deadly embrace." The suicide bomber positions himself
on the same "side" as his victims—with them. Reports from scenes
of suicide bombings inevitably describe the dismemberment of bodies and the mixing of limbs with one another (to the point that it is
impossible to identify their owners). Accordingly, we might add, the
suicide bomber commits "great deeds" not "with the dead" but with
his own life. The title of Christoph Reuter's history of suicide bombing

(one of the books that Rose reviews), *My Life Is a Weapon*, points up this paradoxical instrumentality. Rather than use a weapon to impose separation and distance, the bomber uses the "suicide weapon" in order to demonstrate the unavoidability of "being-with" (to use or abuse Heidegger's term, *Mitsein*), the exposure of life to life.[36]

Intimacy, then, is inseparable from vulnerability—both in the case of suicide bombing and in Goya's "A heroic feat! With dead men!" Such an allegorical reading of Goya's inexhaustible image might find confirmation in another of Goya's *Disasters*: *Para eso habeis nacido* (For this you were born; see figure 3.8). Not unlike Robert Capa's iconic and controversial photograph, *Falling Soldier*, this image captures a man in mid-collapse; he is tumbling forward and vomiting onto a heap of dead bodies, apparently about to join them. Utterly bleak as this image may be, its caption speaks of birth rather than death; and, once again, the caption emphasizes an important distinction. (Goya called these etchings *caprichos enfáticos*—perhaps because they each underscore such a subtle distinction). Rather than a *dying* man, Goya shows us a *helpless* man. The caption ironically evokes such helplessness both as the origin and the destiny of human existence.

The question of vulnerability figures at the heart of Adriana Cavarero's reflection on contemporary violence in *Horrorism*. Although Cavarero does not discuss Goya, her conclusions about the nature of violence would support such an allegorical reading of "A heroic feat! With dead men!" It is important to note that the English and Italian subtitles of *Horrorism* are different. The English, *Naming Contemporary Violence*, announces Cavarero's concern with the intimate relationship between war and the word. "As violence spreads and assumes unheard-of forms," she writes, "it becomes difficult to name in contemporary language. Especially since September 11, 2001, the procedures of naming, which supply interpretive frameworks for events and guide public opinion, have to constitute an integral part of the conflict. One thing is certain: the words 'terrorism' and 'war' evoke concepts from the past and muddle them rather than give them fresh evidence."[37] The book's title itself, *Horrorism*, represents Cavarero's own attempt to name emergent forms of violence. Rather than simply indexing the problem of naming, by contrast, the Italian subtitle, *Ovvero della violenza sull'inerme* (Or, Violence against the Helpless), designates the *object* of this violence. Her guiding thesis—not a hypothesis but an underlying certainty—is that contemporary war is

Figure 3.8. Francisco Jose de Goya y Lucientes (1746–1828), *Para esto hebeis nacido* [This is what you were born for], plate 12 of *Los desastres de la guerra* [The Disasters of War], 1810–14, pub. 1863, etching. 16.3 x 23.7 cm. (Private Collection)

no longer war, or even terror, in the classical sense because the vast majority of its victims are helpless civilians. No matter the directives of international humanitarian law, which commands that every effort should be made to minimize civilian casualties, it is time to admit that war, today, is nothing but a systematic exercise in producing collateral damage. In order to understand this new violence, then, it is necessary to identify what Catherine Malabou calls "the new wounded,"[38] to shift focus from warriors and their alibis to the victims of war. Cavarero writes, "If we observe the point of the helpless victims rather than of the warriors, though, the picture changes here too: the rhetorical façade of 'collateral damage' melts away, and the carnage turns substantial. More than war, what stands out is horror."[39]

Following Hannah Arendt rather than Goya, Cavarero privileges the newborn as the figure of vulnerability and helplessness.

> If, as Hannah Arendt maintains, everyone is unique because, exposing herself to others and consigning her singularity to this exposure, she shows herself as such, this unique being is vulnerable by definition. Arendt does not dwell on this vulnerability, perhaps because she has little interest in the body. But in emphasizing birth as the decisive

category of the ontology of the unique person, she does illuminate the first scene on which the vulnerable being presents itself. Even though, as bodies, vulnerability accompanies us throughout our lives, only in the newborn, where the vulnerable and the defenseless are one and the same, does it express itself so brazenly. The relation to the other, precisely the relation that according to Arendt makes each of us unique, in this case takes the form of unilateral exposure. The vulnerable being is here absolutely the exposed and helpless one who is awaiting care and has no means to defend itself against wounding. Its relation to the other is total consignment of its corporeal singularity in a context that does not allow for reciprocity.[40]

What brings Cavarero's reflections on contemporary violence especially close to my own reading of Goya is that she explicitly distinguishes violence and killing. In the context of a discussion of torture, she writes succinctly: "Death may come at the end, but it is not the end in view."[41] The object of violence is not the living being but the helpless victim—or, more specifically, the *body* of the victim. It would make sense to conclude that the body is vulnerable because it is alive; and, therefore, that it is vulnerable to death. But the defining attribute of the body, Cavarero underscores, is neither life nor death; it is rather *singularity*. Beyond attacks upon the life of the body, then, it is vulnerable to violence that specifically threatens this singularity.

This claim becomes the basis for Cavarero's distinction between terrorism and horrorism. Terrorism revolves around the prospect of violent death and the instinctual fear that it provokes. The paradigmatic manifestation of this fear is flight. "The important point lies in what we might call the instinctual mobility associated with the ambit of terror. Acting directly on them, terror moves bodies, drives them into motion. Its sphere of reference is that of a menace to the living being, which tries to escape by fleeing. This menace is directed, substantially, at life itself; it is a threat of violent death. He who is gripped by terror trembles and flees in order to survive, to save himself from a violence that is aiming to kill him."[42] For this reason, Cavarero incisively concludes, terror converges with the Hobbesian doctrine of war. "Terror is a part of war; more than a strategic weapon, it is its essence."[43] Horror, on the other hand, names an experience of *immobility* that extracts the subject from the logic of war and terror; it provokes revulsion or repugnance rather than fear.

> Violent death is part of the picture, but not the central part. There is no question of evading death. In contrast to what occurs with terror,

in horror there is no instinctive movement of flight in order to survive. . . . Rather, movement is blocked in total paralysis, and each
victim is affected on its own. Gripped by revulsion in the face of a
form of violence that appears more inadmissible than death, the body
reacts as if nailed to the spot, hairs standing on end.[44]

The object of horror is "a violence that appears more inadmissible
than death," and, Cavarero continues, the paradigmatic instance of
such violence is the undoing, disfigurement, mutilation, or dismemberment of the human body. These forms of violence strike the body
as body. Rather than extinguish the life of the body, she specifies,
dismemberment "offends its dignity" or destroys its "figural unity."

> The human being, as an incarnated being, is here offended in the
> ontological dignity of its being as body, more precisely in its being
> as singular body. Death may transform it into a cadaver, but it does
> not offend its dignity or at any rate does not do so as long as the dead
> body preserves its figural unity, that human likeness already extin-
> guished yet still visible, watchable, for a period before incineration
> or inhumation. . . . What is unwatchable above all, for the being that
> knows itself irremediably singular, is the spectacle of disfigurement,
> which the singular body cannot bear. As the corporeal symptoms tes-
> tify, the physics of horror has little to do with the instinctive reaction
> to the threat of death. It has rather to do with the instinctive disgust
> for a violence that, not content with killing because killing would be
> too little, aims to destroy the uniqueness of the body, tearing at its
> constitutive vulnerability. What is at stake is not the end of human
> life but the human condition itself, as incarnated in the singularity of
> vulnerable bodies.[45]

Disfigurement, Cavarero repeatedly claims, entails a violence whose
extremity is measured by the fact that it goes further than killing; it
is "not content with killing because killing would be too little." And
yet the scene of this violence always takes place within the time of life.
We are supposed to understand that, in objective terms, horrorism
always stops short of killing. Cavarero assumes—along with the philosophy of war and terror that she opposes—that the dead are no longer vulnerable. Nor are the living vulnerable to attacks upon the dead.
There is no point at which she equates—as Goya does or seems to
do—violence that *exceeds* death with violence *after* death or violence
with the dead. "As a body," she writes, "the vulnerable one remains
vulnerable as long as she lives."[46] Throughout her book, the exemplary figure of vulnerability remains the newborn—a figure that she
explicitly adopts from Hobbes rather than Freud. Since Cavarero does

not consider the dead to be vulnerable, she never explicitly decides to privilege the case of the newborn over that of the dead. But this is, in fact, what she does; and this decision is legible at key moments in her text. For example: "The dead body, no matter how mutilated, is only a residue of the scene of torture. . . . As every torturer knows, the vulnerable is not the same as the killable. The latter stands poised between death and life, the former between the wound and healing care."[47] Despite her attempts to distinguish vulnerability from mere life, then, Cavarero's analysis ultimately supposes a novel definition of life that she never articulates as such. According to this definition, *life would be distinguished—or perhaps "singularized"—by its exposure to violence that doesn't stop at death.*

The allegorical reading of Goya's "A heroic feat! With dead men" would thus save us from claiming that the dead are vulnerable and measuring the political consequences of this claim. But do we want to be saved? Might it be *necessary* to consider the status of the dead in any political ontology that revolves around the problem of vulnerability? It certainly seems necessary at certain moments of Cavarero's own argumentation. When the question of limits arises in her discussion of torture, for example, she postulates death as the only hard limit: "That the vulnerable one is defenseless makes things easier because, since [torture] is unilateral, the violence can unfold as something irresistible, even unlimitable, except that the death of the vulnerable one . . . always does constitute a limit. And this is precisely the limit against which . . . horror measures the peculiarity of its crime and, in competition with terror, founds its dominion."[48] On the one hand, she claims, death is always the ultimate limit upon violence. On the other hand, horror derives its peculiar meaning from the brazen way in which it defies this limit. Would not great feats with dead men or women be one way or perhaps even *the* exemplary way of defying this limit? Doesn't Cavarero's turn to the newborn (as the figure of the gap between the wound and healing care) need to be supplemented with reflection upon "the dead" (as the figure of the gap between the instant of death and burial or, more generally, the work of mourning)? In the passage on the vulnerability of the body to disfiguration, for example, Cavarero claims that death as such transforms the living being into a cadaver but does not offend the body's dignity. But then she qualifies this statement: "at any rate does not do so as long as the dead body preserves its figural unity, that human likeness already

extinguished yet still visible, watchable, for a period before incin-
eration or inhumation."[49] This passing reflection explicitly recognizes that there is such a thing as violence that offends the dignity
of the dead; that attacks the figural unity and uniqueness of the
dead body, destroying its likeness, make it impossible to identify or
even to recognize *as human*. Cavarero acknowledges the existence
of such violence, and yet she does not consider it to be essential to
the category of horror.

The rigor of Cavarero's argumentation—a rigor that opens possibilities beyond its own explicit conclusions—suggests, therefore,
that it is necessary to consider the dead as vulnerable, and futher,
that "the dead" provide a better example of vulnerability than the
newborn. "Only in the newborn," Cavarero writes, "where the
vulnerable and the defenseless are one and the same, does [vul-
nerability] express itself so brazenly."[50] Along similar lines, she
will state: "Bound to the other and dependent on the other for its
very existence, the newborn infant is not a combatant." But she
adds that the infant is "already characterized by its effort to survive."[51] Doesn't the agency of this effort to survive already bear
witness to something in the newborn that is not absolutely helpless? Doesn't Cavarero's emphasis upon dependency underestimate
the infant and overestimate the omnipotence of the mother? Gilles
Deleuze provides an account of the baby that might help rethink
such basic assumptions: "The will to power certainly appears in
an infinitely more exact manner in a baby than in a man of war.
For the baby is combat, and the *small* is an irreducible locus of
forces, the most revealing test of forces."[52] Despite the measure of
provocation mixed into Deleuze's assertions, they effectively suggest that the newborn might not be the most appropriate figure of
vulnerability; or, at the very least, that vulnerablility might not be
tantamount to nursling dependency or helplessness; and that, consequently, there is a vulnerability that is foreign to the dialectic of
desire and the fantasy of seduction that it implies.

Newborns are, of course, factually helpless. But this does not
mean that they offer the best figure for their own helplessness. In
every respect, "the dead" are a better figure, even for the helplessness of the newborn itself. To the extent that the living beings are
helpless, we might say, they are already dead: from the moment of
birth, there is something in a life that is exposed to being treated

as something dead. Every birth is a virtual stillbirth. As soon as a
being can die, "to be dead" becomes a position within life beyond
life; and, indeed, the many ways of occupying this position (e.g.,
"to play dead," "to be left for dead," "to be dead in the water")
bear witness to the condition of radical helplessness. At the
limit, what Goya's seer intimates and mourns is this inescapable
anachronism—or symbolism—at the heart of singular existence.

CHAPTER FOUR

War, Word, Worst

Reading Samuel Beckett's Worstward Ho

Worst, **adj.** *and* **n.** A. adj. *Used as a superlative of the adjs. bad, evil, or ill. 1a. Most bad or evil, in regard to moral character or behavior; most vicious, wicked, cruel, etc. 2a. Most grievous, painful, unlucky, uncomfortable, unpleasant, unfavorable, etc. 2b. Hardest, most difficult to deal with. 3a. Most wanting in the good qualities required or expected; least good, valuable, desirable, or successful; most inferior; meanest or poorest in quality; least considerable or important. B. 3a. What is most grievous, unlucky, painful, hard to bear; a state of things that is most undesirable or most to be dreaded. 3b. A course of action ill-advised in the highest degree. 3c. The worst part, degree, or phase of. 5a. at the worst: In the most evil or undesirable state that can be; at the greatest disadvantage; fallen to the lowest degree of badness, illness, or misfortune. 6. (to do) the worst or one's worst: the utmost evil or harm possible. 7a. The harshest view of judgment; as to speak or think the worst (of a person or thing). 7c. to make the worst of: to regard or represent in the most unfavorable light. 8. Defeat in a contest.*

Worst, **v.** *1a. To make worse, impair, damage, inflict loss upon. 2a. To defeat, overcome, get the better of (an adversary) in a fight or battle.*

—*Oxford English Dictionary*

Syria Massacre: Over 90 People Killed in Worst Violence since UN Ceasefire Started[1]
Worst Violence in 2 Years Kills 28 Arabs and 3 Israelis[2]
Burma Unrest Escalates in Worst Violence in Years[3]
Mogadishu Rocked by Worst Violence in 15 Years[4]
Loyalists Blamed for Worst Violence[5]
Egypt Clashes See Worst Violence[6]
Athens Sees "Worst Violence in Months" as MPs Pass Austerity Plan[7]
Kazakhs Vote for New Parliament after Worst Violence in 20 Years[8]
The 5 U.S. Cities with the Worst Gang Violence[9]
Rome Counts Costs of Worst Street Violence in Years[10]

And so on.

Worstward ho. For each headline transcribed above, in accordance with current bibliographic practices, I have included a note giving both its original publication date and the date (July 9, 2012) on which I accessed it on my personal computer. The list was selected from the results obtained from a single Google search using the search terms "worst violence." The headlines are presented in the order in which they appeared on my computer screen—that is, in no particular order, chronological or otherwise. They place outbursts of violence side by side in a manner that utterly disregards the specificity of historical context. The point, however, is not to provide an abbreviated history of twenty-first-century war and death but quite simply to record the results of a search—an almost capricious Internet search; an experiment designed to test the capacity of a single word to traverse time and place; a search for "the worst" wherever and whenever it occurs. Such a search can find violence everywhere, every day, because it pinpoints an omnipresent trope in modern journalistic discourse—perhaps even the trope of journalistic omnipresence.

The following discussion of Samuel Beckett's 1983 narrative has everything and nothing to do with this survey of perpetually contemporary headlines. Many writers and theater directors have cited or staged the words of Beckett's broken-down characters in order to give unadorned voice to the experience of contemporary war. In his brief introduction to a selection of Gillian Laub's photographs of maimed survivors of suicide bombings, for example, David Rieff cites the famous last words of *The Unnameable* in order to give voice to the "common wisdom" to which Laub's portraits bear witness:

> It is easy to romanticize death and almost impossible to make an ideological fable out of having one's legs blown off or one's face burned. *Dulce et decorum est pro patria mori*: sweet it is to die for one's country. Those words have adorned countless war memorials in Europe, Canada, and the United States. But one can't make a poem out of walking on prostheses for the rest of one's life or becoming aphasic—not a patriotic poem anyway.
>   The bravery of the photos in this series is that they show what even funerals do not show: the true horror of war and terrorism. They do so in a way that does not seek to turn the young portrayed into types or leech them of their beliefs and prejudices—of their human specificity, in other words. To consider them is to be reminded not just of human cruelty and human stupidity but also of human tenacity. *I can't go on, I'll go on.* The words are Samuel Beckett's, but the wisdom they reflect is the common wisdom of everyone portrayed here, whatever else divides them.[11]

This is just one example of a widespread reading of Beckett's texts as "wisdom" that readily applies to contemporary situations—from scenes of mayhem to teenage angst. As a text that promises to voyage out in search of the worst, then, *Worstward Ho* also promises to confirm the wisdom of such readings. The title is a siren's call. It is an expansive, garish, history- and tradition-bound phrase—almost a slogan—affixed to a few pages of the sparest imaginable prose. Rather than lead the text outward, however, *Worstward Ho* lures the reader in. Into what? In "Trying to Understand *Endgame*," Theodor Adorno examines how Beckett's literary works transcribe to what he calls "the object decay of language," which reduces all language to what the capitalist marketplace makes of it: slogans, stereotypes, trademarks, echoes. The language that remains is what Adorno calls "the second language of those who have fallen silent, an agglomeration of insolent phrases, pseudo-logical connections, and words galvanized into trademarks, the desolate echo of the world of advertisement, is revamped to become the language of a literary work that negates language."[12] Since this second language only opens deeper into the issueless universe of language itself, it does not provide those who have fallen silent with an opportunity to speak. Precisely by giving them more than enough words to replace those they have lost, it locks them irrevocably within their silence, depriving them of any word that might evoke this silence itself.

Rumors of the worst have been greatly exaggerated. Neither the minimal language nor the enigmatic subject matter of Beckett's prose has anything to do with war and violence. Nowhere in the text is the word *war* used or implied; nor does it represent any war-related or warlike events. Beyond the fact that the text was published thirty years ago and could have nothing to do with today's news, it also refuses any relation to any "contemporary" historical moment whatsoever. It is perhaps the most intransigently antimodern work ever written.[13] The text opens with a series of self-canceling paragraphs, among which we read:

> All of old. Nothing else ever. Ever tried. Ever failed. No matter. Try again. Fail again. Fail better.[14]

That said, the language of *Worstward Ho* remains the language of war. As my procession of contemporary headlines suggests, the category of the worst is absolutely central to journalistic, psychoanalytic, and philosophical discourse on the history of war and violence—to such an extent that discourses on war often tell us very little about war and a lot about the worst. Rather than describe experiences or events, analyze causes, elaborate structures, and so forth, these discourses merely add their content to a portrait of the worst. This claim easily can be demonstrated in a literary experiment. Not by accident, it is possible to construct a chain of persuasive statements about war—relevant across the disciplines—simply by linking together elements from the definitions of the word *worst* that appear in the *Oxford English Dictionary*. The propositions that compose the following paragraph are not quotations—either from the dictionary or from any actual discourse on war—but they are recognizable, logically irreproachable, and even true.

War is the *most evil, dreaded, unbearable, undesirable, vicious, wicked, and cruel* social and political eventuality; it entails *grievous* injury, *maximum pain* to soldiers and civilians, widespread *misfortune, discomfort,* and *unpleasure.* Moreover, war provides the *most unfavorable* conditions for the free and creative development of community and the social bond. War is *hard,* and those who endure it have *difficulty dealing* with their experiences for the rest of their lives. What could possibly be cherished about war? It utterly *lacks the least good quality, anything valuable, desirable, or successful.* Even the most glorious victory is predicated upon the *utter failure* to achieve political ends through nonviolent means. Anything valuable that comes from war is permanently tainted with the fact that it was achieved using the *most inferior* means and will be haunted by war's ongoing legacy of *illness, poverty, and trauma.* As Elaine Scarry postulates in *The Body in Pain,* war is primarily a matter of injuring— which is to say, *making worse, impairing, damaging, incurring loss.* Using such violent means, the goal of war is to *defeat, overcome, outdo,* or *get the better of* the enemy.[15]

Discourses on war employ the category of the worst, after the fact, to represent, to judge, to describe, or to analyze history. But my experiment reveals that the reverse is also the case: in fact, such discourses do not speak about war in order to say anything about war but rather to name the worst and to provide this hyperbole with a referent. The entire world of war and violence (if not the world *tout court*) exists—we might say, echoing Mallarmé—to end up in a discourse on the worst. Worstward ho.

War, as a result, is all we know of the worst. Despite the increasing scope and complexity of war in our world and the "richness" of its impact upon every sphere of ethical and political experience, war discourse represents the unrelenting impoverishment of the language of the worst and thereby, perhaps, of language itself. It is not by accident that Beckett's *Worstward Ho* does not ever name war. This omission is purposeful. It is, in fact, more than an omission. The underlying project of Beckett's text, I would argue, is to systematically save the category of the worst—and the entirety of language along with it—from the war that is always in the process of engulfing it. Rather than an object or event, the worst—like the West—evokes a field of possible experience that is larger than war and violence. Certainly larger than any dictionary definition of the worst. Even larger than evil.

The rhythm and texture of Beckett's prose parodies the banality of discourses on evil—which contradicts their implicit claims to novelty and urgency ("All of old"). From headline to headline, writer to writer, and region to region, journalism grounds the worst in the world, but the category never "sticks" to the horrors that it names. No sooner is one event lifted to the status of the worst than another even worse arises to usurp its position. Worsts occur simultaneously in multiple places at once—each, in its context, legitimately called the worst. The staccato rhythm of *Worstward Ho* hops from failure to failure. I have already cited the most famous lines from the text. Again:

> All of old. Nothing else ever. Ever tried. Ever failed. No matter. Try again. Fail again. Fail better.

Later, an analogous series of assertions turns upon the self-defeating pragmatics of the worst.

> The body again. Where none. The place again. Where none. Try again. Fail again. Better again. Or better worse. Fail worse again. Still worse again. Till sick for good. Throw up for good. Go for good. Where neither for good. Good and all.[16]

And again:

> All of old. Nothing else ever. But never so failed. Worse failed. With care never worse failed.[17]

Beckett's minimal sentences, often without verbs, make his prose feel cramped. To some extent, *Worstward Ho* belongs to the series of his late works that scholars have classified as "closed space" narratives. For example, the tone and themes of this text could be shown to recall *The Lost Ones*—the paradigmatic closed space narrative—which opens thus: "Abode where lost bodies roam each sending for its lost one. Vast enough for search to be in vain. Narrow enough for flight to be in vain. Inside a flattened cylinder fifty meters round and sixteen high for the sake of harmony."[18] And yet, as the implicit boatman's call in its title would suggest, *Worstward Ho*'s shorthand actually supposes a "long view"—perhaps a very long view, a view that encompasses the entire globe. Rather than narrate events that occur in rapid succession, Beckett's language operates a hyperbolic contraction of vast stretches of time and space. He linguistically juxtaposes events that might either be incredibly close or hopelessly distant. In the final image of the narrative, three pins converge within one pinhole and yet remain "vasts apart":

> Enough. Sudden enough. Sudden all far. No move and sudden all far. All least. Three pins. One pinhole. Vasts apart. At bounds of the boundless void. Whence no farther. Best worse no farther. Nohow less. Nohow worse. Nohow naught. Nohow on.[19]

From the beginning, we realize, Beckett's language already pertained to this boundless void. Only on the basis of such a wide view would it be possible to assert: "All of old. Nothing else ever."

The problem, however, is not that saying the worst always fails. In its very failure, the category is all too successful. Attempts to say the worst fail in the same way everywhere; but such attempts are everywhere. Nothing is more common. Perpetual pragmatic failure is what makes the category both so "local" and so "global," both responsive to historical change and universally applicable, both infinitely rich and utterly impoverished. The word for the "most evil," strangely, becomes the basis for what might be called universal juris-diction: a "saying of law" that reaches beyond the sphere of constituted law, that consists in nothing but the minimal arraignment of the extreme in language.

The dictionary says that the worst is simply the "most evil." But what does this mean? On the one hand, the "most evil" would be situated at the far end of a graduated scale of ever-increasing evil. It would be the most by comparison with a series of lesser evils. On the other hand, the "most evil" is not on the same footing as the evils to which it is compared. To compare the worst and lesser evils, then, is to compare the comparable and the incomparable. Lesser evil is measured with respect to the worst, but the reverse is not the case. In principle, at least, the worst is that evil *to* which other evils are compared, but it does not compare itself to them in turn; it is simply itself, the incomparable within the space of comparison. The appearance of the worst, even if it is determined by measurement, entails an immediate leap beyond measure. In this sense, the worst simply names evil as such, undiminished evil, evil whose evil can never be contested. To claim that someone or something is the worst is to designate the presence of evil incarnate.

No matter its hyperbolic intensity, however, the worst is also an inherently comparative term. It supposes that the leap beyond all measure can be repeated. Even if the worst cannot be determined by comparison with lesser evils, it can be compared to other worsts. The worst is only the maximum for a time, the worst so far. As soon as the worst appears as such, it opens the possibility of comparing the incomparable. The category of the worst diminishes rather than hypostasizing the evil that it names. The worst thus turns out to be another name for what Hannah Arendt called "the banality of evil." Writes Alexander Garcia Düttmann in an essay on Arendt's *Eichmann in Jerusalem*:

> The worst is always less bad, it is better than the worst, not because it is not bad enough but on the contrary, because it appears and manifests itself as the worst. This is what accounts for the paradoxical aspect of its logic. Where something deserves to be called the worst, there are already two evils competing. One evil is lesser than the other and announces it so that the worst remains still to come. Both evils can be identified, yet their comparison also thwarts the identifiability of the other evil.[20]

Düttmann evokes the possibility of a competition among evils: "Where something deserves to be called the worst, there are already two evils *competing*." Another name for such competition is simply war. With its incessant passage from extreme to extreme, death to death, atrocity to atrocity, war is nothing other than the comparison of the incomparable. For this precise reason, jurists and philosophers find it necessary—in order to sustain the singularity of the worst—to distinguish acts of genocide from acts of war, war from war crimes. Beyond everything that happens in specific wars, all the strategies and technologies squandered and all the damages incurred, war consists in nothing but the displacement of limits that had previously seemed stable. Further, the paradigmatic passage to the extreme is the passage from word to action—the explicit and calculated rejection of language and its limits as the basis for the social bond. The category of the worst, then, would represent the indispensable task of arraigning this hyperbole, of folding into the space of language actions that explicitly reject limits of language.

During the time that he was writing *Worstward Ho,* Beckett is known to have annotated all the references to "the worst" in his copy of *King Lear.*[21] Edgar's series of asides in act 4, in particular, articulate the performative contradiction that structures such universal jurisprudence:

> Oh gods! Who is't can say 'I am the worst'?
>   I am worse than e'er I was.
>
>   . . .
>
>   And worse I may be yet; the worst is not
>   So long as we can say 'This is the worst.' (act 4, scene 1, lines 27–30)

The judgment, "This is the worst," is inseparable from the judgment, "This is bad," which implicitly precedes it. This is bad; this is worse (or the worst, if one says that, between this and that, this is the worst). The two judgments differ in kind, however. The sentence, "This is bad," can function as a predicative proposition, asserting that "bad" is an essential attribute of the thing it designates. Someone says, "This is bad," in principle, because this *is* bad, for the reasons elaborated by the speaker. (Although the designation "bad" can, in the last instance, only be defined in opposition to the good, this opposition does not simply involve comparison, but constitutes the logical structure that makes predicative judgment possible.) However, no one ever says "This is the worst" because this *is* the worst. The reverse is the case: this is only ever the worst because someone *says* that it is such: not simply because someone judges it to be such, but rather because someone openly speaks this judgment at a specifiable time and place. The worst is always the worst *here and now,* judged in the present to be the worst among a specific set of seeable or foreseeable options. (Options that are not necessarily bad. Because "the worst" is simply a comparative term, many if not all of them could be "good," or comparatively good.) The judgment upon the worst does not propose the essence of the thing but merely exposes the vision of a hypothetical judge.

Because of the pragmatic failure that is built into the category of the worst, it is less a matter of judgment than prejudgment or even prejudice. It opens toward rather than resulting from judicial procedure. It is an accusation rather than a verdict.

What is an accusation? One valence of accusation appears in considering the French verb *accuser*, which, before it refers to the act of calling someone to account for some crime, simply refers to an act of phenomenological reduction: the act of casting something into relief, manifesting its presence, or calling attention to it. Even in a judicial context, accusation posits but remains incapable of proving guilt. It does nothing but name a crime or a cause for complaint and thereby call someone to take responsibility for it. Accusers can be vehement or hyperbolic; but such performative bluster belies the essential modesty of accusation itself. In every case, the act of accusation is double: it accuses someone of something and at the same time accuses itself. The act of calling attention also calls attention to itself. The act of accusing someone of a crime also proleptically accuses itself of a crime: the crime of false accusation. Indeed, to the precise extent that an accusation remains structurally open to the claim (or the counteraccusation) of its falsity, it is hyperbolic. As Edgar makes clear, hyperbole is less a matter of exaggeration than of an inversion of temporal order; it is an attempt to speak the truth before it is true. It is an utterance of the truth whose very articulation compromises its veracity. The function of a trial, then, is to both adjudicate the guilt of the accused person and the validity of the accusation itself, if not the validity of the legal statute in whose name the accusation is lodged.

Unlike a declaration of war, which suspends the law, an accusation is an act that willingly inscribes itself within the space of the law—even a law that remains to come; it is precisely the mode in which the law regularly comes before the law, opens itself to systematic contestation. "This is the worst," however, is not a juridical utterance. No person can bring another to trial for "the worst." And yet the idea of accusing some person or entity of the worst isn't senseless—at least not today, especially in the sphere of international law. The hypothesis of such an accusation bears witness to the necessity for the legal system to turn to the extreme, to name crimes before they are crimes, and thereby to call itself to account and into question.

Within this juridical and linguistic horizon, the category of the worst functions as the conventional name for the extreme. Everywhere, at any time, and in any voice, the worst is always the same; and, paradoxically, it is precisely this sameness that endows it with the mobility to circumnavigate the globe in order to "accuse" the most incommensurable horrors. Although the category of the worst offers no concrete description of these horrors, it manifests and openly heeds the demand to speak at the exact point where the destructive acts have abandoned the openness of language. Within the space of this virtual tribunal, then, "the worst" is always already deemed the best word for the occasion—or, at least, the least worse word. A minimal word. A word instead of no word. Instead of eternal peace, we have the perpetual arraignment of horror. Instead of binding promises in language, we have unquestioned faith in the promise of language itself.

This excessively long excursus helps us to grasp more clearly the parodic dimension of Beckett's language in *Worstward Ho.* The English word *ho,* which calls out from the title of Beckett's *Worstward Ho,* can be read as a sort of accusation. *Ho,* the *Oxford English Dictionary* tells us, calls without calling to any specific action; it comes "after the name of a thing or place to which attention is called: used by boatmen, etc., to call attention to the place for which they are starting; hence, generally, with a sense of destination." "Ho" would thus be the interpellation that does no more than place the addressee into relation (or recalls his already existing relation) to a destination before the project of any specific trajectory might be undertaken. Rather than point to something in the world, it opens the world as such. In Beckett's title, then, "ho" functions to call attention to this accusatory dimension of the category of the worst and to its global scope. Echoing an aspirational seafaring motto, "Westward Ho," the title parodies the linguistic optimism that inevitably hinges upon the predication of the worst and hints at the imperialistic dimension of this optimism. Systematically eschewing war for speech, the geopolitical language game elevates the worst to an object of desire: a horizon to be reached, a task to be accomplished, a language to be forged, an occasion for yet more speech. The worst turns into the best. Perhaps even a transcendental Good.

But "Westward Ho" is not the only possible variant of Beckett's odd invitation to the voyage. *Worstward Ho* relays a further call: *Worst-word Ho.* Rather than carry the speaker toward the worst in the world, this exhortation calls attention to the word itself as a destination. Much like war, *Worstward Ho* itself demands a word. Despite the text's apparent sobriety and minimalism, every word bears witness to the urgency of this underlying demand and thereby to its own failed attempts to satisfy it. Also, much like war, this urgent demand for a word arises in response to a break in the chain of discourse. Such a break opens a stretch of time that only a consequential word can bring to an end and that feels unutterably long until such a word is said. However, the occasion for *Worstward Ho* is not war; it is not evil, horror, atrocity, injustice, effraction, the event, or the instant. The urgency of its demand has nothing to do with speed and politics. The break in the chain of discourse to which this text responds from the very first word is, paradoxically, the continuity of the word itself. With a single word, Beckett articulates a linguistic state of emergency:

> On. Say on. Be said on. Till nohow on. Said nohow on.[22]

The word *on* says the going on of discourse without a word. This single word says the absence of a word that could extract itself from this continuity in order to say it and thereby to interrupt it. The imperative to "say on," then, represents the promise of such an interruption; the promise that speech can interrupt the wordless continuity of the word in order to repair the chain of discourse. Once said, however, the imperative folds the saying that it commands into the same continuity that it aims to break: "say 'on'" becomes "say on" (and on). The following imperative—"be said on"—attempts, then, to halt this rapidly intensifying predicament. It is often said that Beckett begins from the middle. But it would be more accurate to say that his texts begin with the promise of such a beginning, a promise that they proceed to show can never be fulfilled. *Worstward Ho* never begins because it can never successfully designate the middle. The word *on* itself is, in a sense, the worst word because it enacts the absence of any word (even "the worst") for the wordlessness of language. The *middle* itself proves to be the chimerical goal toward which *Worstward Ho* sets sail.

For Beckett, the worst word is the only word worthy of the name. The essence of the word, then, can be revealed only through the repeated experience of its unresponsiveness to the demand for a consequential word that would reestablish the chain of discourse. This experience leaves the speaker exposed to an implacable demand to say the unsayable. "Say bones. No bones but say bones. Say ground. No ground but say ground. So as to say pain."[23] Grasped from another angle, however, the same experience simply exposes the fact that the word is essentially immune to the demands that are placed upon the speaker to say everything. Within contemporary journalistic and philosophical discourse, the category of the worst always returns the word to the same place: war. Beckett's project, then, is to reinvent the word by dislodging it from the responsiveness to which it has been consigned. Rather than endow words with new poetic scope and elasticity, however, the task is to stage their unresponsive inanity. "The words too whosesoever. What room for worse! How almost true they sometimes almost ring! How wanting in inanity! Say the night is young alas and take heart. Or better worse say still a watch of night alas to come. A rest of last watch to come. And take heart."[24] Only then would it be possible to save the word from the tyranny of the new.

"Try again. Fail again. Fail better." This series of imperatives can be read in two related ways. On the one hand, the exigency of failure can be linked to the attempt to free language from the project of representation, to empty the word of any determinate signification. Thanks to its urgent referentiality and its constitutive failure, "worst" thus stands as the exemplary word—the real word (other than "word") for "word." As I have suggested, however, this failure is inseparable from spectacular success. The very emptiness of the word *worst* (which makes it both the worst and the best word) allows it to found a regime of universal jurisdiction. The failure of the word liberates it from the shackles of representation but not from the sovereign optic of a judge. On the other hand, this very predicament bears witness to another sort of failure. The fact that the "worst" never names what it claims to name (the worst) does not prevent it from always naming War. Precisely because the worst "is not," it can always refer—beyond the name—to a referent that is never named as such. In Beckett's language—the unnameable. But the point is precisely that Beckett does not accept the identification of the unnameable with War (or, for that matter, any such transcendental signified). War remains too bound up with the optimism that identifies law with the promise of language. Beckett's imperatives imply that linguistic failure is always too facile; it makes too much possible. This failure itself must be failed, they demand. And this further failure must be different from the first. It is not any longer a matter of emptying language of representation. Words fail us not only because they do not name anything but also, perhaps more intriguingly, because they become riveted to one very specific referent. A word can fail because it is used to name everything but the one thing for which it is reserved. The mobility of the word, then, is not a function of its empty abstraction; it is a consequence of silence imposed upon this singular referent. Whenever it is spoken, the word would at once signify and—perhaps secretly—evoke this other thing. Paradoxically, the attachment of the word to this one object—which is never named as such—liberates the word from and for representation. In the case of the worst, the global attempt to fold this category into the space of war functions to prevent the unspeakable object from ever being evoked as such. The task that Beckett's fiction pursues, then, is to dislodge the worst from the world of war in order to allow it to evoke—once again or perhaps for the first time—the object whose muteness underlies its freedom.

Interestingly, Beckett makes explicit that this task entails both work upon language itself (reduction, repetition) and a discipline of imagination. Only by force of imagination, as we will see, is it possible to usurp the position of war as the universal occasion to speak. Throughout Beckett's work, the faculty of imagination is essential to his experimental method. "Imagination dead imagine," he writes at the opening of *All Strange Away*.[25] Only imagination makes it possible to think beyond war; to *see* what cannot be said, to say what cannot be imagined, and thereby to stage the cause of word's failure to respond.

WORD

There are times when a word is required. A word and nothing else. Not just any word, but the right word. At such times, there is no acceptable nonlinguistic substitute for *a* word; and there is no word that would be an acceptable substitute for *the* word. The theory of the performative utterance, in large measure, constitutes the most persistent attempt to understand the nature of this demand to find words. In *How to Do Things with Words*, for example, J. L. Austin provisionally limits his investigation to what he calls "conventional procedures" such as the marriage ceremony, the baptism of a ship, the postmortem bequeathing of a legacy, or the laying of a bet. Such procedures prescribe and revolve around the anticipation of a *moment* when the appropriate person (the woman or man to be married, the celebrant, the legator, the gambler) utters the appropriate word. Among the conditions that define a felicitous performative utterance, Austin specifies, "the procedure must be executed by all participants both correctly and completely."[26] If the moment to speak passes or the requisite participant takes too long to "complete" the utterance, then the utterance is null and void. The marriage vow, for example, must be uttered on the spot. A solemn pause might be acceptable, but the bride or groom cannot take all day or all year—not to mention all hour. Were bride or groom to impose such a delay, to withhold the necessary word or to utter an irrelevant word, the performative would not only be "infelicitous," but entire ceremony would be held up, perhaps immemorially suspended. This reserve would plunge all parties to the event, including the speaker himself or herself, into a time of ongoing silence, a time whose passage is defined negatively as a time without the required word. Further, this time would not merely be a waiting period. It would be worse. Of course, the required word might some day be said. Eventually, the appropriate person might get around to uttering it. On that day, however, the word would have lost its relevance long ago; it became permanently inapposite *at the very moment when it was not spoken.* Those who experienced the disappointment of such a lost moment would be plunged into a distended time during which the necessary word can no longer be hoped for, a time perhaps rife with words but not the right word, words whose profusion only accuses the absence of the one that was never spoken; the inane continuity of an unbroken afterlife.

Austin's concept of the conventional procedure helps to isolate and formalize the demand to find words, but it certainly does not provide the last word, as it were, on this demand. The convention provides the illusion that there are words appropriate to every occasion or historical conjuncture. But there are other types of situations—emergent historical, political, ethical, or amorous conjunctures—that hinge upon the utterance of a word. These situations cannot be formalized before they occur. Nor can it be determined in advance which word they require, who should utter it, and how (or whether) any of this would become known.

In July 1917, for example, Lenin wrote a pamphlet, "On Slogans," that denounced political parties' reliance upon old slogans in new historical situations. "Too often has it happened that, when history has taken a sharp turn, even progressive parties have for some time been unable to adapt themselves to the new situation and have repeated slogans which had formerly been correct but had now lost all meaning—lost it as 'suddenly' as the sharp turn in history was 'sudden.'"[27] Lest the vanguard lapse into redundancy and bureaucracy, the new historico-political situation demands a new word—a word that will bring about what Deleuze and Guattari have called an "incorporeal transformation."[28] Moreover, the precise word that the new situation requires can only be derived from an alert analysis of the situation as it develops. "Every particular slogan must be deduced from the totality of specific features of a definite political situation."[29] Lenin's courage and his genius consist in the perspicacity of his analysis and his unflinching readiness to take responsibility for its political consequences.

The history of the Russian Revolution provides an example of what can happen when the right word is found on time. However, European history is not lacking in situations whose historical and political legacy consists in the fact that an event occurred for which no one ever found the right words—catastrophes. The most unavoidable among such events is the Nazi extermination of European Jews during World War II. For the most trenchant thinkers of this event—Hannah Arendt, Paul Celan, Maurice Blanchot, Philippe Lacoue-Labarthe—it is not only defined by the systematic destruction of uncountable lives but also by the fact that this destruction proceeded unabated for an ongoing period without any response—during the war and afterward—without so much as a single consequential word ever being uttered even to call it into question. It is possible that this "period" hasn't yet come to an end. The legacy of the Shoah—literary, philosophical, ethical, and political—consists in various attempts to measure and assume responsibility for the consequences of this lost moment.

For Paul Celan, the failure to speak has catastrophic effects upon language itself and, in particular, upon the German language—the language in which the extermination took place and from which a timely word would have borne the most weight. The irreversible loss of the moment to speak renders the survival of the German language inherently problematic. As Hannah Arendt said in a more affirmative tone, the experience of surviving the war as a German speaker is inseparable from a confrontation with the fact that "the language remains."[30] In his Bremen address, Celan writes:

> Only one thing remained reachable, close and secure amid all losses: language. Yes, language. In spite of everything it remained unlost. But it had to go through [hundurchgeben durch] its own lack of answers, through terrifying silence, through the thousand darknesses of murderous speech. It went through and gave no words for what was happening, but it went through it. Went through and could resurface, 'enriched' by it all.
>
> In this language I tried, during those years and the years after, to write poems: in order to speak, to orient myself, to find out where I was, where things were going, to chart my reality.
>
> It meant movement, you see, something happening [Ereignis], movement [Bewegung], being under way [Unterwegsein], it was an

> attempt to find direction. And when I ask about the sense of it, I feel
> I must tell myself that this question also speaks to the question as the
> sense of the clock's hand.[31]

The language may remain unlost, but it is no longer the same. By virtue of going through its own forms of answerlessness (*Antwortlosigkeiten*), terrifying silences, and "the thousand darknesses of death-bringing discourse" (*tausend Finsternisse todbringender Rede*), Celan writes, with a heavy note of irony, that it came through this ordeal "enriched." The German word translated by "enriched" is *angereichert*. Especially placed in proximity to his reference to the *thousand* darknesses of death-bringing discourse, which evokes the Nazi *Tausendjähriges Reich*, it becomes difficult not to read "Reich" at the heart of this word. In what sense, then, could language be *enriched* and *enreiched* at the same time?

The historical and political failure to give words at any moment that would have mattered brings about an irreversible rupture between "the language that remains"—the language now defined by its answerlessness and complicity with extermination—and a supposedly ideal language—a language that would have lived up to one's hopes, a language whose vigilant speech unto itself would have made the "final solution," both name and thing, impossible. This rupture would enrich language to the precise extent to which it restores language to itself—perhaps to its essential finitude, or materiality, but, more precisely, once again to use Celan's own word, to its answerlessness. Celan thus wagers—and herein resides the singularity of his position and his poetics—that even and especially such a language must become the basis for relation, dialogue, and life in common. The very failure of the German language to give words for what happened enriches language by making its finitude inescapable. Rather than free language, failure binds language permanently to the unspoken event. Precisely because language can no longer be conceived as an abiding treasury or providential mother tongue that releases the words we need when we need them, because, on the contrary, language shows itself to be inseparable from the possibility of unthinking disregard for any conjuncture or turning point and neglect of any responsibility, it becomes necessary to struggle with and against language in order to reinvent its words as words worthy of the name.

To begin with, the continuity of language without answers itself constitutes an open conjuncture that must not go without a word.

What is this continuity? Is it an event or a nonevent? How is it possible to name it? Celan wrote poems in this unlost language, he writes, "in order to speak, to orient myself, to find out where I was, where things were going, to sketch for myself a reality. It meant, as you see, something happening [*Ereignis*], movement [*Bewegung*], being under way [*Unterwegsein*], it was an attempt to find direction." Continuity has no direction. But it might be possible to approach this continuity itself as a presupposition ("to find out where I was"). Celan evokes the "the sense of the clockhand," which embodies both the possibility of marking time and the empty circularity of time without answers. This emptiness simply means this: no one (not even language itself) can respond in my place; it is up to me to both invent the word and, perhaps more important, the demand to which it responds.

WORST

J. L. Austin does not develop an explicit reflection on the possibility of designating the worst; nonetheless, a colloquial usage of the term arises, in passing, at a key point in his essay, "The Meaning of a Word." In this text, Austin extends the theory of the performative utterance to speech situations that are not determined in advance by ritual or conventional procedures. At the point in his discussion where the reference to the worst occurs, Austin is discussing the relationship between languages and what he calls "extraordinary cases." Whereas ordinary language tends to "break down," an ideal language would always find itself to the measure of the extraordinary:

> Ordinary language breaks down in extraordinary cases. (In such cases, the cause of the breakdown is semantical.) An ideal language would not break down, whatever happened. In doing physics, for example, where our language is tightened up in order precisely to describe complicated and unusual cases concisely, *we prepare linguistically for the worst*. In ordinary language we do not: *words fail us*.[32]

Of course, Austin does not deal with the utterances "I am the worst" or "This is the worst." To prepare linguistically for the worst is certainly not simply to be prepared to designate the worst at the right time. Nonetheless, these utterances demonstrate the belief on the part of the speaker that he speaks an ideal language. Were anyone to speak an ideal language, the *mark* that this language had arrived would perhaps be sudden undeniable truth of the sentences, "I am the worst," "This is the worst." In other words, these are the sentences in which an ideal language would *advertise* itself (perhaps not coincidentally, the language of the best and the worst is integral to the function of advertising and popular media). The (unbreakable) function of the ideal language, and, it would seem, language as such, is to describe cases when they arise: to fulfill the jurisdictional function of saying what is the case in absolutely every single case. The worst case (the extraordinary case, the limit case) thus becomes the test case that, were it to arise, would allow such a language to manifest its adequacy. The ideal language would indeed have to begin with envisioning such a case, "in order precisely to describe [it] concisely" when it happens.

Ill seen ill said. Read against the grain of its most obvious "Beckettian" sense, the title of the work that immediately precedes *Worstward Ho* in Beckett's late "trilogy" concisely formulates the structure of an ideal language constitutively prepared for the worst. On the one hand, the title does indeed mark an "ill" that afflicts both seeing and saying. The ill of the first is inseparably the ill of the second in accordance with what Blanchot calls the "optical exigency" of the Western tradition that subordinates thought to the metaphor of vision (and thereby makes saying dependent upon the said, the signifier dependent upon the signified). If the said should correspond to the seen, a disturbance of seeing will necessarily upset the relation between saying and the said. On the other hand, the title can also be understood in exactly the opposite sense: it posits an absolute homology between the seen and the said, a homology that appears with reference to their common object, the "ill." The French version of this title, *Mal vu mal dit,* makes the necessity for this other reading even clearer, because *mal* functions at once as an adverb—meaning "ill" or "badly"—and as a substantive noun—meaning "evil." Indeed, the homology is underscored by the suggestion of a temporal coincidence between the seen and the said; rather than the one being the consequence of the other, the two belong to the same instant. Between them, a linguistic prudence that speaks at the speed of sight. No sooner seen than said:

> Enough. Quicker. Quick see how all in keeping with the chair. Minimally less. No more. Well on the way to inexistence. As to zero the infinite. Quick say. And of her? As much. Quick find her again. In that black heart. That mock brain.[33]

The imperative ("Quick see . . . Quick say . . . ") is thus a discrete and hyperbolic version of the optical exigency, in that it does not simply require that saying follows from seeing, but rather that they should happen at the same time or, better, *at once*, which—meaning "this instant," "right now"—is a synonym for *quick*. The title would then announce the accomplished fact of this coincidence, or even the fulfillment of the law from which the imperative would derive (in the same way that, in Kant, the imperative presupposes the positing of an archetype outside of time). The elision of the imperative would thus bear witness to the speed of an accomplishment (quicker than quick) withdrawn from the retarding condition of extended time; and thus also to the position of language inseparable from a vision of the whole.

"The worst" always refers or defers to the presence of a judge in the form of his synoptic vision. Hence, Edgar opens his asides with the exclamation invoking the presence of a transcendental instance (or, interestingly, instance*s* in the plural)—"oh gods!" And the *here and now* inseparable from the designation of the worst is exclusively the here and now that pertains to the judge's discretion. If one asserts the worst as the designation of an absolute hyperbole, therefore, this assertion implies the possibility of a synopsis that encompasses all possible options, from the position of which it would be possible to designate the absolute worst among all the bad and all the good.

In *Worstward Ho*, Beckett will figure the position of this eternal present as an encompassing stare. At first, the stare appears alone, directed at a series of "shades" that phase in and out of the "dim void": "Clenched staring eyes. All in the dim void shades. One astand at rest. One old man and child. At rest plodding on. Any others would do as ill. Almost any. Almost as ill."[34] Always, the text designates the eyes that stare as "clenched"—a word that is idiomatically associated with the teeth, or a hand formed into a fist, but that Beckett applies to the eyes—in order to mark that the stare is a function of the eyes in the head rather than in the face. Behind the eyelids, the head stares by itself, regardless of the face and what the face tries not to see or turns away from. (Indeed, clenched implies an anxious effort not to see.) Moreover, the blink of an eye, the *Augenblick*, is the figure for the instant, for the blindness, the syncope, or the elision of the punctum, constitutive of time that passes. Blindness—or perhaps blinkeredness—to what happens while this eye is briefly shut but also to what other eyes see, both while this eye is shut and while it remains open. The now of the clenched staring eyes would therefore consist in one blink that gathers what the spacing of time excludes or separates. "All at once in that stare. Clenched eyes clamped to all."[35] Beckett eventually has the stare shift away from the eyes altogether, to emerge in the form of the head itself, or "That head in that head . . . The sunken skull."[36] The skull becomes the *imago dei*. "Away. Full face from now. No hands. No face. Skull and stare alone. Scene and seer of all."[37]

In principle—to answer Edgar's question from *King Lear*: "Who is't can say 'I am the worst'"—God is the only one who can say (or who can *rightfully* say) "I am the worst." The spatio-temporal condition of any finite being (perhaps even of one of the *gods*) prevents him from speaking the truth, since there might be another "worst" that he cannot see because of its separation from him in space or, as Edgar says, he might become worse than him-self at a future time that, for now, remains constitutively inaccessi-ble. These conditions thus make the pronunciation of the judgment upon the worst into an act of hubris, since the utterance puts its speaker into an unattainably elevated position for anyone but God himself. Hubris punished through the bounds that it attempts to transcend: imagining that I am the worst, or that I am in a position to judge myself the worst, I allow myself to remain unconscious of the *passing* time during which I become still worse than I ever was. As Edgar says: " . . . the worst is not/ So long as we can say, 'This is the worst.'"

According to this tradition, therefore, the worst is associated with the finitude of discourse and the failure of language that it entails. This failure appears in the form of a discourse that confesses its own finitude. Whereas God is the only one who could rightfully claim, "I am the worst," "I" am the only one who can *cite* the proposition, "I say 'I am the worst,'" and, thus, the one who can openly wonder *who* is it that can say, "I am the worst." Citation instantaneously converts an act of hubris into an act of humiliation and supplication. As soon as I attempt openly to call myself the worst, and thus to elevate myself to the level of one who can judge his own being, I will always end up *citing* myself before the God whose position I sought to occupy, exposing the turn whereby my act of hubris becomes the form of my abjection. However, this abjection will not in turn appear as evidence that, after all, I am the worst, that I am the worst precisely for having tried to usurp the right to call myself the worst. As in Edgar's case, this abjection consists merely in the simple, openly articulated obser-vation that I am *not* the worst; that, as long as I am there to say it, the worst will never name what it seems to name.

The negation of the hyperbole has an indeterminate effect: it can either mean that I am better than the worst or (as Edgar claims) worse than the worst. In either case, the worst itself *is not*. To be worse (or better) than the worst is to be in a position from which one cannot say what one is. This is a position of abjection, not simply because it occupies a very low rung on the scale of malignity, but because it renders one incapable of speaking what God can see. To supplement this failure of language, one must confess it to God so that he might reveal himself in place of what cannot be spoken.

The relation between the worst and its negation thus starts to function differently than the relation between the worst and the bad, or between the worst and the good. Excluding the position of God, there is no such thing as *the* worst. One can always say, "This is the worst," but the worst named will always remain *this* worst. Whereas God would have access to the entire axiological scale that runs from best to worst, the being who must contend with spatiotemporal limitations can only establish such a scale based on available experience, such that "the worst" always becomes merely the worst *so far*.

> First one. First try fail better one. Something there badly not wrong. Not that as it is it is not bad. The no face bad. The no hands bad. The no—. Enough. A pox on bad. Mere bad. Way for worse. Pending worse still. First worse. Mere worse. Pending worse still. Add a—. Add? Never. Bow it down. Be it bowed down. Deep down. Head in hat gone. More back gone. Greatcoat cut off higher. Nothing from pelvis down. Nothing but bowed back. Topless baseless hindtrunk. Dim Black. On unseen knees. In the dim void. Better worse so. Pending worse still.[38]

The worst takes its place both at the limit of the axiological scale and within a potentially unlimited series of *worsts*, the perpetuation of which testifies to the fact that the worst itself is not, and thereby manifests the withdrawal of the position from which it could be spoken. The series is constituted through the compulsive lurching of language from one act of hubris (or one citation of its failure) to the next.

Accordingly, the undecidability of the title, *Ill Seen Ill Said*, articulates both the ideal of language and its compromise. The imperative that seems to have been instantly gone beyond continues to exert itself precisely in the initial "ill" that upsets the homology between the seen and the said. In his important reading of *Worstward Ho*, Alain

Badiou has suggested that this ill, in fact, does not afflict saying but positively manifests the *autonomy* of *saying* with respect both to the seen and to the said. Moreover, this autonomy is a basic axiom of Beckett's poetics, inscribed in his works precisely in the form of the imperative to speak (*l'impératif du dire*)—or rather, the imperative *to say*. I cite a rather long passage to give a sense of the style of Badiou's argumentation.

> It is necessary to understand fully that 'to say is to ill say' establishes an essential identity. The essence of saying is ill saying. Ill saying is not a failure of saying, but the precisely the contrary: All saying is, in its very existence as saying, an ill saying.
>
> 'Ill saying' is implicitly opposed to 'well saying.' What is 'well saying'? 'Well saying' is a hypothesis of adequation: The saying is adequate to the said. But Beckett's fundamental thesis is that the saying that is adequate to the said suppresses saying. Saying is a free saying, and in particular an artistic saying, only to the extent that it does not coalesce with the said. 'Saying is under the imperative of saying, it is under the imperative of the 'on,' and it is not constrained by the said.
>
> If there is no adequation, if saying is not subject to the prescription of 'what is said,' but is only submitted to the rule of saying, then ill saying is the free essence of saying, or rather the affirmation of the prescriptive autonomy of saying. One says to ill say. And the height of saying—that is, poetic or artistic saying—is precisely the controlled regulation of ill saying, which fulfills the prescriptive autonomy of saying.[39]

Although Badiou is the only one to have attempted to give the imperative the importance that it holds throughout Beckett's work, it seems that he misrecognizes—or fails to remark on—certain essential aspects of the imperative to say. I emphasize three points.

1. Before saying (*le dire*) involves a relation of adequation to "what is said" (*le dit*), it is the saying of the *word*. The first word of Beckett's text could not be more overdetermined. It is an imperative, an example of obedience to another imperative (inscribed in the next phrase), a description (of a beginning without beginning that happens without regard for any imperative). Nonetheless, the repetition of "on" in the imperative to "say on" opens a reading of the word as nothing more than a word. The imperative cites the word, remarks the word as word. If saying is ill saying (or rather, missaying) then this ill does not so much affect the relation between saying and what is said as it does the relation between saying and the said word. Saying is something other than pronouncing or speaking—hence, Beckett's systematic translation of words about speaking into words

about saying (e.g., "to misspeak" becomes "to missay"). What then would it mean to "missay" a word? What if the word itself is the ill that afflicts saying?

These questions take us back to Austin's conclusion, "words fail us." Austin's work has in common with *Worstward Ho* its preference for the problems of saying over those of speaking, and its love for the word: how to *do* things with words but also how to *say* things with words. The distinction between the performative and the constative breaks down once it becomes clear that saying, to the extent that it has to do with the word, is itself already doing. The word, for Austin, is a constitutively praxic unit. If the question of the thing, or the "case," arises for him, it would be in terms of this praxis. What is the difference between speaking and saying? Whereas speaking foregrounds the role of the voice in signification, saying subordinates the voice to the word; whereas speaking implies an ability to speak or even a need to speak, saying merely implies either the chance to say something or precisely the imperative to say something. Both the chance and the imperative to say demand words regardless of—or even beyond—one's ability to speak.

The problem of the imperative to say in Beckett, then, can be further elaborated in terms of the saying of the performative utterance. Performative conventions command that specific words be openly cited in certain speech situations. In such situations, the "imperative to say" would be the imperative to say the word that "now" must "be said." As Beckett writes: *say for be said*. Like "quick," the passive construction structurally binds saying to a situation, to an unmarked right here and now.

2. The imperative to say is the imperative to say within a certain space of time—perhaps even in *no time*. The performative speech situations that require that certain words be said are condensed affairs that hinge upon a highly charged instant, such that they also implicitly require that the saying happen at a given time, while time still remains, and then quickly, all at once. To get married, for instance, one cannot say "I" today and "do" tomorrow. In this sense, the imperative to say itself cannot have the abiding status of a categorical imperative because it emerges within the same situation—if not the same instant—as the saying that it requires. The paradox of Beckett's imperative "quick say" is that the utterance bespeaks an urgency that usurps the very time for saying to which it enjoins its addressee. It

urges: say no later than "now" at this very instant in which you are commanded to say.

3. The situation that calls for a word does not have to be juridico-conventional; it can be defined by a singular thing or an event—what Austin calls a "case." Idiomatically, saying retains an essential link with the case or the example: the imperative form, "say," is often used to improvise an example in the midst of a discourse (" . . . if an animal—say, a cat—one day decides . . . "). Not only conventional but also emergent occasions demand that words be said on the spot. Throughout his essay, Austin imagines himself into situations that require someone to say something in response to exceptional events. Just before invoking the ideal language that would be prepared for the worst, Austin writes:

> Suppose that I live in harmony and friendship for four years with a cat: and then it delivers a philippic. We ask ourselves, per-haps, 'Is this a real cat? Or is it not a real cat?' 'Either it *is*, or it is *not*, but we cannot be sure which.' Now actually, that is not so: neither 'It is a real cat' *nor* 'It is not a real cat' fits the facts semantically: each is designed for other situations than this one: you could not say the former of something which delivers philip-pics, nor yet the latter of something which has behaved as this for four years . . . With sound instinct, the plain man turns in such cases to Watson and says 'Well now, *what would you say?*' 'How would you *describe* it?' The difficulty is just that: there is *no* short description which is not misleading: the only thing to do, and that can easily be done, is to set out the description of the facts at length.[40]

The imperative to say that impinges upon the witness in such extraor-dinary cases does not make itself felt simply as the demand to say something, to offer a description, but more in the demand to be *brief*. Something like an ethics of *wit*, whose soul lies in brevity, subtends this entire scene. It is the imperative to say something "in a word"; for this is the demand that confronts the witness with the inadequacy of his language to the situation. As Austin stresses, the point is not that there is no possible description of the situation but that there is no *short* description—and, perhaps beyond description, no word, no *idiom* appropriate to the situation. After giving the properly *unheim-lich* example of knocking at a man's door "just after" he has died ("home" or "not home"?), Austin concludes: "A new idiom might in odd cases be demanded."[41]

The imperative to say that pertains especially to the odd case is the demand for an idiom: both a language with a word for the case and, more important, a language that corresponds to the dimensions of the encounter. An idiom is per definition concise—and sight provides the measure of its concision: "But supposing I happen *first* to think of the situation when I call on [a man] just after he had died: *then I see at once* it would be wrong to say either [that he is home or not]" (my emphasis). [42] Austin's ideal language (prepared for the worst), one might recall, would be that language which is "tightened up in order precisely to describe complicated and unusual cases *concisely*." It would be a language of total idiomaticity, seamlessly responsive to the demands imposed on it by even the worst situations as they arise— and thus insulated against the anxiety that infuses a discourse that goes helplessly on in search of the idiom that would have rendered it unnecessary, nipped it in the bud, but whose moment—now—is long gone. Despite the relative brevity of his essay, Austin worries to his readers about its length: "It is divided into three parts, of which the first is the most trite and the second the most muddled: all are too long." [43] The breakdown of ordinary language, therefore, makes us *go on* (or "say on") too long; it leaves us irresponsible before the demand for an idiom.

What is extraordinary about Austin's text is its drive *to see what cannot be said*—to see the worst when language itself prevents him from saying it. *Worse* than the breakdown of ordinary language in the worst cases is the way in which its constitutive ill preparation prevents us even from seeing the worst. No thanks to the blinkers of language, we fail even to recognize situations in which an idiom is demanded of us, to measure the failure of language, and thus the degree of our own irresponsibility.

To prepare for the worst is not only a matter of taking measures against its incursion; it also solicits the worst. What characterizes sciences like physics is their ability to elaborate a language that itself opens toward the worst; they begin with (and function as a permanent access to) the demand for a new idiom. With ordinary language, however, access to such a demand remains contingent upon the emergence of odd cases. Even then, the oddity of the case will likely escape us to the very extent that we rely exclusively on words to apprehend it. The oddity of the odd case is liable to appear *as such* only insofar as we find a way to see what cannot be said (e.g., we become curious, interested).

The capacity for this curiosity or interest lies in what Austin calls *imagination*—which is precisely what makes it possible to see (and thus to seek) the oddity of the odd, the singularity of the singular. The question of the relation between language and the power of imagination arises at key points in Austin's paper. On the one hand, the power of imagination is hindered by words: "I think I can see that there are difficulties about our powers of imagination, and about the curious way in which it is enslaved by words."[44] On the other hand, it is precisely the kind of sight afforded by imagination—limited as it may be—that makes it possible to grasp the difficulties that hamper its power. Imagination is the act whereby one constructs and projects oneself into a (real or fictional) situation—to address the case but also to address it to oneself—to say "now" to oneself. To mark time through exhortation: such is the essential—albeit feeble—power of the imagination.

> Ordinary language *blinkers* the already feeble imagination. It would be difficult, in this way, if I were to say 'Can I think of a case where a man would be neither at home nor not at home?' This is inhibiting, because I think of the ordinary case where I ask 'Is he at home?' and get the answer, 'No': when certainly he is not at home. But supposing I happen *first* to think of the situation when I call on him just after he has died: then I see at once it would be wrong to say either. So in our case, *the only thing to do is to imagine or experience* all kinds of situations, and then suddenly round on oneself and ask: there, *now* would I say that . . . ? A new idiom might in odd cases be demanded (my emphasis).[45]

The power of imagination constitutes a demand for an idiom—perhaps even an idiom beyond language or a language of the instant itself. The first word and syntagm of Beckett's text, we recall, is "On." This word inscribes the twin imperative to fail and to go on that always drives language beyond the possibility of an idiom. If the imperative to "say on" founds the autonomy of saying, then the words of language always veer into discourse away from any situation in which they would still matter. Language as such turns away from the concision of the idiom. At the same time, Beckett's entire text is marked, and disarticulated, by an extraordinary concision. Its peculiar language manifestly results from a concerted attempt to make syntax into a function of the word or series of words, and even of the idiom. The shards of recognizable syntactical elements that punctuate the text usually form variations upon idiomatic phrasing (e.g., "Try again. Fail again. Fail better"; "Any other would do as ill"; "Something here is badly not wrong"). The very phrase that highlights the disjunction of word and idiom is itself already oriented toward the case ("the worst") that would call for its utterance. Beckett's language subordinates emergent singularity of concrete situations to the desire—which traverses language—to name the once in order to access the onceless. Those "worsening" words that always leave language short (or long) of the worst are also those that seek the worst in order to see that which is worse than the word.

CHAPTER FIVE

The Translation of a System
in Deconstruction

Jacques Derrida and the War of Language against Itself

If I had to risk a single definition of deconstruction, one as brief, elliptical, and economical as a password, I would say simply and without overstatement: *plus d'une langue*—both more than one language and no more of one language.

—Jacques Derrida, *Mémoires: for Paul de Man*

One of the most ingrained presuppositions of translation theory is that the need for translation results from what Wilhelm von Humboldt called the "diversity of human language construction"[1] (*die Verscheidenheit des menschlichen Sprachbaues*) and that, at the limit, translation constitutes a congenitally failed attempt to overcome this diversity. Even Walter Benjamin's inexhaustible essay, "The Task of the Translator," presumes that this task is defined in terms of the problem of linguistic diversity. In large measure, Benjamin inherits this presumption from Mallarmé—whom he cites in the original French:

> Les langues imparfaites en cela que plusieurs, manque la supreme: penser étant écrire sans accessoires, ni chuchotement mais tacite encore l'immortelle parole, la diversité sur terre, des idioms empêche personne de proférer les mots qui, sinon se trouveraient, par une frappe unique, elle-même materiellement la verité.[2]

Benjamin inserts this passage in his own discourse without translating it. For the sake of commentary, however, I would venture the following translation:

> Languages imperfect because several, the supreme is lacking: thinking being writing without accessories, or muttering but ever tacit immortal speech, the diversity on earth, of idioms prevents anyone from

proffering the words which, otherwise would be found, with a unique
coinage, itself materially the truth.

If there are any at all, there are not many theories of translation that
do not define the task of the translator in terms of this mythical construction of its problem. This construction is inseparable from a series
of basic presuppositions that clarify and give meaning to the task of
the translator: the object of translation is foreign language; what is
"foreign" about a language is linguistic (i.e. it can simply be identified
with the words of the language); translation is the solution both to
the epistemological and to the political problems posed by the diversity of languages; the goal of translation is understanding or transparency; translation is a hermeneutic process; the goal of translation
is to eliminate the need for translation; translation constitutes a utopian enterprise; translation is impossible. Most theories of translation
adopt one or another of these claims and thereby inscribe themselves
in the heritage of the Babel narrative—or, at least, a certain reading
of this narrative.

I would like to argue, however, that the work of Jacques Derrida
represents perhaps the only attempt to put into practice and to elaborate (in that order) a theory of translation that reframes the very problem of the task of the translator.

CONFUSION

From "Des Tours de Babel" to "Two Words for Joyce" and "What Is
a Relevant Translation?," Derrida distinguishes between untranslatability and foreignness. In an important essay on translation as the
"passage into philosophy," Marc Crépon has established that Derrida
consistently privileges what Roman Jakobson, in "On the Linguistic
Aspects of Translation,"[3] has called *intralinguistic* translation, translation that operates within the confines of a single language. But there
are two different concepts of such translation.

The first concept, which Crépon elaborates at length, has to do with
the work of formalizing language that is inseparable from the project
of philosophy itself. Translation, in this sense, refers to the process—
which Crépon calls "originary intralinguistic translation"—whereby
structurally equivocal signifiers are stabilized, endowed with a univocal meaning, forcefully embedded in conceptual hierarchies, and
thereby raised to the level of transmissible philosophemes.[4] Intralinguistic translation, in this sense, lays the groundwork for the project

of interlinguistic translation. Only after the words of each language have been formalized as univocal philosophemes does translation from one language to another become possible. Derrida's own philosophical project, Crépon argues, begins by calling into question the validity and authority of this original intralinguistic translation. Deconstruction is inseparable from a "counter-project of translation" that opens "the question of the *possibility* of *another passage* into philosophy or of a *passage into something other* than philosophy— that is, simultaneously, the question of an *other* project and an *other* concept of translation, or even still of an *other* thought and an *other* practice of tradition."[5]

The second concept of intralinguistic translation, as Derrida problematizes it, emerges from the fact that each supposedly foreign language—foreign with respect to another language—incorporates words that do not, strictly speaking, belong to it; and that, consequently, will not have been foreign (to an eventual translator's target language). Although this concept of intralinguistic translation is essential to Derrida's reading of Babel, his construction of confusion or untranslatability, and to his counterproject of translation, Crépon does not explore it. Like the vast majority of translation theory, in fact, Crépon's analysis ultimately defines its problem in terms of the diversity of languages. "At the very moment when it demands an other thought of translation," he writes, "deconstruction cannot dispense with a thinking that is linked to the diversity of languages and idioms—to that which happens to language, to the relation between languages and to the works of the tradition, written in a given language, through translation."[6] True enough. However, precisely because deconstruction demands an other thought of translation, it also requires an other thought of the diversity of languages, a thought that would no longer rely upon the mythical construction of this diversity.

In order to appreciate this aspect of Derrida's reflections on translation, it would be useful to compare the examples that he privileges to examples that belong to the traditional reading of the Babel narrative. The most famous such example can be found in Benjamin's essay: "Without distinguishing the intended object from the mode of intention, no firm grasp of this basic law of a philosophy of language can be achieved. The words *Brot* and *pain* 'intend' the same object, but the modes of this intention are not the same. It is owing to these modes that the word *Brot* means something different to a German than the word *pain* to a Frenchman, that these words are not interchangeable for them, that, in fact, they strive to exclude each other."[7] In their simplicity, then, these little words make legible the echo of the Fall whereby languages and peoples continue to be dispersed or "strive to exclude one another." The examples that Derrida privileges, however, embody the inclination of languages to *include* one another. In "Des Tours de Babel," he shows that, strictly speaking, the *proper name* does not belong to any one language. "At the very moment when pronouncing 'Babel' we sense the impossibility of deciding whether this name belongs, properly and simply, to *one* tongue."[8] Even within the language where the name "first" appears, the proper name will have already been transferred, transported, or translated, so that it cannot simply be translated as a word "of" this language.

In "Two Words for Joyce," Derrida's reflections revolve around two words from *Finnegans Wake*—HE WAR—that are written both in English (war = to war) and in German (*war* = past tense of the verb *sein*) at the same time so that they must be translated in order to be read. Finally, "What Is a Relevant Translation?" discusses the translatability of the "French" word *relevante*. This word is untranslatable, Derrida claims, precisely because it remains impossible to determine its source language. "It is impossible to decide the source language to which, for example, the word 'relevante' answers. . . . Nor the language to which it belongs at the moment when I use it, in the syntagms or phrases where I move to reinscribe it. Does this word speak one and the same language, in one and the same language? At the same time, we don't even know if it is really one word, a single word with a single meaning, or if, homonym or homophone of itself, it constitutes more than one word in one."[9] As Derrida stresses, what is at stake here is the unity and unicity of language. Is it possible legitimately to claim that any language is *one and the same* and therefore foreign to all other languages?

Any reading of the Babel narrative turns upon the way in which one interprets the central event of the "confusion" or (in Alter's version) "bafflement" of language. This event is inseparable from another event: the scattering of peoples across the earth. The two are in fact one and the same event so that the interpretation of confusion depends largely upon the way in which one understands its relation to the dispersion that occurs with it. The traditional reading privileges the moment of rupture, shattering, scattering, dispersion, divergence, or diaspora, understanding confusion as the inevitable result of the ensuing diversity. The presumption is that confusion refers to the condition of a person confronted with another person speaking a language that he does not understand—a "foreign" language—and that translation is an inevitably failed attempt to transcend this condition.

To a certain extent, Derrida's approach to the Babel narrative does not depart from this traditional reading. In "Des Tours de Babel"—a title that the translator, Joseph F. Graham, leaves untranslated in order to emphasize the "turn" or "trope" in the French word *tour*, which also means "tower"—Derrida's elaboration of translation as "trope" presupposes the multiplicity of tongues as privation or interdiction. In telling the story of the "inadequation of one tongue to another" and thus of the "need for figuration, for myth, for tropes, for twists and turns, for translation inadequate to supplement what multiplicity forbids us [*traduction inadequate pour suppléer à ce que la mutiplicité nous interdit*]," the narrative becomes "the myth of the origin of myth, the metaphor of metaphor, the narrative of narrative, the translation of translation, and so on."[10]

Although the Babel narrative never explicitly evokes the task of translation, it is itself, qua narrative, an allegory of translation; it tells the story of the need for the figuration-translation that it already institutes. Regardless of its abyssal complexity, however, this allegory presupposes that figuration emerges and circulates in the space (of interdiction) between languages in the plural; it presupposes that these languages are *languages*, which, in turn, supposes both a certain concept of language and, perhaps more significantly, a certain concept of dispersion. In "Two Words for Joyce," Derrida offers an elementary analysis of this concept of language and the concepts of translation and dispersion that it implies: "The current concept of translation is still regulated according to the *twice one*, the operation of passing from one language into another, each of them forming an organism or a system the rigorous integrity of which remains at the level of supposition, like that of a body proper."[11]

To postulate a language as "foreign," Derrida suggests, is to suppose that it is a "dispersed" but self-enclosed organism or totalizable system, "a body proper"—such that it is always possible to distinguish the words of one language from those of another. Dispersion, in this sense, might shatter the unity and coherence of an original language, but it would leave untouched the supposition that various postlapsarian languages constitute monadic *corps propres*.

In his essay on translation, Roman Jakobson distinguishes between three forms of translation: intralingual translation, interlingual translation, and intersemiotic translation or transmutation. In his brief commentary on this essay in "Des Tours de Babel," Derrida observes that Jakobson's categories revolve around the supposition that interlingual translation—translation *between* languages or "post-Babelian" translation—corresponds to translation proper and, therefore, that the other two categories constitute figurative uses of the word *translation*:

> But in the case of translation 'proper,' translation in the ordinary
> sense, interlinguistic and post-Babelian, Jakobson does not translate:
> he repeats the same word: 'interlingual translation and translation
> proper.' He supposes that it is not necessary to translate; everyone
> understands what that means because everyone has experienced it,
> everyone is expected to know what is a language, the relation of one
> language to another and especially identity and difference in fact
> of language. If there is a transparency that Babel would not have
> impaired, this is surely it, the experience of the multiplicity of tongues
> and the 'proper' sense of the word 'translation.'[12]

In opposition to this experience of the multiplicity of tongues, then, Derrida will elaborate another experience of the post-Babelian state of confusion. The Babel event, for Derrida, does not only divide "immortal speech" into a number of mutually incomprehensible languages; it also baffles language as such, preventing each separate language from consolidating itself as a self-identical individual. In a certain respect, Derrida takes post-Babelian "confusion" more literally than any other reader. Rather than mere opacity or incomprehension, "confusion," for Derrida, means interpenetration, mixture, hybridization. After Babel, no language would be constituted as a separate language without being deconstituted as an individual; the singularity of language would consist of an unpredictable mixture of grafts and borrowings from several other languages.

Derrida's "Two Words for Joyce," for example, consists of a lengthy commentary on the problems that beset the translator when he confronts two little words from *Finnegans Wake*: "He war." It could legitimately be claimed that Joyce's work is written in English. At the same time, even a cursory reading of Joyce's "book of the dark" reveals that it relentlessly exploits the elective affinity of the very "letter" of the English language with an open series of other languages. Derrida's two words, "he war," could be said to be written in English and German at the same time, such that it is impossible to read them "in English" without translating them. The very body of each language is never its own. Rather than evoke the incomprehension that results from multiplying tongues, then, "confusion" results from the deconstruction of language as *corps propre*. Translation, he writes at one point, is the "translation of a system in deconstruction."[13] The key to the allegory of this deconstruction lies in what is strangely the most overlooked aspect of the Babel narrative: the tower itself. Not only does the tower—in French translation—silently name trope (*tour*); it is also literally a tower (*tour*), an edifice or construction doomed to incompletion.

> The 'tower of Babel' does not merely figure the irreducible multiplicity of tongues: it exhibits an incompletion, the impossibility of finishing, of totalizing, of saturating, of completing something on the order of an edification, architectural construction, system and architectonics. What the multiplicity of idioms actually limits is not only a 'true' translation, a transparent and adequate interexpression, it is also a structural order, a coherence of construct. There is then (let us translate) something like an internal limit to formalization, an incompleteness of the constructure. It would be easy and up to a certain point justified to see there the translation of a system in deconstruction.[14]

Ultimately, Derrida does not stop at the assertion that languages are hybrid bodies shot through with unspoken fragments of other languages. If languages are incomplete, it is not merely because they contain more than one language but also, more intransigently, because they contain *more than language*. There is an internal limit of formalization because each language, in its very constructure, already entails an innumerable series of translations that transfer something into language that does not strictly speaking belong to language.[15]

Unlike other readings of the Babel narrative that revolve around the "negative" moment of dispersion or scattering, Derrida's reading emphasizes the "positive" moment at which Yahweh gives the name "Babel" for the first time. It is precisely this act of giving the name, he contends, that sows confusion. According to the order of the biblical narrative itself, the naming of the city constitutes a secondary event. *First* God baffles the language of the people and scatters them across the earth, *and then*—as a kind of memorial to his own intervention— he gives the name "Babel" to the terminally unfinished city. "And the LORD scattered them from there over all the earth and they left off building the city. Therefore it is called Babel, for there the LORD made the language of all the earth babble. And from there the LORD scattered them over all the earth" (Genesis 11:8–9). But what exactly does it mean to "baffle" or "confuse" a language? How is it possible to divide a single unproblematic language into several languages that constantly confront their speakers with the problem of translation?

We do not have answers to these questions because of the elliptical nature of biblical discourse. And we do not seek answers to these questions simply because we presuppose—based on a set of unquestioned theological principles—that God can and should do whatever he wishes. The narrative order of the biblical text itself, which evokes the act of God but does not represent it, supports such a presupposition. To the extent to which translation theory accepts the diversity of languages as a first principle, then, it upholds the order of scriptural narrative—or rather, upholds narrative order itself as scriptural. Working with and against the tradition of translation theory, Derrida's reading of Babel inverts the temporal order of biblical narrative; he claims that the posthumous or memorial event of naming is a representation of a primary event held in reserve.[16] The name "Babel"—which, Alter tells us, constitutes a pun on the Hebrew verb *balal* ("to confuse," "to confound," "to baffle")— means confusion. The text of the Bible explains that the name was chosen because of its meaning: "Therefore it is called Babel, for there the LORD made the language of all the earth babble. And from there the LORD scattered them over all the earth." Cities are frequently defined by events that happen both in them and to them.[17] According to the order of scriptural narrative, then, Babel would be named *after* such an event, the event of its incompletion, in the wake of this event, with a name that explicitly refers to it as a historical turning point in the life of the city and the people. In Derrida's reading, however, the act of giving the name—which, at a certain point in his essay, he calls the "Babelian performance"—itself constitutes the event to which it would refer. Much like performative utterances that do what they say (e.g., "I declare the session officially closed"; "time of death: 12:43PM"), it is the act of naming the city "confusion" that sows confusion and dooms the people's endeavor to remain unfinished. In this manner, Derrida reads the text of the Bible against the grain of its own scriptural order and thereby breaks with the mythical presuppositions that doom translation theory to reduce translation to a nostalgic resignation to misunderstanding, imperfection, and finitude.

More remarkably—and all the more disconcerting to the extent that Derrida does it without remarking on it—Derrida does not shy away from exposing and analyzing the act of God. For Derrida, the essence of God does not lie in his withdrawal from human knowledge or his omnipotence but rather, very much to the contrary, in the way in which he exposes or even deposes himself through his *acts*. The history to which translation belongs does not revolve around Man and his Fall but rather God and his deconstruction. Aligning himself with Hegel on this point, Derrida turns to Jakob Böhme's God of anger: "And the name of God the father would be the name of the origin of tongues. But it is also that God who, in the action of his anger (like the God of Böhme or of Hegel, he who leaves himself, determines himself in his finitude and thus produces history), annuls the gift of tongues, or at least embroils it, sows confusion among his sons, and poisons the present (*Gift-gift*)."[18]

How, then, does giving the name sow confusion or poison the present (the "present" in both temporal and economic senses)? The answer is deceptively simple. The gift of the name "Babel" sows confusion precisely because it is a proper name that corresponds to a common noun ("Bavel"). From the moment that this synthesis—an apriori synthesis—is forged, the language in which it appears—which Derrida calls the "tongue of Genesis" (*la langue de la Genèse*),[19] without otherwise identifying it[20]—is defined by the problems of translation that it poses. "'Babel' could be understood in one language as meaning 'confusion.' And from then on, just as Babel is at once proper name and common noun, confusion also becomes proper name and common noun, the one as the homonym of the other, the synonym as well, but not the equivalent, because there could be no question of confusing them in their value. It has for the translator no satisfactory solution."[21] The question, for Derrida, is not merely *how* to translate Babel, by which word or phrase to translate it. Confronted with the gift of this name, the translator must consider *whether* to translate it at all. According to the usual practice of most translators, in fact, proper names are not translated. Unlike common nouns, these words are simply transferred or transposed. A character named Pierre in a French novel will also be named Pierre in the English translation of the novel just as a person named Pierre does not change his name when he travels from Paris to London. The proper name is "proper" not because it belongs to a specific language but rather because it belongs to a singular being to whom it was given and who, as it were,

carries it around with him or her;[22] it is "the reference of a pure signifier to a singular being." In a translation, then, the proper name often
has the same status as that of foreign words or citations in the original text—which are most often left untranslated or, in cases when
the translation is liable to render these words invisible because they
are drawn from the target language, accompanied by a note (e.g., "in
English in the original"). At the same time, as Derrida underscores,
a proper name can also be—and structurally speaking always is—
distinguished by the fact that it is the homonym of a common noun.
The point is not that this homonymy endows the proper name with a
supplementary meaning but that it is an essential trait of the signifier
itself. In order to grasp or transmit the signifier "Babel," in order to
show that this signifier is characterized precisely by the way in which
it functions as both proper name and common noun, it is necessary
to translate it.

What is singular about Derrida's exposition of this problem of
translation, as I have suggested, is the way in which he uses it to
distinguish between the foreignness of language and untranslatability. Based on his analysis of Babel as a homonym, it would be possible—continuing to think within the scriptural order of the Babel
narrative—to conclude that the proper name's correspondence to a
common noun is what makes it specifically Hebrew. Or, alternately,
what characterizes Hebrew as a distinct language is the fact that
in it the proper name Babel can also be understood to mean confusion, that such correspondences in any language (such as *pierre/
Pierre* in French) are what define the untranslatable foreignness of
that language. To a certain extent, such conclusions are legitimate.
For Derrida, however, confusion makes it impossible to identify the
specificity of any given language or indeed to identify any language
whatsoever. While the proper name seems to be the most idiomatic
and untranslatable element in any language, it circulates, even in the
language to which it supposedly belongs as a fragment of a foreign
language. The proper name is never at home in any language, Derrida
insists throughout "Des Tours de Babel": "The noun *pierre* belongs
to the French language, and its translation into a foreign language
should in principle transport its meaning. This is not the case with
Pierre, whose inclusion in the French language is not assured and is
in any case not of the same type. 'Peter' in this sense is not a translation of Pierre, any more than Londres is a translation of 'London.'"[23]
No proper name as such can with any assurance be ascribed to any

identifiable language, to any supposedly self-enclosed linguistic system (e.g., "French"). This does not mean, however, that the proper name can be ascribed to some other foreign language, or that it constitutes the point at which two "different" languages become inextricably confused. The proper name is foreign without belonging to any identifiable foreign language. The fact that languages in their diversity seem to include proper names, Derrida pursues, is an effect of an originary form of intralingual translation.

In Crépon's reading of Derrida, intralingual translation consists of the philosophical consolidation and stabilization of the lexicon. According to Derrida's reading of the Babel narrative, however, such translation is at work on an even more basic level; it consists in the metaphoric operation whereby a proper name, "Babel," is transferred into the language of Genesis:

> For in the very tongue of the original narrative there is a translation [*une traduction*], a sort of transfer [*une sorte de translation*] that gives immediately (by some confusion) the semantic equivalent of the proper name which, by itself, as a pure proper name, it would not have. As a matter of fact, this intralinguistic translation operates immediately; it is not even an operation in the strict sense. Nevertheless, someone who speaks the language of Genesis could be attentive to the effect of the proper name in effacing the conceptual equivalent (like *pierre* in *Pierre*, and these are two absolutely heterogeneous values or functions); one would then be tempted to say first that a proper name, in the proper sense, does not properly belong to the language [*n'appartient proprement à la langue*]; it does not belong there, although and because its call makes language possible [*bien et parce que son appel la rend possible*] (what would language be without the possibility of calling by a proper name?); consequently it can properly inscribe itself in a language only by allowing itself to be translated therein [*par conséquent il ne peut s'inscrire proprement dans une langue qu'en s'y laissant traduire*], in other words, interpreted by the semantic equivalent: from this moment it can no longer be taken as a proper name.[24]

According to the classical reading of the Babel narrative, confusion consists in the mutual incomprehensibility of diverse languages. It is the situation that demands what Jakobson calls *inter*linguistic translation. For Derrida, however, it is a primordial act of *intra*linguistic translation that produces the state of Babelian confusion. Derrida's reading of Babel thus opens the question whether any language is ever self-identical. Through his analysis of the way in which the proper name Babel is transferred into the language of Genesis, Derrida shows, at the very least, that it is difficult to distinguish *intralinguistic* translation and *interlinguistic* translation; the proper name is the essential weak point at which every language incorporates a foreign element into its "own" system. But it is also necessary to say more. The proper name "in the proper sense" does not merely belong to a foreign language; it is foreign to language as such.

This is an extremely delicate point that has been somewhat obscured by the translation of Derrida's text. Throughout the passage in question, Joseph E. Graham's translation introduces an ambiguity that obscures the radicality of Derrida's thinking. In question is the translation of the definite article. In translation from French to English the definite article is often dropped. To refer to language as such or the very concept of language in French, one always uses the definite article: *la langue*. In English, however, this is not the case: one says simply "language" or "language as such." Not "the language." "The language" always refers back to a specific language such as "the English language." When Derrida writes that a proper name, in the proper sense, "*n'appartient proprement à la langue*," it would be logical and appropriate to translate this final phrase as "does not properly belong to language." But Graham retains the article: "does not properly belong to the language." The resulting translation suggests that it is merely a matter of the proper name belonging to a specific language, the language of the Babel narrative, the language of Genesis; that the proper name *first* belonged to some other language and was *then* introduced into this language. At this point in his argument, in fact, Derrida goes further: his claim is that the proper name does not belong to any specific language because it is foreign to language as such. The proper name is essential to language, but it isn't properly linguistic. It constitutes the point at which language itself opens itself to and turns upon the incorporation of the nonlinguistic; the proper name is the point at which the *corps propre* of language is divided from itself. Arguably, Graham's translation is appropriate to the extent to which, in fact, the proper name only ever appears in the context of a specific language; that which is foreign to language is only ever registered as an element heterogeneous to the system of a language. And yet this is a point at which the translator's hypervigilant insistence upon potential linguistic nuances in the original tends to soften the categorical thrust of the argument. The supposition is that, especially in order to be faithful to a "deconstructive" text, it is necessary to convey the maximum linguistic overdetermination when, in fact—at this juncture in the text in question—the deconstructive dimension of Derrida's thinking lies in the most uncompromising assertion possible. The nuanced translation highlights the potential ambiguity of Derrida's language and thereby insists upon the aspect of his argument that itself insists upon linguistic ambiguity or polysemy. Accordingly, such a translation promotes the common—and not entirely distorted—supposition that deconstruction hinges upon a linguistic turn. In fact, as Derrida's reading of Babel itself demonstrates, deconstruction turns upon the deconstruction of language itself as an autonomous system.

The "program" with which Derrida opens *Of Grammatology*—the book often cited to support the claim that deconstruction is a version of the linguistic turn—clearly asserts that, even as it doubles language, what Derrida calls "writing" remains something other than language, larger or more comprehensive than language, liable to destroy it from within:

> By a hardly perceptible necessity, it seems as though the concept of writing—no longer indicating a particular, derivative, auxiliary form of language in general[,] . . . no longer designating the exterior surface, the insubstantial double of a major signifier, *the signifier of the signifier*—is beginning to go beyond the extension of language. In all senses of the word, writing thus *comprehends* language. . . . The secondarity that it seemed possible to ascribe to writing alone affects all signifieds in general, affects them always already, the moment they *enter the game*. . . . The advent of writing is the advent of this play; today such a play is coming into its own, effacing the limit starting from which one had thought to regulate the circulation of signs, drawing along with it all the reassuring signifieds, reducing all the strongholds, all the out-of-bounds shelters that watched over the field of language. This, strictly speaking, amounts to destroying the concept of 'sign' and its entire logic.[25]

Writing *comprehends* language, Derrida writes, in all senses of the word *comprehend*. What are the senses of this word? In English, the *Oxford English Dictionary* tells us, the obsolete senses of *comprehend* evoke a chase or a hunt: to seize, to grasp, to lay hold of, to entrap, to overtake, to attain, to compass. In English (*comprehend*) as in French (*comprendre*), the less untimely senses of the word refer to a moment of internalization or enfolding: "to take in, comprise, include, contain"; "to lay hold of all points of (any thing) and include them within the compass of a description or expression; to embrace or describe summarily; summarize; sum up"; "to enclose or include *in* or *within* limits." Both in English and in French, the most common meaning of the word refers to the act of grasping or encompassing something with the mind: "to grasp with the mind, conceive fully or adequately, understand." In English, comprehending is often considered to be synonymous with understanding. But such a synonym does not exist in French. According to the Littré, to comprehend is to apply the principle of reason: *se rendre raison d'une chose, se l'expliquer.* To render reason to oneself for something, explain it to oneself. If writing comprehends language, then, this means that writing has always already laid hold of language, snared it, entrapped it—as if writing were somehow *earlier* or *faster* than language; language has always been caught up in writing; writing has always contained language as one of its possibilities or effects, so that the possibilities or effects that we habitually ascribe to language can ultimately only be understood in terms of writing; writing allows us to render the very principle or reason of language.

Beyond laying hold of language quickly, however, writing is everywhere. Comprehending language, it's both fast and vast. Larger than language and perhaps even larger than the world. And yet, as Derrida shows in his writings on translation, the economy of writing only ever appears in the form of the punctual upsurge. A discrete or minimal verbal body. A single name or word or, at most, two words. To the extent that it always belongs both to no language and to more than one language—"*plus d'une langue*"—the proper name embodies the economy whereby language "itself" comprehends more than language. In "What Is a Relevant Translation?," Derrida calls the word *relevant* (itself always between languages) a "translative body."[26] As Freud abundantly demonstrated in *Interpretation of Dreams*, before language functions as signification, it is characterized by its powers of substitution and displacement; and further than these, it operates in the service of synthesis, condensation, and overdetermination.

For both Derrida and Freud, such economy is political economy. If the act of God in the Babel narrative consists in the gift of the proper name, then the "confusion of tongues" is less a matter of dividing the supreme language into diverse languages than of what Derrida calls, in a reading of Joyce's construction of the Babel narrative in *Finnegans Wake*, "war in language and on language and by language." The body of the word itself—the singularity of its untranslatable synthesis—is an act of war. War in what sense? The next task is to address this question.

WAR

Up to this point, I have established a simple but easily misrecognized point—that the object of translation, the problem that the task of the translator addresses, is not foreign language but rather something foreign to language inscribed within the language upon which it works. Even this manner of posing the problem, however, remains potentially misleading. The supposition that translation takes place between languages obscures the role of the literary work in the theory and practice of translation. But this is not surprising since the prevailing rhetoric of translation remains grounded in a mythical vision of translation as the reconciliation of the world's languages, overcoming man's foreignness to man. This rhetoric distinguishes the "object" language from the "target" language; it designates the translator as a specialist in a specific language (e.g., the "award-winning Spanish-to-English translator"); it accounts for the work of the translator in terms of the work's original, "foreign" language (e.g., "translated from the French by the author"). Likewise, when we speak of literary works, we identify them with the national language in which they were originally written, often considering them to be a contribution to the history of this language. And yet this same rhetoric also implicitly acknowledges a fact that even the slightest acquaintance with the practice of translation should make unavoidable: the translator translates works, not languages. The question is not which English words should be used to translate Flaubert's French, for example, but rather how best to translate Flaubert—full stop.[27]

Benjamin's essay on the task of the translator is a decisive contribution to translation theory precisely because it refuses to separate the problem of translation from the study of literature. He introduces the problem of translation with a series of assertions about the relation or nonrelation between the artwork and its receiver. "In the appreciation of a work of art or an art form, consideration of the receiver never proves fruitful. Art . . . posits man's physical and spiritual existence, but in none of its works is it concerned with his response. No poem is intended for the reader, no picture for the beholder, no symphony for the listener."[28] These claims lay the groundwork for his subsequent claim that the object of translation is not the meaning of the literary work, which might be determined on the basis of its grammar and lexicon, but what Benjamin calls its *Uberleben* (survival) or its *Fortleben* (afterlife, continued life, living on).

By virtue of its translatability the original is closely connected with
the translation; in fact, this connection is all the closer since it is no
longer of importance to the original. We may call this connection
a natural one, or, more specifically, a vital connection. Just as the
manifestations of life are intimately connected with the phenomenon
of life without being of importance to it, a translation issues from the
original. Not so much from its life as from its afterlife [*Zwar nicht
aus seinem Leben so sehr denn aus seinem 'Überleben'*]. For a translation comes later than the original, and since important works of
world literature never find their chosen translators at the time of their
origin, their translation marks their stage of continued life [*das Sta-
dium ihres Fortlebens*]. The idea of life and afterlife in works of art
[*Der Gedanke vom Leben und Fortleben der Kunstwerke*] should be
regarded with an entirely unmetaphorical objectivity. Even in times
of narrowly prejudiced thought there was an inkling that life was not
limited to organic corporeality. . . . The concept of life is given its due
only if everything that has a history of its own, and is not merely the
setting for history, is credited with life. In the final analysis, the range
of life must be determined by history rather than by nature. . . . The
philosopher's task consists in comprehending all of natural life
through the more encompassing life of history. And indeed, is not the
continued life of works of art far easier to recognize than the contin-
ual life of animal species?[29]

Even for Benjamin, however, the work ultimately becomes an occasion for translation that operates between languages. As radical as
Benjamin's concept of life may be, it is what allows him to reduce
the work to its language. In his reading of the essay, Derrida claims
that what Benjamin calls *Überleben* cannot be reduced to *Fortleben*;
that "sur-vival" is not merely a matter of naturally or supernaturally
extended or expanded life. "Such sur-vival gives more of life, more
than a surviving. The work does not simply live longer, it lives more
an better, beyond the means of its author."[30] For Derrida, the work is
a gift, not a seed. Its survival is contingent upon transmission rather
than transmutation or growth. Ultimately, however, Benjamin's argument tends to confuse what Derrida separates. He explicitly entrusts
the survival of works to what he calls "the holy growth of languages,"
"*jenes heilige Wachstum der Sprachen*." What lives on in the work is
its language; the life of the work thus becomes a moment within the
ongoing growth of languages.

> Translation thus ultimately serves the purpose of expressing the
> central reciprocal relationship between languages. . . . In the indi-
> vidual, unsupplemented languages, meaning is never found in rela-
> tive independence, as in individual words or sentences; rather, it is in

a constant state of flux—until it is able to emerge as pure language from the harmony of all the various modes of intention. Until then, it remains hidden in languages. If, however, languages continue to grow until the end of time [*aus das messianische Ende ihrer Geschichte wachsen*], it is translation which catches fire on the eternal life of the works [*ewige Fortleben der Werke*] and the infinite renewal of language [*unendlichen Aufleben des Sprache*]. Translation keeps putting the hallowed growth of languages [*jenes heilige Wachstum der Sprachen*] to the test. How far removed is their hidden meaning from revelation, how close can it be brought by knowledge of this remoteness?

   This, to be sure, is to admit that all translation is only a somewhat provisional way of coming to terms with the foreignness of languages [*sich mit der Fremdheit der Sprachen auseinanderzusetzen*].[31]

Benjamin's easy passage—without noticeable transition—from discussion of the work of art to discussion of the relationship between languages reveals that his theory of translation rests upon a traditional concept of the relationship between work and word. Rather than merely translate works, then, the translator "intends language as a whole, taking an individual work in an alien language as a point of departure" (Ihre Intention geht . . . auf eine Sprache im ganzen von einem einzelnen Kunstwerke in einer Fremden aus).[32] The life and afterlife of the artwork bears witness to the messianic horizon toward which it strives: the reconciliation of languages toward which the work's own language contributes by virtue of its singular intervention within history. "The intention of the poet is spontaneous, primary, graphic; that of the translator is derivative, ultimate, ideational. For the great motif of integrating many tongues into one true language is at work."[33]

   According to Derrida's transformative reading of Benjamin, these organicist or geneticist metaphors—despite their prevalence—are powerless to determine the sense of his text. Rather than understand translation in terms of organic life, he argues, Benjamin demands that we understand life in terms of translation—or, more radically, the "contractual" relationship between a translation and the original work. This reading has obvious consequences on the level of critical practice. In all his work on translation theory and practice, including the essay on "The Task of the Translator," Derrida never passes—as Benjamin explicitly does—from problems of translation to the problem of language in general. To a remarkable degree, Derrida is always concerned with translation as a practical problem posed by specific texts or, more often, single words or phrases in those texts. Rather than accept the parameters of a sedimented understanding of the Babel narrative, Derrida provides a fresh reading of translation in the biblical text itself; in "What Is a Relevant Translation?," his reflections on translation, sovereignty, and the theologico-political revolve stubbornly around the problem that confront the translator of a few words from Shakespeare's *The Merhcant of Venice*; and finally, as the title suggests, "Two Words for Joyce" revolves around the very practical questions of translation raised by exactly two words from *Finnegans Wake*. Whereas Benjamin conceives of the relationship between the artwork and language in terms of perpetual life (growth, harmony, and ultimate reconciliation), Derrida construes this relationship in terms of perpetual war. Working within the framework of the traditional reading of Babel, Benjamin never doubts that the object of translation is language and that the task of the translator is to work toward the integration of the earth's diverse languages. For Derrida, the work is defined by an originary translation that hybridizes languages; and that, more radically, bears witness to something foreign to language—the economy of writing, the body of the word—at work within the system of language that prevents it from being consolidated as language. In the work, the translator discovers not foreign language but something foreign to—and at war with—language as such.

"HE WAR." In Derrida's reading of Joyce's Babel myth, these two words (telegraphing the act of God that divides language and disperses peoples) both proffer a declaration of war, the announcement of an act that precedes the act, and posit the act itself—a war "in language, on language, and by language." Derrida works these words through rhapsodic series of "translations" that culminate in an inversion whereby a declaration of war and the act of war change places. The declaration, it turns out, is already the war that it should merely precipitate.

HE WAR

> I spell them out: H E W A R, and sketch a first translation: HE
> WARS—he wages war, he declares or makes war, he is war, which
> can also be pronounced by babelizing a bit (it is in a particularly
> Babelian scene of the book that these words rise up), by Germanizing,
> then, in Anglo-Saxon, He war: he was—he who was ('I am he who is
> or who am,' says YHWH). Where it was, he was, declaring war, and
> it is true. Pushing things a bit, taking the time to draw on the vowel
> and to lend an ear, it will have been true, *wahr*, that's what can be
> kept [*garder*] or looked at [*regarder*] in truth.

> He is 'He,' the 'him,' the one who says I in the masculine, 'He,'
> war declared, he who was war declared, declaring war, was he who
> was, and he who was true, the truth, he who by declaring war veri-
> fied the truth that he was, he verified himself, he verified the truth
> of the truth by war declared, by the act of declaring, and the act of
> declaring is an act of war, he declared war in language and on lan-
> guage and by language, which gave languages, that's the truth of
> Babel when YHWH pronounced its vocable, difficult to say if it was
> a name . . .
>
> I stop here provisionally, through lack of time; other transforma-
> tions are possible, a great number, about which I'll say another two
> words later.[34]

Language already does what it seems merely to promise. This temporal inversion structures each of the transformations to which Derrida subjects Joyce's words. When Derrida reads "war" as the past
sense of the German verb *sein*, when he translates "he war" as "he
was" (or, in French, using the preterit, *il fut*—an important detail to
which I will return in a moment), he insists that this past does not
correspond to the passage of a former present; it is an immemorial
past that, as it were, *was* without ever *having been*. God was before
he ever was. In Joyce's text, the biblical sentence, "And he war,"
appears immediately after an explicit reference to Babel that stages
the proper name opposite its palindrome: "And let Nek Nekulon
extol Mak Makal and let him say unto him: Immi ammi Semmi.
And shall not Babel be with Lebab? And he war."[35] Even as this palindrome overturns the tower, it plays with the letters and the meaning of being.

> Once this war is declared, he was it (*war*) by being himself this act of
> war which consisted in declaring, as he did, that he was the one who
> was (*war*). The God of fire assigns to the Shemites the necessary, fatal
> and impossible translation of his name, of the vocable with which
> he signs his act of war, of himself. This palindrome . . . overthrows
> the tower but plays too with the letter, the meaning of being and the
> letters of being, of 'being,' BE, EB (baBEl/lEBab), as it does with the
> meaning and the letter of the name of God, EL, LE.[36]

In passing, Derrida evokes the "God of fire." In French, the expression is *le Dieu de feu*. *Dieu* rhymes with *feu*; God rhymes with fire.
Thanks to the letter, fire inhabits the very name of God. Likewise, *feu*
(fire) comes very close to *fut* (war, was), so that it becomes the trope
of passage without passage, passage beyond being. *Dieu sans l'être*.
A few paragraphs later, Derrida returns to the God of fire, making

more explicit that it is the angry or jealous God who bans translation no less than graven images.

> So what happens when one tries to translate 'he war'? It is impossible not to want to do it, to want violently—and reading itself consists, from its very first movement, in sketching out translation. 'He War' calls for translation, both orders and forbids transposition into the other language. Change me (into yourself) and above all do not touch me, read and do not read, say and do not say otherwise what I have said and which will have been; in two words *which was*. For the 'he war' also tells of the irreplaceability of the event that it is, which is that it is, and which is also unchangeable because it has already been a past without appeal which, before being, was. So that's war declared. Before being, that is being a present, it was: was *He, he flees*, the late god of fire the jealous god [Avant d'être, c'est-à-dire un présent, cela fut, fut Il, fuit, feu le dieu de feu le dieu jaloux].[37]

HE WAR is a singular, irreplaceable event. It is the event of a singular performative utterance—a declaration of war. At the same time, it is idealistic to imagine that a declaration of war could take the form of a performative, that one could declare war by doing things with words. Even if the declaration of war is already considered to be an act of war in its own right, even if the word bears the force of law, the entire concept of the verbal declaration of war still supposes that the conduct of war can and should follow a certain order; that words should precede acts of outright violence; that each party to the conflict should openly and honestly declare their intentions before attacking in order to allow the other side enough time to muster a counterattack. The declaration of war might be an act of war in that it sets in motion a process that culminates in death and destruction, a process that leads beyond words; but the meaning and importance of such a declaration supposes that it manifestly takes place in language and as language. War, then, is something else. Most—if not all—wars are undeclared in the sense that they begin with acts rather than words. Moreover, through these acts they declare not that war will imminently begin but that it has already begun. It has begun without anyone being alerted that it would happen; this is already it, and there is no going back now.

For Carl Schmitt, as for an entire tradition, killing is the *passage-à-l'acte* that defines war. There are numerous points in Schmitt's work that underscore that killing is always linked to the decision to end diplomacy and discussion, to pass from word to act.[38] Derrida's reading of Joyce, however, shows that there are other forms of passage to the act and that killing might not be the ultimate and definitive act of war. The words HE WAR are untranslatable because they are written in more than one language at the same time. For the very same reason, they constitute an act of war. They are not words. They are a kind of nonverbal performative—a poetic or graphic event whose force lies not in its *well-timed utterance* but rather in its *untimely economy*. Economy of what Derrida calls the mark.

> The German *war* will only have been true in declaring war on English, and in making war on it in English. The fact of the multiplicity of languages, what was done as confusion of languages can no longer let itself be translated into *one* language, nor even into *language*. To translate 'he war' into the system of a single language . . . is to erase the event of the mark, not only what is said in it but its very saying and writing, the mark of the law and the law of its mark.[39]

This economy is less a matter of exchange, circulation, or capitalization than of extreme condensation, the condensation of numerous languages in a countable number of words. And this economy constitutes an act of war by virtue of its immeasurable speed—the speed whereby writing "comprehends" language; that makes it possible to write in multiple languages *at the same time*. This *same time*, however, is not the present but an unrecoverable past, a past that can never be translated into the present precisely because, for structural reasons, it can only be *represented* in one language at a time. Even in order to be read, HE WAR must be translated *first* into English and *then* into German or vice versa, but there is no word in any language that captures its peculiar synthesis of English *and* German. That which is simultaneous on the level of writing can only be translated in the form of a diachronic sequence.

If we approach rhetoric as the constitutive form of temporality, as Paul de Man did in "The Rhetoric of Temporality," Joyce's writing would point up the constitutively allegorical dimension of all translation. "The fundamental structure of allegory," de Man wrote in his reading of Wordsworth's "A Slumber Did My Spirit Seal," lies in "the tendency of [a] language toward narrative, the spreading out along the axis of an imaginary time in order to give duration to what is, in fact, simultaneous within the subject."[40] There is also an ineluctable tendency of translation—which would ideally contain an identical number of words as the original—to veer into narrative, paraphrase, parentheses, translator's notes, commentary, even memoir. Relying perhaps too heavily upon the translation of the word *trans-lation* or

Über-setzen as "meta-phor," theorists of translation have generally failed to emphasize this allegorical dimension.[41] In this respect, once again, Derrida proves to be the exception. As Derrida's readings of Genesis and Joyce demonstrate, the word is never merely a unit of meaning but also an overdetermined node, a point of extreme condensation, or even what Freud called the "navel" of a dream.

Against Lacan's determination of the dream's navel as a hole or gap, Derrida—claiming to read *The Interpretation of Dreams* more closely—shows that Freud describes the navel as a knot or meshwork: "Whatever exceeds the analysis of the dream is indeed a knot that cannot be untied, a thread that, even if it is cut, like an umbilical cord, nevertheless remains forever knotted, right on the body, at the place of the navel. The scar is a knot against which analysis can do nothing."[42] This place, Derrida later adds, would be "a knot or a tangled mass of threads, in short, an unanalyzable synthesis."[43] It is precisely the economy of such an absolute synthesis that Derrida discovers in Joyce's two words. The resistance of this synthetic knot to analysis is inseparable from its resistance to translation. It cannot be translated without a critical or allegorical narrative that breaks this knot down into distinct threads (first English, then German) in order to display their synthetic relationship to one another.

There is always at least a minimal—most often much more than minimal—aesthetic difference between the original and the translation. In "What Is a Relevant Translation?," Derrida explains that the act of translation always entails a singular negotiation between two hyperboles, two principles of economy. The principle of translation is less a matter of linguistic differences than what Derrida, referring to Kant, calls "aesthetic difference" between the original and the translation.

> If to a translator who is fully competent in at least two languages and two cultures, two cultural memories with the sociohistorical knowledge embodied in them, you give all the time in the world, as well as the words needed to explicate, clarify, and teach the semantic content and forms of the text to be translated, there is no reason for him to encounter the untranslatable or a remainder in his work. If you give someone who is competent an entire book, filled with translator's notes, in order to explain everything that a phrase of two or three words can mean in its particular form . . . there is really no reason, in principle, for him to fail to render—without any remainder—the intentions, meaning, denotations, connotations, and semantic overdeterminations, the formal effects of what is called the original. Of

course, this operation, which occurs daily in the university and in literary criticism, is not what is called translation, a translation worthy
of the name, translation in the strict sense, the translation of a *work*.
To make legitimate use of the word 'translation' (*traduction, Über-
setzung, traducción, translaciôn*, and so forth), in the rigorous sense
conferred on it over several centuries by a long and complex history
in a given cultural situation (more precisely, more narrowly, in Abra-
hamic and post-Lutheran Europe), the translation must be quantita-
tively equivalent to the original, apart from any paraphrase, explica-
tion, analysis, and the like. . . . No translation will ever reduce this
quantitative or, in a Kantian sense, this aesthetic difference, since it
concerns the spatial and temporal forms of sensibility.[44]

The translator is consigned to negotiate between these extremities,
Derrida could have added, because of the "extreme" economy of
the work itself. The fact of this economy—embodied in Joyce's two
words—demands that the translator find a word not only for each of
the words in the original, or even for all the words that these words
contain, but also a word (the "best" word) that translates as precisely
as possible that which in the original exceeds the languages that it
inscribes—which is to say, its inscription itself. The Derridean task
of the translator consists in the demand to transmit as economically
as possible the singular economy of the work. It is, in other words, to
find a word for that which in language remains foreign to language, to
find a word for the very work of the work, its "inscription," its "writing," its "body," or its "event."

Despite the emphasis of Derrida's entire philosophical enterprise
on the letter or trace, on that which can never be vocalized because
it does not belong to any one language, his writings on translation
reveal the imperative that orients this enterprise from beginning to
end: *one must not economize on economy; one must not pass over in
silence what remains mute*. Albeit in passing, he explicitly articulates
these prescriptions in "Two Words for Joyce": "Despite the need to
'phonetize,' despite the book's appeal for reading out loud, for song
and for timbre, something essential in it passes the understanding as
well as the hearing: a graphic or literal dimension, a muteness which
one should never pass over in silence. You can't economize on it, and
this book cannot be read without it."[45] These prescriptions return us
to demand, which Mallarmé articulates, to discover a "unique coinage, itself materially the truth." The task of the translator, if not the
philosopher, is not a matter—even at the utopian limit—of reconcil-
ing languages by translating one into another. Instead, it entails the

attempt to find words that supplement the lack of any supreme language, words that function to name—to break silence without voicing—the truth of language.

In his reading of Joyce, then, Derrida insists that the imposition of this truth—precisely to the extent that it is unspeakable—constitutes an act of war. The task of the translator, in this case, is not only to find words that do justice to the economy of Joyce's words, but, more generally, to name this war and thereby the truth that it harbors. Joyce's truth can only be named if the war whereby it imposes itself is recognized as war. Derrida's fundamental gesture—in this reading of Joyce and in other texts such as *Voice and Phenomenon* or "Le facteur de la verité"—is to name war where no war has yet been acknowledged; to discern the implicit declaration of war, and thereby explicitly to declare and enter into this war himself; to speak in the now explicit name of war, to measure its stakes and its limitations, to denounce its compromises and uphold its promise.

This entire scene of reading presupposes that it is not always obvious when wars happen precisely because they do not always break out; they often get started in silence and remain underground or unconscious for years, if not centuries; their existence is often denied for political reasons by at least one of the parties involved in the conflict, if not both. In an extremely illuminating essay on war, "What's in a War? (Politics as War, War as Politics)," Étienne Balibar observes that wars always have proper names and that the naming of war is itself always a decisive moment: "It has to do generally with the problem of naming the event, war being in a sense the archetypal 'event' in history, at least in national histories, and we know that to name the event is at the same time to decide that there is an event, an operation in which subjects are themselves part of the object they are considering."[46] However, beyond the problem of giving wars proper names, there is the more formidable problem of "*naming the war a war*, i.e., granting it the character of a war." "Not every war is acknowledged as a war," Balibar continues, "and this is clearly a question of decisive political importance, as is the fact that at some point, or after the event, for a combination of motives which concern either the magnitude of the engagements, or the legal status of the adversaries, or both, something that was not called a war becomes a war. And perhaps we may have to consider also the reverse case, of 'wars' which are not exactly wars."[47] This, then, is precisely Derrida's gesture.[48] Reading the muteness of Joyce's HE WAR, he declares it a declaration of war, not only a war that is represented in the narrative of *Finnegans Wake*, but a war that would silently encompass the Babelian performance of the entire work, a war that might not be recognized as such precisely because it takes the form of a literary work, or because both its object and its subject are language itself.

The function of this gesture is twofold. On the one hand, as I have just suggested, it aims to contest the validity of the cultural and ideological interests at stake in failing to recognize the status of this war as war. To provide a somewhat reductive summation of what's at stake for Derrida in naming war, we could say that it is a matter of upholding the "good" (perhaps even the hyperbolic Good beyond being) of a mark that inscribes multiplicity without subordinating it to the hegemony of the One. On the other hand, Derrida suggests that we need to examine the transformations of war—analyzing the way in which historical circumstances give rise to wars that cannot be understood in terms of any extant concept of war and, more generally, the way in which war "itself" might he inherently metamorphic, defined by periodic changes in logic and form.

Joyce's works constitute, in Derrida's words,

> a hypermnesiac machine, there in advance, decades in advance, to compute you, control you, forbid you the slightest inaugural syllable because you can say nothing that is not programmed on this 1000th generation computer—*Ulysses, Finnegans Wake*—beside which the current technology of our computers and our micro-computerized archives and our translating mechanisms are of a slowness incommensurable with the quasi-infinite speed of the movements of Joyce's cables. How could you calculate the speed with which a mark, a marked piece of information, is placed in contact with another in the same word or from one end of the book to the other?[49]

As readers of Clausewitz, we assume that war entails the escalating deployment of ever greater force. In the first and last instance, however, the extremity of war goes beyond the interaction of forces. The force of force lies not in its magnitude but in its capacity to threaten. Conflict does not become war unless force represents a threat or an act of hostility; and force cannot threaten the enemy unless it can breach his defenses. Speed, then, is inseparable from war because it is precisely that which in various ways endows force with the capacity to breach defenses. Weapon design, for example, always revolves around considerations of speed. A sword is no threat unless its bearer can swing it quickly and accurately. A bullet is harmless without the gun that makes it travel at a certain velocity. On a more complex level, since war takes place between living beings who are by definition mobile, any hostile deployment of force must move faster than its target—not only faster than the target's body but also faster than his mind, faster than his mind can calculate the speed of the force directed against him in order to defend against it. This is precisely the dimension of war to which traumatic experience bears witness.[50]

Cathy Caruth, in her influential construction of traumatic experience, stresses the way in which the traumatic event happens too fast for the mind to grasp it: "the wound of the mind . . . is not, like the wound of the body a simple and healable event, but rather, like Tancred's first infliction of a mortal wound on the disguised Clorinda in the duel, is experienced too soon, too unexpectedly, to be fully known and is therefore not available to consciousness until it imposes itself again."[51] Speed is inherently traumatogenic. This is why, before World War I, traumatic neurosis was associated primarily with railway accidents.[52] In this sense, however, trauma proves to be an integral dimension of war. There is no war without trauma because there is no act of hostility that does not attempt to break down or break through the enemy's defenses in order to kill him. There is no killing without wounding or effraction. Precisely because trauma is predicated upon the absence of any physical wound, it is predicated upon the separation of force and the speed whereby it is delivered and turns deadly; and thus it bears witness to the absolute hostility—the pure will to harm—at the heart of war. Even more than bloodshed, trauma would manifest the passage to the extreme whereby war comes into its own as war.

Derrida's reading of Joyce goes further than Clausewitz and even further than the theory of war as trauma. Without explicit reference to the use of force, the hypermnesia of the mark alone constitutes a primordial effraction. In order to read Joyce, Derrida contends, we must play the losing game of entering into his memory—performing the painstaking process of reconstructing the entire system of overlapping references encoded in each of his vocables. But the more we play this game, the more we are confronted by the dizzying economy of Joyce's text, by the fact that it has already done in less than an instant what it takes us much too long to accomplish.

> Being in memory of him: not necessarily to remember him, no, but
> to be in his memory, to inhabit his memory, which is henceforth
> greater than all your finite memory can, in a single instant or a single
> vocable, gather up of cultures, languages, mythologies, religions,

philosophies, sciences, history of mind and literatures. I don't know
if you can like that without resentment and jealousy. Can one pardon
this hypermnesia which a priori indebts you, and in advance inscribes
you in the book you are reading? One can pardon this Babelian act
of war only if one knows it happens already, from all time, with each
event of writing.[53]

If celerity implies hostility even in the absence of force, then the lag
time between the speed of the mark and the distension of reading
implies an exposure to violence without possible defense.

Such violence is the motive for Derrida's confessed resentment and
ambivalence with respect to Joyce. Unlike an author who "writes in
order to give, in giving, and therefore in order to give to forget the gift
and the given, what is given and the act of giving [*qui écrit pour donner, en donnant, et donc pour donner à oublier le donné et la don-
née, ce qui est donné et l'acte de donner*],"[54] Joyce (himself as author)
refuses to be forgotten—enters into a duel with the reader, demanding that he never stop remembering the author and everything that he
remembers, cruelly forcing him to assume a memory that will never
be his own. Isn't one of the cruelest outcomes of war the fact that
it leaves behind wounds that compel the survivors to remember the
hands that inflicted them, both the violence and the violator? Derrida's reflections on this point distinctly recall Nietzsche's genealogy of
morals, with its emphasis upon the cruelty of mnemotechnics. "Perhaps thee is nothing more terrible and strange in man's prehistory,"
Nietzsche writes, "than his *technique of mnemonics*. 'A thing must be
burnt in so that it stays in the memory: only something that continues
to hurt stays in the memory'—that is the proposition from the oldest (and unfortunately longest-lived) psychology on earth. . . . When
man decided he had to make a memory for himself, it never happened without blood, torments and sacrifices."[55] Implicitly building
upon such premises, Derrida suggests that the cruelty at the basis of
memory does not merely belong to prehistory, but remains susceptible
to being reactivated at any time. As Joyce demonstrates, it is always
possible to transmit or transpose—through writing, for example—
the cruelty within one's own memory upon an other, to compel an
other to bear this violence in one's place. This is the source of the
resentment (again, a concept from *The Genealogy of Morals*) that the
reader cannot help but feel with respect to Joyce. As Derrida writes,
it is only possible to forgive Joyce for inflicting this violence upon the
reader if one presumes that he, too, was subject to the same ordeal;

that the peculiar economy of his own writing constituted an attempt to outstrip some "sadistic demiurge" who left him no peace. "One can pardon it only if one remembers too that Joyce himself must have endured this situation. He was its patient, and what's more that's his theme or, as I prefer to say, his scheme. He talks about it often enough for there to be no simple confusion between him and a sadistic demiurge, setting up a hypermnesiac machine, there in advance."[56] Such forgiveness is also what makes it possible to read Joyce otherwise.

To the extent to which war is inherently traumatogenic, to the extent that this revolves around the speed of a passage to the act, it is also inherently mute. Mute, not silent. The din or noise of war is legendary. But such clamor is nothing but the sound that rises in the absence of speech. It is thus necessary to amplify the basic definition of war. Beyond an armed conflict between living beings, war is a conflict between speaking beings who have ceased speaking. Language always functions as a retarding factor—the prelude to or the deferral of an act. However, the turn from speaking to acting does not merely result from the momentary need to concentrate, to gather one's forces and project oneself upon the instant. To pass to the act is to abandon the possibility of speech once and for all. The return from war is not the return to speech. War leaves behind vast regions of unclaimed and unspeakable experience. In the famous preamble to his essay "The Storyteller," Benjamin asks: "Was it not noticeable at the end of the war that men returned from the battlefield grown silent—not richer, but poorer in communicable experience?"[57]

In his extended commentary, beyond Joyce's two words, on the passage from *Finnegans Wake* in which they appear, Derrida underscores his pun on *Lord* and *loud*. Derrida writes, "I read very aloud [*je lis à voix très haute*]," and then cites (among others) the following lines from the *Wake*:

> Great is him whom is over Ismael and he shall mekanek of Mak Nekulon. And he deed.
>   Uplouderamainagain!
>   For the Clearer of Air from on high has spoken in tumbuldum tambaldam to his tembledim tombaldoom worrild and, moguphonoised by that phonemanon, the unhappitents of the earth have terreumbled from firmament unto fundament and from tweedledeedumms down to twiddledeedees.
>   Loud, hear us!
>   Loud, graciously hear us![58]

Precisely because this Lord is the angry God who wars, the God of fire, Joyce characterizes him by the height of his volume ("Loud," "Uploud") rather than the authority of his voice. Commenting on these lines, Derrida aligns it with questions of the relation between voice and phenomenon that captured his attention in his first published book on Husserl: "let us limit ourselves, if one can say this, to all that passes through the voice and the phenomenon, the phenomenon as phoneme: at the center of the sequence, hear then 'phonemanon.'"[59] But, as Joyce explicitly specifies, this "phonemanon" is less a matter of voice than noise; more than phonic, it is megaphonic ("moguphonoised by that phonemanon").[60] Unlike the singular tone or timbre of the voice, the magnitude of its sound is mute: like the boom that arises upon a body's transgression of the sound barrier, the voice becomes megaphonic as it exits speech and language.

This booming, however, is nothing less than the noise of language itself. Language, for Derrida, is always too loud: for those with ears to hear, it is shot through with the clamor of its imperialistic intent. There is no unraised voice. Even an inner voice can only be called a voice to the extent to which it has been raised, albeit raised without making a sound. Psychotic subjects, for example, complain of being relentlessly persecuted by voices that no one hears. The voice as such—one's own voice, the voice of the other, the voice of conscience, any voice—is an agent of war. Against the imperialism of the voice, Derrida sides with the mute economy of writing not only because writing is better than the voice (there are too many places to enumerate where Derrida identifies writing with the highest Good) but also because it makes legible the imperialism whereby the voice strives to repress anything that threatens to disrupt its hegemony.

His lecture on Joyce is thus punctuated by moments at which he raises his own voice only to highlight its elevation and thereby to underscore what remains mute in the voice itself—the violence of the One that endows the speech act itself with its unquestioned ethical, social, political, and even libidinal value. In this way, Derrida reactivates the primal scene of Joyce's own writing, which, despite its hyperbolic Babelism, demands (impossibly) to be spoken and sung in English and is celebrated as English prose. *Finnegans Wake*, in Derrida's reading, "is" war, war without or beyond being. And to read *Finnegans Wake*—or, indeed, to read in general—is to enter into this war one way or another. Derrida's own manner of entering it—his parti pris—is (1) to take the side of writing against the imperialism of

the Voice; and thereby (2) to take the side of war itself, to insist that
the polemic that joins and divides voice and writing not be passed
over in silence.

> For a little while, I've been speaking out loud. In proffering 'he war,'
> I entrust myself to this truth, so often recalled: in this book, in this
> event worked on by the confusion of languages, multiplicity remains
> controlled by the dominant language, English. Now despite the need
> to 'phonetize,' despite the book's appeal for reading out loud, for
> song and for timbre, something essential in it passes the understand-
> ing as well as the hearing: a graphic or literal dimension, a muteness
> which one should never pass over in silence. You can't economize on
> it, and this book cannot be read without it. For the Babelian confu-
> sion between the English war and the German war cannot fail to
> disappear—in becoming determined—when listened to. It is erased
> when pronounced. One is constrained to say it either in English or
> else in German, it cannot therefore be received as such by the ear. But
> it can be read. . . . The event is linked to the spacing of its archive and
> would not take place without it, without being put into letters and
> pages. Erase the typeface, mute the graphic percussion, subordinate
> the spacing, that is, the divisibility of the letter, and you would again
> reappropriate *Finnegans Wake* into a monolinguism, or at least subju-
> gate it to the hegemony of a single language. Of course this hegemony
> remains indisputable, but its law only appears as such in the course
> of a war through which English tries to erase the other language or
> languages, to colonize them, to domesticate them, to present them for
> reading from any one angle.[61]

By virtue of the irreducible economy of Joyce's writing, his English is
divided from itself by "a graphic or literal dimension, a muteness that
one should not pass over in silence." No matter its discrete position in
Derrida's exposition, this prescription clearly summarizes Derrida's
entire ethics and politics of reading. On the one hand, the voice offers
no access to the constitutive Babelism of Joyce's writing precisely
because it represents the ineluctable drive to reduce its overdetermination, to remember each of its "parts" one at a time and thereby
violently to dismember it, to erase once and for all the singular economy of its mark. On the other hand, Derrida insists, "one should
never pass over in silence" the muteness of this graphic dimension.
We have a basic ethical and political responsibility not to pass over in
silence that which does not and cannot speak for itself—something
in language that does not strictly speaking belong to language: the
spacing of the archive, the undecomposable numerousness of inscription. Moreover, if speech and language are themselves the preeminent

forms of the silence whereby writing is doomed to immemorial disappearance, then never passing writing over in silence means something other than speaking it aloud or lending it a voice. Derrida's ethics and politics thus constitute a break with "voice" as the privileged figure for the process of enfranchisement. In large measure, rather than speaking it is *reading* that breaks the silence that hangs over the muteness of writing.

The classical representation of war revolves around a more or less straightforward division between word and act. The word as a symbolic pact or promise is aligned with the horizon of peace, while war constitutes an act that would break this promise or rupture this horizon (always *too soon* with respect to the prospect of unending peace). For Derrida, however, war takes place *in language on language and by language*. The act of war takes the form of writing or the mark; it might be nonverbal but it is not external to the symbolic field. War is not tantamount to a regression, in Lacanian terms, to the imaginary or the real; or, in Hobbesian terms, to the state of nature. To verify this claim, it is not necessary to go any further in the analysis of HE WAR than we have gone so far. Rather than brutal destruction or annihilation, this act of war takes the positive form of a poetic invention or work of art; rather than take something away, it posits something new. Rather than break all social and political bonds, transgress interdictions and conventions, this act of war inaugurates a bond more exigent that the bond of language itself.

Afterword

Thus arose the almost monstrous demand that I should behave continually as if I myself were a corpse.

—Daniel Paul Schreber, *Memoirs of My Nervous Illness*

ON IMMOBILITY

At various points throughout this book, I observed that war is a matter of mobilization and speed, the traversal, distribution, and occupation of space. Without movement, potential movement, or perhaps even emotion, there would be no war. There would only be conflict without passion, departure, attack, struggle, strike, clash, or contest. Kant's satiric projection of a pacified world as the vast graveyard of the human race offers a precise image of the opposite of war: stasis and separation for eternity. War on earth necessarily ends when all movement stops (save the movement of the earth itself). There is no war among stones or plants—or at least plants of the noncreeping or noninvasive variety such as trees. Accordingly, Wordsworth's "A Slumber Did My Spirit Seal" turns upon a line that associates absence of motion and absence of force: "No motion has she now, no force:/ She neither hears nor sees;/ Rolled round in earth's diurnal course/ With rocks, and stones, and trees." How is peace possible, we might ask along with Kant, that does not cancel life? What is movement that does not open a conflict or pose a threat? Perhaps Kant's reflections on hospitality offer a potential response to this question. For the sake of peace, he proposes, we must learn to distinguish between attack and arrival, vector and approach. And yet *War after Death* claims that the relationship between war and movement is not so clear-cut; it does not necessarily begin with mobilization and end with demobilization. Focusing on violence with the nonliving, this book proposes the opposite thesis: the ultimate stakes of war can only be grasped starting from immobility; war constitutes a relationship between the quick and the dead, the mobile and the immobile, and perhaps even between the immobile and the immobile, or the dead and the dead; and, further, the problem of peace must also be reframed starting from an elaboration of these counterintuitive displacements.

Chapter 1 revolves around the Taliban's massacre, in March 2001, of the twin Buddhas of Bamiyan. Confronted with contemporary transformations of war—including the very recent expansion of drone warfare programs around the world—I claim that we have more to learn from this event than from the attacks of September 11, 2001. The antihero of chapter 2 is propped up in plain sight: the effigy of a white man for whom Jean Genet proposed that *The Blacks* be played (in the unlikely event that a theater books an all-black audience). This immobile figure is ultimately a placeholder for Genet himself, and it recurs—albeit discreetly—in his late political writings. At the stilled heart of chapter 3 lies Goya's depiction of the disasters of war—in particular, his etchings of mayhem committed with bodies after death. These images raise questions about both the tendency and the goal (in Clausewitz's language, *der Zweck* and *das Ziel*) of war. Is violence committed after death, violence inflicted upon the enemy's body after he is dead and immobilized, violence that keeps going when the enemy stops moving, can such violence be discounted as a rare form of atrocity? Or mustn't we see in it an extremity that opens beyond and always haunts the customary extremity of war and death? One of Goya's "black paintings," *Duelo a garrotazos* (Duel with Clubs), fantasizes a brutal conflict between fighters wielding cudgels, their legs buried up to the knees in the earth. The two men are rooted like trees in the ground where they stand and cannot run from one another's blows. Another of Goya's paintings, the haunting *El Perro*—sometimes designated with the title "Half-Buried Dog"—might also bear witness to the painter's preoccupation with immobilized life. Immobility precedes death, the image suggests; and thus death precedes death. Rather than take place between living beings that rush toward death and immobility, war would transpire between "sitting ducks" that expose one another to violence without any natural limit. Even war between living beings is already war after death.

Parallel to this discrete meditation on immobile bodies, this book is concerned with the way in which acts of war can have an impact on language and law. In his famous editorial in the *New York Times*, "A New Kind of War," Rumsfeld explains to the reading public how the war on terror explicitly evokes and displaces the traditional language of war. In much the same way, journalists and political leaders who commented on the destruction of the Buddhas of Bamiyan openly struggled to make the language of war fit the event. Genet claims that his late political writings establish a "discipline of the real" that breaks from the "discipline of grammar" that characterized his earlier novels and plays; and this break becomes legible at key moments in these writings. Among these moments, I examine how Genet's projection of a theatrical and political space where the dead appear alongside the living, where effigies figure among animate bodies, displaces the grammar of life in common. When Genet writes about his visit to the Shatila refugee camp very soon after the Phalangist massacre, he searches for the appropriate manner of articulating the peculiar form of community that links him to the dead bodies at his feet. Rather than describe himself standing *with* or *amid* the tortured corpses, he decides to write that he found himself alongside them (*auprès d'elles*). Interestingly, on the very first page of *Prisoner of Love*, his memoir of his experiences with the Palestinians in the 1970s and 1980s, he insists precisely that he didn't spend time *with* these groups but—once again—*alongside* them *("auprès—et non avec eux—des Palestiniens")*. He articulates his relation to the living using—decidedly so—the same preposition that he used to articulate his relation to the dead; he insists upon a modality of relation that does not distinguish between the living and the dead, the mobile and the immobile, the body and the image. In addition to greatly expanding and displacing the usual sense of community, this manner of articulating relation demands that we discover another grammar for the critique of violence. Such a project, then, underlies my reading of the caption—"A heroic feat! With dead men"—that Goya affixes to his vision of mayhem. The "with" in "great deeds with the dead," the preposition that articulates the relation between war and its object, cannot be understood as the "with" whereby people or the people grasp their own being-together—with-or-against, with-and-against one another. Because the violence that appears in this image transgresses the limits of death and thus the limits of regular war, it can no longer be articulated in terms of the duel in which friend mobilizes *with and against* enemy, enemy *with and against* friend, or brother *with and against* brother.

Chapters 4 and 5 take a somewhat different approach to the questions that specific acts of war raise about language and the social bond. Both Beckett's *Worstward Ho* and Derrida's essay on Joyce and translation are texts that think war—and language itself—in terms of speed rather than movement. More precisely phrased, they presuppose a reflection on the ways in which speed complicates or even nullifies the role of movement in war. Armed conflict between mobile bodies tends inexorably to arrest movement. Each fighter aims to bring about—to borrow the title of a novel by Maurice Blanchot—an *arrêt de mort*: a "death sentence," as Lydia Davis translates the phrase, but also, more literally, the arrest, stay, or stasis of death. The goal is to immobilize the enemy once and for all and thereby to eliminate the threat that he represents. The role of technology in war, however, makes it more difficult if not impossible to evaluate threats based on the distinction between mobility and immobility. An immobile sniper who fires from a distance can be more dangerous than a soldier running with an unsheathed sword. In order to fire his weapon most effectively, the sniper stays as still as possible. Accordingly, the greater the speed of a weapon, the more it renders irrelevant the target's lesser or greater mobility. In relation to the velocity of a bullet, for example—or perhaps even something faster—a body in flight might as well be standing still. Immobility, in this sense, is something other than the opposite of mobility; it bears witness to the fact that the other's speed has eliminated movement as a means of escape.[1]

I show that Beckett's prose in both *Ill Seen Ill Said* and *Worstward Ho* is animated by an unarticulated demand to say a word as quickly and concisely as possible. Quick. Quicker. Quick see. Quick say. It is no accident that "quick" is a synonym for life—as if, in order to stay alive, life must keep moving and move quickly. Since the speed of eye and tongue outstrips that of the body, image and word become the highest manifestations of life. And yet both of Beckett's texts are punctuated by the word *still*. "Try again. Fail again. Better again. Or better worse. Fail worse again. Still worse again." The ill that ultimately condemns seeing and saying to fail, preventing them from responding to the imperative to act quickly enough, lies quite literally in this word. In English, *still* refers both to *motionlessness* and *perpetual motion*. Beckett's prose, we might say, remains caught in a state of *perpetual motionlessness*: it never stops coming to a halt; it advances without ever moving. In his long essay on *Worstward Ho*, Badiou calls this odd form of movement "immobile migration."[2]

Rather than mere cessation or absence of motion, this motionlessness is the perspectival effect of speed. Eye and word are quick but, it
would appear, never quick enough. Confronted with the quickness of
the object to which they must respond, their quickness is no different
from paralysis, their life indistinguishable from death.

Woven through my reading of Beckett is a discussion of J. L. Austin's essay, "The Meaning of a Word" (unless the former is woven
through the latter). Thanks to Austin, this chapter and perhaps
the entire book revolve around an uncanny example that it never
addresses at length. Much like Beckett, the philosopher finds ordinary language uniquely unprepared for the worst. When he imagines someone calling at the home of a man who has just died, no
word is right to describe the situation. In this case, the immobile
host catches the importunate guest off guard—rather than vice
versa (the usual case)—because the complex event of his death at
home outstrips his linguistic resources. The English language—or
perhaps any language—contains no word that prepares the speaker
to act quickly enough to confront this situation and incorporate into
his experience. Without a single move, the dead host paralyzes the
living guest; his immobility, paradoxically, opens a period of perpetual war, an epoch of waiting that defies the right word ever to arrive,
a time that proves every word of every language—and perhaps language as such—to be ill said.

The immeasurable acceleration of Beckett's language mimics the
rhetoric that rises to greet the disasters of war with "the worst"
whenever and wherever they occur; the rhetoric that implicitly but
openly declares war on this very word—and by extension on language itself—forecloses the possibility that it would have time to
name anything other than war. The immobility of Beckett's prose,
it turns out, displaces language more quickly than it can be halted
by the urgency of current events. In its brevity, the word—the minimal unit of language—brings the mobility of discourse to a standstill.
Beckett's staccato wit, then, wages war upon the imperious discourse
of war in order to open language to objects that this discourse functions to repress.

Like Beckett's fiction, Derrida's reading of Joyce turns upon the
citation of two minimal words from *Finnegans Wake*. Like Austin's
unlucky visitor, the reader of these words immediately finds himself
paralyzed—once again, on the level of language. Even to begin reading these words, written in at least two languages at once, he must

become a translator; and the task that he confronts is impossible. The words can be reduced to one language at a time and then translated one after the other. When read in English, "he war" becomes "he wars." When subsequently read in German, the sentence becomes "he was." What cannot be translated—and thus becomes the specific object of translation—is the graphic economy that allows Joyce to write in several languages at the same time. In this case, the linguistic difference (the "foreignness") that divides the original from its translation is less significant than what Derrida calls "aesthetic difference." There is no translation that can do justice to the economy— speed and compactness—of Joyce's prose. The form of the reader's paralysis is, paradoxically, a discourse that goes on too long, that unfolds in succession what occurs simultaneously in Joyce's text. Stasis, in this instance, consists in the inability to halt the movement of language. The impossibility of translation means that it's impossible for it not to go on too long.

Finally, Derrida's reading of Joyce suggests, the aesthetic difference between original and translation entails an elementary political differend. The speed whereby Joyce's writing silently collapses multitudes into the space of a single mark constitutes an originary act of war, the war that Yahweh wages against Shemite imperialism, what Derrida calls "the war of language against itself." Joyce calculates and exploits the effects of an element in language—the mark—that is foreign to language as such but allows for the computation, centralization, hybridization, transmission, and archivization of languages. Precisely this element, in Joyce's two words, perpetually wars against any single language that would position itself as the One into which all other languages would be translated. The object of translation— translation that eschews the imperial project to which it succumbs far too often—is not foreign language but the mark that inhabits and divides every language from itself. The task of the translator, in Beckett's words, is to go on without being able to; to continue struggling long after the war is lost, not in the hope of finally destroying the enemy, but in order to do justice to his or her (or even, perhaps, its) singular polemic.

ON RAPE

In the final stages of writing this book, I was increasingly led to the conclusion that "war after death" is synonymous with a crime that

I rarely name. In a word, rape. Many of the examples that I privilege in this book explicitly feature the destruction of the male body—not only violence against inanimate or dead bodies, bodies defined by their immobility, but also violence against manifestly—often garishly—sexed bodies. The Buddhas of Bamiyan are colossal male figures. The corpses on display in Goya's etchings are all male. Moreover, the specific acts of violence committed "with" many of these bodies—that is, castration—negatively highlight their sex. Finally, Genet's open letter to the enemy—an enemy who might be no more than an effigy—largely consists in the promise to sexually abuse and dismember the unknown figure whom it addresses. "I'll give him all I've got: whacks, slaps, kicks, I will have him gnawed by starving foxes, make him eat English food, attend the House of Lords, be received at Buckingham Palace, fuck Prince Phillip, get fucked by him, live for a month in London, dress like me, sleep where I sleep, live my stead: I seek the declared enemy."[3] In contemporary wars, however, there is no shortage of such outrages. In April 2012, for instance, the *Los Angeles Times* printed photographs of American soldiers posing with the dismembered limbs of Afghan suicide bombers.[4] Focusing exclusively upon such examples, however, risks forestalling the question of the relationships between war, violence, and the feminine. The most symptomatic and explosive examples of war after death, in fact, are instances of what feminist scholars do not hesitate to call the "war against women." The upsurge of systemic rape in the age of globalization ultimately provides a much clearer index of the changing relationship among war, violence, and the social bond. Horrifying as the mutilation of the male body may be, it can always be mistaken for an isolated act that remains within the frame of war; it breaks with the limits of war, but it does not challenge the political and cultural conditions of representability. More often than not, in fact, the crime of mayhem takes place in representation. Representation functions as the coup de grace. Because of the traditional role of men in war, the male body—in its vulnerable exposure to death—functions to incarnate a fundamental limit, the very principle of political economy. "Great deeds" with the male body—deeds that reduce it to a sexual thing—deliberately seek to flaunt this limit and to threaten the social, political, and cultural institutions that depend upon it. War after death is perhaps already rape to the precise extent that it aims at something in the body beyond its life. In "Faith and Knowledge," Derrida explicitly aligns rape with the emergence of what he calls a "new cruelty" that attacks not the life of the victim but his or her "body proper."

> Double rape. A new cruelty would thus ally, in wars that are also
> wars of religion, the most advanced tehnoscientific calculability with
> a reactive savagery that would like to attack the body proper directly,
> the sexual thing that can be raped, mutilated or simply denied, desex-
> ualized—yet another form of the same violence.[5]

Derrida does not explicitly address questions of the relationship between violence and the feminine. Nor does *War after Death*. Nonetheless, I would argue that this book is a necessary prolegomenon to further work on questions of rape and the political; for, in order to grasp the centrality of rape as a form of the gravest violence, it is first necessary to extricate the critique of violence from traditional narratives of war and death. *War after Death* is thus only a preliminary fragment of broader and necessarily collective work that would explicitly address emerging questions of war, violence, and the feminine. In conclusion, then, I would like to raise some questions and sketch out paths for future research. These remarks, of course, will necessarily remain too formal and hesitant; but it is always best, I think, to raise questions even if they can only be left open.

Not coincidentally, feminist scholars who have studied the role of sexual violence against women in Western culture and politics are also those who have taken most seriously the problem of war after death. What becomes especially clear in this scholarship is the complex historicity of rape as the exemplary form of war after death. Many authors—such as Susan Brownmiller, Catherine MacKinnon, Ruth Seifert, Rhonda Copelon—uphold what initially appears to be a hyperbolic postulate: that rape perpetrates and perpetuates nothing less than an ongoing war of men against women. Despite the extremity of this hypothesis, it effectively articulates the complex structural and historical dimension of rape. Historically, rape always accompanies war; but the official and unofficial histories of war never suffice to explain the act of rape. Nonetheless, because rape brings sexual difference into play, it is never simply an isolated crime. It is a historical event that irrevocably transforms bodies, families, and societies. Rape would be the manifestation of an untimely—intersubjective—war that is larger and longer than anything that philosophical and historical discourse would call "war"; it is a mode of war without war, war beyond war, war before war, and war after war. There is rape in marriage, rape in dating, and rape in war. More than any "peacetime" preparations for future wars—which Kant considered the gravest threat to eternal peace—rape would be the most intransigent threat to any peace worthy of the name.

As this scholarship clearly shows, the most effective way to call into question the narrative of war-and-death is to call attention to the fact that systematic rape—especially but in no way limited to the rape of female civilians by male soldiers—has always been an essential dimension of the political enterprise of war. In her lucid contribution to a volume of essays on rape in the Bosnian War, *Mass Rape: The War against Women in Bosnia-Herzegovina*, Ruth Seifert argues that rape should be included among the de facto "rules" of war. In principle, she claims, rape never factors into official military strategy; but, in fact, it never fails to occur and therefore should be considered a form of preordained crime.

> War is a ritualized, finely regulated game. I use the word "game"—a strange word given the lethal context—because behavior in war follows specific "rules of the game." . . . In war well-defined armies are present, the enemy is clearly identifiable, and there are recognizable procedures at the front, with a clear order of command. When looking back through history we find much to suggest that within this ritual one rule of the game has always been that violence against women in the conquered territory is conceded to the victor during the postwar period. We have no evidence that any negotiations have ever been carried out to halt this outrage against women. It also seems to have made no difference whether women's bodies were at soldiers' disposal in other quarters—in brothels, for example. As a member of the highest military court in the United States explained, a rape in a war zone has no relation to available women or prostitutes. That means that in the "open space" of war, many men simply prefer to rape: it has nothing to do with sexuality, but rather reflects the exercise of sexual, gender-specific violence.[6]

Despite the "lethal context" of war, Seifert persists in calling it a ritualized game. Indeed, as I have attempted to show throughout this book, killing—precisely because of its lethality—is an indispensable moment within the ritual of war, no less conventional than the soldier's uniform. Even if conflict does not end upon any single death, the rule of death always functions to declare the fact that war is an end-oriented enterprise. Even if a given war continues indefinitely, each death in battle prefigures the end of war. One death, some day, will be the last in this war; and every death could be this ultimate death. As Seifert underscores, however, rape is a "postwar" phenomenon: it tends to happen in the wake of conflict and conquest, as a supplement to it, rather than as the central activity. "When looking back through history we find much to suggest that within this ritual one rule of the game has always been that violence against women in the conquered territory is conceded to the victor during the postwar period." If the violence of this "postwar period" belongs to the rules of war, then the narrative of war and death ceases to be valid. Taking rape seriously as an act that is integral to war as such, it becomes necessary to presume that the "postwar" moment does not simply happen "after" the end of any specific war. The sexual violence that—on an empirical level— appears to perpetuate a single war, or even war in general, would be the untimely continuation of an "older" war that is more difficult to situate within history. Consequently, any given war must be considered to be a much longer, more complex, more comprehensive, and indeed more violent undertaking than the official, historiographical beginning and end dates would suggest.

But rape does have a strategic function, Seifert claims. It is a necessarily paradoxical and inconsistent function but one that ultimately brings us closer to the essence of war—its horror—than narratives of death and sacrifice. Indeed, Seifert effectively shows that the ultimate strategy of war becomes legible only through consideration of sexual violence. It is precisely because rape pertains to a war that is larger and older than war that it becomes a powerful weapon within political conflicts between nations and peoples, enemies and brothers. Such wars might begin with hopes of ending one day in victory or defeat, but, as Seifert claims, they can only reach a conclusion by threatening *never to end*, disregarding the rules of war, destroying both people and culture.

> In "dirty wars" it is not necessarily the conquest of the foreign army, but rather the deconstruction of a culture that can be seen as the central objective of war actions, for only by destroying it—and that means by destroying people—can a decision be forced. . . . We see an additional aspect of cultural destruction in the fact that the female body functions as a symbolic representation of the body politic. . . . This also means that the violence inflicted on women is aimed at the physical and personal integrity of the group. This in turn is particularly significant for the construction of the community. Thus the rape of the women in a community can be regarded as the symbolic rape of the body of this community. Against this background, the mass rapes that accompany all wars take on new meaning: by no means acts of senseless brutality, they are rather culture-destroying actions with a strategic rationale.[7]

If rape is the exemplary act of war, rather than military conflict, then the outcome of war no longer hinges upon the prospect of an ultimate deathblow. Rather than test the strength or intelligence of the parties to the conflict, *war instead aims to strain a group's emotional capacity to tolerate the destruction of the social bond itself*—what Seifert calls the "physical and personal integrity of the group." Foremost among the constituents of this group integrity, I would argue, figure the rules of war themselves. There is no social bond without rules of war. For precisely this reason, however, the social bond as we know it is founded upon a beautiful fiction. If rape plays such an essential role in war, it is because war itself is devoted to the destruction of its own rules, and because, in every case, whether or not rapes actually occur or can be identified, it requires such extreme violence in order to reach any outcome whatsoever.

More radically, perhaps, rape would be perpetrated—much like the massacre of the Buddhas of Bamiyan—explicitly in order to strain a group's capacity to endure symbolic violence—which is always difficult, if not impossible, to categorize in ethical, juridical, or political terms. Rape is not a sexual act, Seifert stresses; it is a symbolic act of violence. It is a symbolic act of violence committed against a real body; but, worse perhaps, it is a symbolic act of violence committed "with" a real body, an act of violence that attacks this body as a symbol, exploiting this body as a proxy or effigy in order to destroy something or someone who may be out of reach, unattainable, or untouchable (such as the "body politic"). For this reason, as many scholars have established, there is a close relationship between rape and genocide.

Sexual violence, then, would be a form, perhaps even the exemplary form, of war after death: violence that opens beyond pain, beyond pleasure, beyond the principle that converts pain into pleasure. Not coincidentally, then, sexual violence is by definition exercised upon an immobile victim. Whereas war, traditionally defined, takes place between animate beings on the move who aim to stop one another in their tracks, sexual violence can occur only after a body has been immobilized. Precisely because rape is sexual violence, it aims at something other and beyond the life of the victim. In this sense, rape always flirts with necrophilia. I would argue, in fact, that it disregards the distinction between the animate and the inanimate, the mobile and the immobile. Alexandra Stiglmayer cites the testimony of a Bosnian woman that underscores this dimension of the act to which she was subjected: "Since the first guy wasn't satisfied with me, he suggested that they switch partners. He took my friend, and I had to go to his friend. Then we had to lie down and, the way they said it, relax and enjoy it. . . . It hurt for a minute. After that all your feelings vanish, you become a stone and do not feel anything."[8]

International law recognizes rape as a war crime but does not classify it among the gravest outrages. In "Resurfacing Gender: Reconceptualizing Crimes against Women in Time of War," Rhonda Copelon explains that rape is systematically categorized as a crime against personal honor or dignity rather than a crime of violence such as murder, mutilation, cruel and unusual treatment, or torture. "Where rape is treated as a crime against honor, the honor of women is called into question and virginity or chastity is often a precondition. Honor implies the loss of station or respect; it reinforces the social view, internalized by women, that the raped woman is dishonorable. And while the concept of dignity potentially embraces more profound concerns, standing alone it obfuscates the fact that rape is fundamentally violence against women—violence against a woman's body, autonomy, integrity, selfhood, security, and self-esteem as well as her standing in the community."[9] Despite the fact that rape does not necessarily jeopardize the life of the victim, however, there is no question that it constitutes a grave act of violence. And yet the failure of international law to recognize rape as a crime of violence is not without reason; for the violence of rape cannot and should not be understood in terms of the traditional concept of violence—which, as I have argued, is dependent upon the narrative of war-and-death. Rape is often committed in tandem with murder (before or after) but, in itself, it does not necessarily lead to death because it implicitly assaults something—call it "honor," "dignity," "the body," "security," "selfhood," "self-esteem," "space," "memory," or "culture"— other than the life of the victim. In order to recognize the specific violence of rape, then, nothing less would be required than a new critique of violence. Such a critique would make it possible to measure the gravity of violence in other terms than life and death and thus to grasp the agency of nonlethal or extralethal violence within supposedly lethal violence itself.

INTRODUCTION

1. Immanuel Kant, *Toward Perpetual Peace and Other Writings on Politics, Peace, and History*, ed. and introd. Pauline Kleingeld; trans. David Colclasure (New Haven: Yale University Press, 2006), 67.

2. It could well be the case that the satiric effect of this picture and its caption derives from the knowledge that the end of the human race would look nothing like a graveyard and would be far from peaceful.

3. Giorgio Agamben, *Homo Sacer: Sovereign Power and Bare Life*, trans. Daniel Heller-Roazen (Stanford: Stanford University Press, 1998), 88.

4. Barack Obama, "A Just and Lasting Peace," www.nobelprize.org/nobel_prizes/peace/laureates/2009/obama-lecture_en.html. Accessed February 28, 2013. Notably, Obama immediately qualifies his affirmation: "And yet this truth must coexist with another—that no matter how justified, war promises human tragedy. The soldier's courage and sacrifice is full of glory, expressing devotion to country, to cause, to comrades in arms. But war itself is never glorious, and we must never trumpet it as such." These truths (war as peace, war as human tragedy) must "coexist," I would argue, precisely because the humanity of this tragedy—death in battle—corresponds to aim and limit of war that ultimately open toward peace.

5. Saskia Sassen, "Anti-war," http://dictionaryofwar.org/node/891. Accessed February 28, 2013.

6. In a recent paper, "Ethics and the Consequences of the Act" (unpublished manuscript delivered as the keynote address at "Narrative, Act, Ethics," Buffalo, NY, March 1, 2012), Danielle Bergeron writes that ethics begins where psychoanalysis ends: 'If a part of the subject's truth is to be discovered in analysis through the signifiers that form the chain of knowledge about the unnamed, another part of this truth will never be named. Lacan said: "the truth can only be half-said." An ungraspable and uncontrollable real will always remain; will "never cease not to be written"; and will continue to act. In the final stage of analysis, then, it is necessary for the analysand to assume, on the basis of the knowledge constructed in analysis, an ethics of the censored.'

7. Sigmund Freud, *The Standard Edition of the Complete Psychological Works of Sigmund Freud,* ed. and trans. James Strachey, 24 vols. (London: Hogarth Press, 1953–74), vol. 8, 36. Hereafter SE followed by volume number.

8. Ibid., 38.

9. Ibid.

10. *The English Bible, King James Version: The Old Testament,* ed. Herbert Marks (New York: W. W. Norton, 2012), 894–95.

11. Freud, SE XVIII, 26.

12. Ibid., 22.

13. Ibid.

14. Torquato Tasso, *Jerusalem Delivered,* trans. Anthony Esolen (Baltimore: Johns Hopkins University Press, 2000), 241.

15. Ibid.

16. Ibid., 242.

17. Ibid., 243.

18. Ibid.

19. Freud, SE XVIII, 27. "This little fragment of living substance is suspended in the middle of an external world charged with the most powerful energies; and it would be killed by the stimulation emanating from these if it were not provided with a protective shield in this way: its outermost surface ceases to have the structure proper to living matter, becomes to some degree inorganic and thenceforward functions as a special envelope or membrane resistant to stimuli. In consequence, the energies of the external world are able to pass into the next underlying layers, which have remained living, with only a fragment of their original intensity. . . . By its death, the outer layer has saved all the deeper ones from a similar fate—unless, that is to say, stimuli reach it which are so strong that they break through the protective shield." Unless, I would add, there are also forces that not only aim to break *through* the dead protective shield, but to destroy the protective shield *itself* and to take, as "collateral damage," the living being along with it.

20. On the shell or garment as the material double, simulacrum, or "body of the body," see Andrzej Warminski, "Facing Language: Wordsworth's First Poetic Spirits," *Diacritics* 17, no. 4 (Winter 1987): 18–31.

21. In all his published work devoted to elucidating the work of Jacques Derrida, Martin Hägglund lucidly analyzes the relationship between the time of life and the structure of the trace. But his most radical articulation of this relationship appears in a recent critique of the work of Quentin Meillassoux. In this essay, Hägglund shows that it is possible "to make explicit a continuity between the nonliving and the living in terms of the structure of the trace." This continuity is synonymous with what he calls "the arche-materiality of time." The relation of life to itself—its care for its own survival or fear for its destruction—is necessarily temporal. Precisely for this reason, this self-relation implies the intervention of a material support. "Given that every temporal moment ceases to be as soon as it comes to be, it must be inscribed as a trace in order to be at all. . . . Every temporal moment therefore depends on the material support of spatial inscription. . . . The material support of the trace,

however, is itself temporal. . . . The trace is always left for an unpredictable future that gives it both the chance to live on and to be effaced." Martin Hägglund, "Radical Atheist Materialism: A Critique of Meillassoux," in *The Speculative Turn,* ed. Levi Bryant, Nick Srnicek, and Graham Harman (Victoria, Australia: Re-press, 2011), 114–29. My concern is to show that the Freudian elaboration of the death drive is implicitly predicated upon such a continuity between the living and the nonliving; that the clarification of this continuity helps to grasp the relationship between the death drive, violence, and primary masochism; and that it destabilizes the presuppositions that found the traditional critique of violence. With respect to the final point, Hägglund remains content to postulate that "the trace is always left for an unpredictable future." I would argue, however, that the future is always both predictable and unpredictable. Thanks to specific historical and textual precedents—and, indeed, thanks to Hägglund's own analyses—it becomes predictable that the future of the trace will entail deliberate attempts to efface or destroy it; and the living can be and will be exposed to attacks upon them that disregard the distinction between the living and the dead. Consideration of such acts of violence, I contend, transforms traditional notions of the goals of war and its role in politics. On a more general note, my critical method differs from Hägglund's in that I am less interested in elaborating the structure of the trace in general—open to an unpredictable future—than in how determinate events and texts bring this structure and its consequences into focus.

22. William Shakespeare, *Sonnets*, ed. Katherine Duncan-Jones (London: Arden Shakespeare, 1997).

23. Jean Genet, *Prisoner of Love*, trans. Barbara Bray (Middletown, CT: Wesleyan University Press, 1992), 328–29.

24. Jacques Derrida, *Chaque fois unique, la fin du monde*, ed. Michael Naas and Pascale-Anne Brault (Paris: Galilée, 2003), 9. My translation. Unless otherwise noted, thoughout this book, the emphasis is the author's.

25. Jacques Derrida, *Archive Fever*, trans. Eric Prenowitz (Chicago: University of Chicago Press, 1996), 11–12.

1. STATUES ALSO DIE

1. Donald H. Rumsfeld, "A New Kind of War," *New York Times*, September 27, 2001.

2. Ibid.

3. Ibid.

4. Martha Gellhorn, *The Face of War* (New York: Atlantic Monthly Press, 1988), 225.

5. Immanuel Kant, *Practical Philosophy*, ed. Mary J. Gregor; trans. Allen Wood (Cambridge: Cambridge University Press, 1996), 317.

6. In *The Least of All Possible Evils* (New York: Verso Books, 2011), Eyal Weizman lays the groundwork for a critique of violence in the age of international humanitarian law (IHC). Despite appearances, Weizman lucidly demonstrates, such law does not function to oppose or even to restrict military violence but rather merely to "moderate" or "shape" it. Rather than

prohibit or denounce military violence as such, IHC goes no further than demanding that "unnecessary" or "disproportionate" violence be kept to a minimum. In this sense, the law even stops short of prohibiting disproportionate violence; it requires only that state and nonstate actors clearly make an attempt to minimize it. In effect, Weizman shows, IHC more or less explicitly permits and legitimizes the use of military violence as long as the extremity of this violence was—and can be shown to have been—calculated in advance. "The moderation of violence is part of the very logic of violence," Weizman writes (3). The measure of humanitarian violence, then, would be what Weizman calls the "principle of proportionality." The concept "proportionality in attack" is implicitly formalized in Protocol 1 (Pt. IV, Art. 51, 5b)—established quite recently, in 1977—of the Geneva Conventions, which condemns "any attack which may be expected to cause incidental loss of civilian life, injury to civilians, damage to civilian objects, or a combination thereof, which would be excessive in relation to the concrete and direct military advantage anticipated." Weizman's analysis, therefore, helps us to see that Rumsfeld's poetics of likelihood and probability is directly related to the humanitarian principle of proportionality in attack. Calculating what is likely to happen in the coming war, Rumsfeld is implicitly justifying the expansion of military violence and the demilitarization of violence (although once deemed excessive) that is not (unfortunately) proportionate to the projected threat.

7. Hart Seely, *Pieces of Intelligence: The Existential Poetry of Donald Rumsfeld* (New York: Free Press, 2009).

8. Ibid., 2. "As we know,/ There are known knowns./ There are things we know we know/ We also know/ There are known unknowns./ That is to say/ We know there are some things/ We do not know./ But there are also unknown unknowns,/ The ones we don't know we don't know."

9. The point, however, is that such calculation is never merely the contrary of artistic production, that one should never be too confident that art is inherently unwarlike.

10. Samuel Weber, *Targets of Opportunity* (New York: Fordham University Press, 2005), vii–viii.

11. Stephen Halliwell, *The "Poetics" of Aristotle: Translation and Commentary* (Chapel Hill: University of North Carolina Press, 1987), 40–41.

12. This aspect of Aristotle's poetics becomes especially clear in the work of one of his foremost modern proponents, Henry James. James's treatise on the art of fiction takes up where Aristotle's *Poetics* leaves off, insisting upon the excess—the movement beyond mere possibility—that constitutes the project of the novel. What Aristotle calls "necessity" or "probability," James calls "life." Railing against "superstitious" or "evangelical" discourses on fiction that reduce it to the status of a joke or make-believe (or even, perhaps, "literature"), he upholds the right of the novel "really to represent life." "The only reason for the existence of a novel is that it does attempt to represent life." The novelist, James, holds firm, must not apologize for telling stories— either by suspending the validity of the entire production by placing it in quotation marks or by employing it as a means to seduce the reader. Anthony

Trollope, for example: "He admits that the events he narrates have not really happened, and that he can give his narrative any turn that the reader likes best." This refusal to apologize is what likens the novelist's discourse to that of the historian, the painter, or the philosopher. The painterly or philosophical dimension of the novel, then, lies in its constitutively historical intention to represent life. In this respect, James appears explicitly to overturn Aristotle's claim that poetry is more philosophical than history. And yet he too ends up conferring top honors upon the novelist because of "his having more difficulty collecting his evidence." The art of fiction is especially difficult because, in order to go beyond fiction toward life, the novelist cannot rely upon mere facts. Beyond recounting what did happen, the novelist tells what might have happened. His narrative is predicated upon an extremely complex calculation of probability; his evidence is hypothetical without being "purely literary." James is thus more faithful to Aristotle than he appears to be. In fact, his treatise on the art of fiction shows that Aristotle's own distinction between poetry and history, rather than oppose these genres of discourse, makes it more necessary than ever to grasp the inextricable relationship between them. The specific intentionality of fiction makes it difficult, if not impossible, to define fiction in its "own" terms. See Henry James, "The Art of Fiction," in *Literary Criticism*, vol. 1: *American Writers & European Writers* (New York: Library of America, 1985), 44–65.

13. For this reason, perhaps, Cathy Caruth calls trauma a "deathlike break." Cathy Caruth, *Unclaimed Experience: Trauma, Narrative, History* (Baltimore: Johns Hopkins University Press, 1996), 87. The traumatic break is "deathlike," presumably, because it is merely like death; it does not actually bring death itself. At the same time, this break is not merely akin to death. More radically, it simulates death; for the trauma "victim" dies without actually dying. The actuality of this death consists in the imposition of a sheer possibility—which becomes all the more crushing because its actualization did not succeed in diminishing or eliminating it. For the living—and perhaps even for the dead—death becomes nothing other than the unbreachable distance from any actuality.

14. Rumsfeld, "A New Kind of War."

15. This comment calls for a more detailed elaboration of Clausewitz's very interesting construction of the time of war in *On War*. In the famous dictum that I cite above the German word commonly translated as "continuation" is *Fortsetzung*—which, in literal terms, is less a matter of uninterrupted temporal flux than of advancing or furthering political interests. This so-called continuation, then, would not entail continuity at all but rather a movement constituted by a violent shift or transference, an abrupt change in means or levels of political problem solving. This shift would only be continuous to the extent that, from one means to another, it maintains and upholds the same political ends. Both politics and war are oriented and intensely strained toward common ends; and the function of shifting from one to the other would be to maintain this intensity—to keep these ends in view and, more important, at stake. As Schmitt forcefully underscored, discontinuous shift from politics to war—or rather, from one political means to another—is

itself essentially political, since, unlike war itself, the time of politics is inherently discontinuous and heterogeneous, constituted of shifts, hesitations, moments of suspension, breakdowns, impasses, accelerations, and so forth. In principle if not in fact, however, the political shift to war also entails a movement beyond politics; for the shift to war consists of an abrupt change of temporal regime. More than an acceleration of events, it brings about a passage from time shot through with discontinuity to the ideal continuity of war. For the continuity of war itself, the continuity of the intensification or passage to extremes that define war itself, Clausewitz reserves the Latinate word *Kontinuität*. Section 14 of the programmatic opening chapter of *On War* is titled "Continuity Would Thus Be Brought about in Military Action and Would Again Intensify Everything." In this text, he writes: "If this continuity were really to exist in the campaign, its effect would again arouse men's feelings and inject them with more passion and elemental strength, but events would follow more closely on each other and be governed by a stricter causal chain. Each individual action would be more important and consequently more dangerous" (Carl von Clausewitz, *On War*, trans. Michael Howard and Peter Paret [Princeton: Princeton University Press, 1976], 83). Although Clausewitz insists that, in actuality, individual wars are characterized by much inaction and misdirection, such states are governed by the ideal of continuous intensification, which would thus exert unrelenting pressure upon every moment of a given conflict and the psyches of those who participate in it. Within the terms of my own argument, the continuity of war would be less a matter of the elemental or logical connection between events on the ground than of the illegibility of war. Continuity would thus characterize the subjective relation to novelty that cannot be discerned as such, because there is no name for it, much less a narrative or conceptual language adequate to the task of describing it. Rather than define continuity as an interconnected sequence, in other words, continuity should be defined negatively as time without an answer, the immeasurable time that transpires before—if ever— the right language (or gesture) can be found to institute a historical break. Or rather, perhaps, to find a place in history for the break that this temporal parenthesis already is (but cannot be experienced as such).

16. Rumsfeld, "A New Kind of War."

17. See Gilles Deleuze and Félix Guattari, *A Thousand Plateaus*, trans. Brian Massumi (Minneapolis: University of Minnesota Press, 1987), 351–423.

18. Saskia Sassen, "Anti-war," http://dictionaryofwar.org/node/891. Accessed February 28, 2013.

19. Étienne Balibar, *Politics and the Other Scene*, trans. Christine Jones, James Swenson, and Chris Turner (New York: Verso, 2002), xi.

20. Attacks upon the frame of war itself are clearly the defining feature of terrorist warfare. This is precisely the reason why the discourse about terrorism—if not the thinking of terrorists themselves—is intensively focused upon the moment of *attack*. Even in classical warfare between sovereign nation-states, an attack can only be successful if it defies the calculations on the basis of which the enemy defends himself; it activates what Rumsfeld

famously called "unknown unknowns," referring to a range of possibilities that the Defense Department has considered irrelevant or incredible or never even recognized as such.

21. Étienne Balibar, "What's in a War? (Politics as War, War as Politics)," *Ratio Juris* 21, no. 3 (September 2008): 372.

22. Ibid.

23. Étienne Balibar, *Violence et civilité* (Paris: Gallimard, 2010).

24. Andreas Huyssen, *Present Pasts: Urban Palimpsests and the Politics of Memory* (Stanford: Stanford University Press, 2003), 162.

25. Ibid.

26. In July 2012, this type of extreme violence emerged once again—this time in Timbuktu, Mali. Ansar Dine, a hard-line Salafi group, commenced destroying a number of centuries-old Sufi mausoleums. The Reuters report published in the *New York Times* emphasizes the group's will to keep on destroying the shrines until there are no more to destroy. "About 30 militants armed with assault rifles and pickaxes destroyed three mausoleums on Saturday and three more on Sunday, witnesses said. The group said it planned to destroy all 16 of the city's main shrines." "Islamist Militants in Mali Continue to Destroy Shrines," *New York Times*, July 1, 2012.

27. Luke Harding, "Taliban Blow Apart 2000 Years of Buddhist History," *Guardian Unlimited*, March 3, 2001.

28. Ibid.

29. Isabel Hilton, "Blaming the Breakers of Statues," *Guardian Unlimited*, March 4, 2001; emphasis added.

30. Barbara Crossette, "Taliban: War for War's Sake," *New York Times*, March 18, 2001.

31. Koichiro Matsuura, "Les crimes contre la culture ne doivent pas rester impunis," *Le Monde*, March 16, 2001. My translation.

32. Ibid.

33. Ibid.

34. Ibid.

35. See Bruno Latour, *We Have Never Been Modern*, trans. Catherine Porter (Cambridge, MA: Harvard University Press, 1993). Notably, Latour followed up his research for *We Have Never Been Modern* with a sustained engagement with the problem of the relationship between the image, critique, and science. He curated an exhibition titled *Iconoclash* (Zentrum für Kunst und Medientechnologie, Karlsruhe, Germany, 2002) and edited the accompanying volume of essays that deal with the logic of iconoclasm in art, science, and religion. See Bruno Latour and Peter Weibel, eds., *Iconoclash* (Cambridge, MA: MIT Press, 2002). Moreover, in his introduction to the volume, Latour explicitly associates the problem of iconoclasm with the attacks of 9/11: "Since September 11, 2001, a state of emergency has been proclaimed on how we deal with images of all sorts—in religion, politics, science, art, and criticism—and a frantic search for the roots of fanaticism has begin." Introduction reprinted in Bruno Latour, *On the Modern Cult of the Factish Gods* (Durham, NC: Duke University Press, 2010), 96.

36. Stanley Idzerda, "Iconoclasm and the French Revolution," *American Historical Review* 60, no. 1 (October 1954): 26.

37. Chris Marker, *Commentaires* 1 (Paris: Seuil, 1961), 9.

38. UNESCO, *Convention Concerning the Protection of the World Natural and Cultural Heritage*, http://whc.unesco.org/archive/convention-en.pdf, 1.

39. Freud, SEXIV, 276.

40. Ibid., 299.

41. UNESCO, *Convention Concerning the Protection of the World Natural and Cultural Heritage*,1.

42. Freud, SEV, 262.

43. Carl von Clausewitz, *On War*, ed. and trans. Michael Howard and Peter Paret (Princeton: Princeton University Press, 1976), 75–77. Elaine Scarry lauds Clausewitz for his unflinching attention to the central role of injuring in war: "Of all writing—political, strategic, historical, medical—there is probably no work that more successfully holds visible the structural centrality of injuring than Clausewitz's *On War*." Elaine Scarry, *The Body in Pain* (Oxford: Oxford University Press, 1985), 65.

44. Carl Schmitt, *The Concept of the Political*, trans. George Schwab (Chicago: University of Chicago Press, 2007), 33.

45. Orlando Patterson, *Slavery and Social Death* (Cambridge, MA: Harvard University Press, 1985).

46. Jean-Luc Nancy, "L'Idôlatrie des Taliban," *Libération*, March 13, 2001. My translation.

47. Clausewitz, *On War*, 13.

48. Immanuel Kant, *Toward Perpetual Peace and Other Writings on Politics, Peace, and History*, ed. and introd. Pauline Kleingeld, trans. David L. Colclasure (New Haven: Yale University Press, 2006), 70–71.

49. Jean-François Lyotard, *Soundproof Room: Malraux's Anti-Aesthetics*, trans. Robert Harvey (Stanford: Stanford University Press, 2001), 67.

50. Søren Kierkegaard, "By a Graveside," in *Three Discourses on Imagined Occasions*, ed. and trans. Howard V. Hong and Edna H. Hong (Princeton: Princeton University Press, 1993), 69–102.

51. Ibid., 71.

52. See Freud, "Why War?" SEXXII, 197–215; *Three Essays on the Theory of Sexuality*, SEVII, 148 ff.

53. Schmitt, *The Concept of the Political*, 26–27.

54. Ibid., 27.

55. Carl Schmitt, *The Nomos of the Earth*, trans. G. L. Ulmen (New York: Telos Press, 2003), 351.

56. Ibid., 329.

57. "The exception in jurisprudence is analogous to the miracle in theology." Carl Schmitt, *Political Theology: Four Chapters on the Concept of Sovereignty*, trans. George Schwab (Chicago: University of Chicago Press, 1985), 36.

2. OPEN LETTER TO THE ENEMY

1. Jean Genet, *The Declared Enemy: Texts and Interviews,* trans. Jeff Fort (Stanford: Stanford University Press, 2004), 1. I have slightly modified this translation throughout this chapter.

2. Ibid., 287–88.

3. Ibid., 287.

4. The *prière d'insérer,* Gérard Genette tells us, is the nineteenth-century forerunner of the *quatrième de couverture,* the elliptical description of a book's contents that often appears on the back cover. Originally, the *prière d'insérer*—which today can still be found in certain French books—was a loose leaf page summarizing the story of a forthcoming novel addressed to newspaper editors, "praying" that they insert the summary in a column of the paper. Needless to say, the situation of this unbound page between book and newspaper could not be more appropriate to the present discussion. See Daniel Bermond, "Entretien avec Gérard Genette," *L'Express,* January 9, 2002. For further discussion of the function of the paratext in general, see Gérard Genette, *Paratexts: Thresholds of Interpretation,* trans. Jane E. Lewin (Cambridge: Cambridge University Press, 1997).

5. A particularly relevant example of such an address appears in Michael Mann's film *Manhunter* (1986), based on Thomas Harris's crime novel *Red Dragon.* At a certain point, jailed serial killer Hannibal Lektor, who is enlisted by the cop who caught him to help hunt down another serial killer, sends clandestine messages in the form of personal advertisements to the "enemy" against whom he is supposedly allied. But one might also point to the recent incidence of sniper "attacks" in and around Washington DC (summer 2002) by John Allen Muhammed and John Lee Malvo. Throughout the search for the duo, the police consistently communicated with them through broadcast press conferences, at times also in the form of a "personal" ciphered code. However, this latter scene was complicated by the fact that the chief of police (named "Moose") agreed to speak in ventriloquized ciphers designed and programmed by their intended addressee: "You have indicated that you want us to do and say certain things. You asked us to say, 'We have caught the sniper like a duck in a noose.' We understand that hearing us say this is important to you." Although the source of this cryptic expression has been traced to a Native American folktale, it seems that its function as an utterance scripted for the mouth of Chief Moose (rhymes with "noose") was to draw the name and authority of the speaker into the play of the letter and thus to show that the "manhunt" was unfolding in a political space determined without other sovereignty than the circulation of the letter itself. It should also be noted that, as long as the identity of the killers remained unknown, the political climate of the time ("post-9/11") made it unclear whether the sniper was merely a criminal or a political enemy; it remained impossible to distinguish between a criminal act and an act of war. The space of this indistinction would be precisely the international media sphere that makes that openness of the address possible, in that the address itself (to the man on the other end of the gun) precedes the possibility of knowing whether he is a criminal or an enemy.

6. Jean Genet, *The Blacks: A Clown Show*, trans. Bernard Frechtman (New York: Grove Press, 1994), 6.

7. Ibid., 4.

8. Jean Genet, *Prisoner of Love*, trans. Barbara Bray (Middletown, CT: Wesleyan University Press, 1992), 18.

9. Genet, *The Declared Enemy*, 241.

10. Ibid.

11. Ibid., 239–40.

12. Kant cites this expression in his article "An Answer to the Question: What Is Enlightenment?" in which he discusses the responsibility of tyrants to avoid interference with the attempts of citizens to publicly clarify their religious ideas. "It indeed detracts from his majesty if he interferes in these affairs by subjecting the writings in which his subjects attempt to clarify their religious ideas to governmental supervision. This applies if he does so acting upon his own exalted opinions—in which he exposes himself to the reproach: *Caesar non est supra Grammaticos*—but much more so if he demeans his high authority so far as to support the spiritual despotism of a few tyrants within his state against the rest of his subjects" (Immanuel Kant, "What Is Enlightenment?," in *Political Writings*, ed. Hans Reiss [Cambridge: Cambridge University Press, 1991], 58). As always in Kant, the contestation of political authority takes place in the name of a higher obedience, obedience to an absolute master, the law of the public sphere as such, which, in this case, is called grammar. Genet's political engagements, therefore, his decision in favor of the real against the imagination, is primarily a rupture with the model of the political that belongs to a constituted public sphere—a public sphere present even in his prison cell.

13. G. W. F Hegel, *Phenomenology of Spirit*, trans A. V. Miller (Oxford: Oxford University Press, 1977), §§58–60, 35–38. In particular, §58: "Argumentation [*das Räsonieren*] is freedom from all content, and a sense of vanity [*Eitelkeit*] toward it. What is looked for is therefore the effort to give up this freedom, and, instead of being the principle of the content that moves by force of will, to sink this freedom in the content itself, letting it move through its own nature, that is, through the self as its own self, and then to contemplate this movement. This refusal to intrude into the immanent rhythm of the concept, either through the will or with wisdom adduced from elsewhere, constitutes a restraint which is itself an essential moment of the concept" (translation modified). And §59: "[Argumentation (*der räsonierenden Verhalten*)] is reflection into the empty 'I', the vanity of its own knowing.—This vanity, however, expresses not only the vanity of this content, but also the futility of this insight itself; for this insight is the negative that fails to see the positive within itself." And §60: "The solid ground which argumentation has in the passive subject (*Der feste Boden, den das Räsonieren an dem ruhenden Subjekte hat*) is therefore shaken, and only this movement itself becomes the object. The subject that fills its content ceases to go beyond it and cannot have any further predicates or accidental properties." Compare to Immanuel Kant, "What Is Enlightenment?," 55. "For enlightenment of

this kind, all that is needed is *freedom*. And the freedom in question is the most innocuous form of all—freedom to make *public use* of one's reason. But I hear on all sides the cry: Don't argue [*räsonniert nicht*]! The officer says: Don't argue, get on parade! The tax offical: Don't argue, pay! The clergyman: Don't argue, believe! (Only one ruler in the world says: *Argue* as much as you like about whatever you like, *but obey*! [räsonniert, *so viel ihr wollt, und worüber ihr wollt; aber* gehorcht!])."

14. Jean Hyppolite, *Logic and Existence,* trans. Leonard Lawlor and Amit Sen (Albany: SUNY Press, 1997), 133.

15. Indeed Tarski's formulation could be read as elaborating Hegel's more forceful "now is night" demonstration in the chapter of the *Phenomenology* on sense-certainty—which also shows that the dependence of a proposition upon an empirical state of affairs both prevents it from ever being true in its own terms and opens the way to the legitimate advent of the truth in the form of self-consciousness.What Hegel's demonstration introduces that Tarski's tautology entirely elides is the element of *time* (the "now"). Whereas Tarski marks the function of the imagination with the use of a counterintuitive predicate, Hegel more discretely, and more rigorously, marks it by marking time itself. See Alfred Tarski, "The Concept of Truth in Formalized Languages," in *Logic, Semantics, and Metamathematics* (Oxford: Clarendon Press, 1956).

16. Genet, *The Declared Enemy,* 208–28. Genet happened to be in Beirut on September 16 and 17, 1982. He witnessed the departure of the American and French forces, and he managed to gain access to the Shatila refugee camp for several hours after the massacre had taken place.

17. At several points in *Prisoner of Love,* Genet suggests the possibility that the memoir had its beginnings in Shatila, only to retract the suggestion immediately each time. "The different lengths of time it can take a viral infection to incubate may be so varied it's impossible to put an exact date not merely to its birth but even to its conception. To the moment when there's a slight biological or other jolt. And just as the origins of a revolution or of a family fortune or dynasty may be lost in minute changes of direction, so I can't really give a date to the beginnings of this book. Was it after Shatila?" (338). "Perhaps the massacres at Shatila in September 1982 were not a turning point. They happened. I was affected by them. I wrote about them. But . . . the act of writing came later, after a period of incubation" (373). For a more detailed account of the events surrounding the writing of "Four Hours in Shatila" and its relation to *Prisoner of Love,* see "Entretien avec Leila Shadid," in *Genet à Shatila,* ed. Jérôme Hankins (Paris: Solin, 1992).

18. Genet, *The Declared Enemy,* 211.

19. Genet, *Prisoner of Love,* 328–29.

20. Hannah Arendt, *Between Past and Future: Eight Exercises in Political Thought* (New York: Penguin Books, 1954), 239–40.

21. Ibid., 238.

22. Ibid., 242.

23. Ibid., 240. Arendt's essay is associated with *Eichmann in Jerusalem,* in that it was written in response to the controversy that surrounded the

publication of that book. And this passage shows the extent to which Arendt
was aware of the dangers attendant upon democratic self-legislation that
become explicit with Eichmann's justification of his actions with reference to
Kant. For discussion of these matters, see Juliet Flower MacCannell, "Fascism and the Voice of Conscience," in *The Hysteric's Guide to the Future
Female Subject* (Minneapolis: University of Minnesota Press, 1999). This
passage also shows the extent to which, for Arendt, the political exceeds the
parameters of both plurality and consensus, and perhaps even of political
philosophy. Alain Badiou largely builds the concept of what he calls political
thought against Arendt's political philosophy, grounding his polemic on the
assertion that her philosophy subordinates the political as such to the regime
of consensus. It seems that her politics are closer to what Badiou calls the
metapolitical than one might initially suppose on the basis both of received
ideas about Arendt's thoguht and of Badiou's arguments. See Alain Badiou,
"Against Political Philosophy," in *Metapolitics*, trans. Jason Barker (New
York: Verso Books, 2005), 10–25.

24. The first section of the chapter, "Mental Activities in a World of
Appearances," is called "Invisibility and Withdrawal" (§9) and deals precisely with the invisibility of mental activity. Hannah Arendt, *The Life of the
Mind* (New York: Harcourt Brace Jovanovich, 1971), 69–80. Paolo Virno
has recirculated the trope of the "life of the mind," understood in very much
these terms of a politics of the invisible, in a way that suggests its relevance
to contemporary political analysis: for him, as for Arendt, politics begins
where the invisible quantities of thought and labor become central to public life. Virno—and the Italian school of political thinkers with which he is
allied—shows that such politics develops from a systematic transformation
of the politico-economic field, from the rise of what he calls "immaterial
labor," whereas the scope of Arendt's analysis is actually more restricted.
She seems to understand the "life of the mind" to mean something more like
what it most obviously connotes: the withdrawn life of the thinker or truthteller himself. Nonetheless, the horizon of her thought is larger than that of
the conclusions she derives from it herself. See Paolo Virno, "Virtuosity and
Revolution: The Political Theory of Exodus," in *Radical Thought in Italy: A
Potential Politics,* ed. Paolo Virno and Michael Hardt (Minneapolis: University of Minnesota Press, 1996).

25. Arendt, *Between Past and Future,* 259–60.

26. Genet, *The Declared Enemy,* 245.

27. Genet, *Prisoner of Love,* 29.

28. Ibid., 3.

29. Ibid., 205.

30. See the landscape photography of Andreas Gursky for an attempt to
produce resemblance without scale, to situate human beings in a landscape
without figuring them as the measure.

31. On the portrait as painting of the absolute, see Jean-Luc Nancy, *Le
regard du portrait* (Paris: Galilée, 2000).

32. The relation of the measure of size to the problem of the simulacrum
perhaps accounts for the importance of the figure of Gulliver in the work of

Pierre Klossowski. For example, in his essay "Protase et Apodose," in *L'Arc*, no. 43 (1970), Klossowski identifies an entire trajectory of his work with the Gulliverian *vision disproportionelle*. For an extensive consideration of the simulacrum in Klossowki and Genet in terms other than those that I am proposing, see Scott Durham, *Phantom Communities: The Simulacrum and the Limits of Postmodernism* (Stanford: Stanford University Press, 1998).

33. With these considerations in mind, it would be interesting to read the film by Pierre Klossowski and Raul Ruiz, *L'Hypothèse du tableau volé*, with Poe's *The Purloined Letter* and Lacan's seminar on the same.

34. Carl Schmitt, *The Concept of the Political*, trans. George Schwab (Chicago: University of Chicago Press, 2007), 27.

35. The demand for the inadequacy of the enemy perhaps comes close to what Pierre Klossowski calls "la pratique du dissemblable." See Pierre Klossowski, *Roberte et Gulliver* (Paris: Fata Morgana, 1987), 14. "Trouver dans les lois de l'optique/ une manière de se conduire envers ses semblables/ et dans les règles de la *perspective*/ la pratique du dissemblable/ c'est l'invention de Gulliver!" Perhaps Klossowski finds in Swift an opening onto another political tradition than the one inaugurated with Rousseau. In the *Discours sur l'origine et les fondements de l'inegalité parmi les hommes*, the mythical invention of the name "man" also revolves around the calculation of a fundamental disproportion. Although, in Paul de Man's analysis, the calculation, which is the basis for civil society, functions as "a lie superimposed upon an error." Paul de Man, *Allegories of Reading: Figural Language in Rousseau, Nietzsche, Rilke, and Proust* (New Haven: Yale University Press, 1979), 155. Swift (and Klossowski and Genet after him) would thus already give the lie to Rousseau's conception of civil society, upholding the uncertainty of a politics of error.

36. Cf. Emmanuel Lévinas, *The Humanism of the Other*, trans. Nidra Poller (Chicago: University of Illinois Press, 2005).

37. For example, Brutus at the end of Shakespeare's *Julius Caesar*: "I shall have glory by this losing day/ More than Octavius and Mark Antony/ By this vile conquest shall attain unto" (vv. 36–38).

38. Cf. Schmitt, *The Concept of the Political*, 28: "The enemy is not merely any competitor or any partner of a conflict in general. He is also not the private adversary whom one hates. An enemy exists only when, at least potentially, one fighting collectivity of people confronts a similar collectivity. The enemy is solely the public enemy, because everything that has a relationship to such a collectivity of men, particularly to a whole nation, becomes public by such a relationship. The enemy is *hostis*, not *inimicus* in the broader sense: *polemos*, not *exthros*."

39. Schmitt's term for the detachment of the political from determinate groupings such as the nation-state and the indeterminacy of the enemy that results from it. "A world in which the possibility of war is utterly eliminated, a completely pacified globe, would be a world without the distinction of friend and enemy and hence a world without politics. It is conceivable that such a world might contain many very interesting antitheses and contrasts, competitions and intrigues of every kind, but there would not be a meaningful

antithesis whereby men could be required to sacrifice life, authorized to shed blood, and kill other human beings. For the definition of the political, it is here even irrelevant whether such a world without politics is desirable as an ideal situation. The phenomenon of the political can be understood only in the context of the ever present possibility of the friend-and-enemy grouping, regardless of the aspects which this possibility implies for morality, aesthetics, and economics" (*The Concept of the Political*, 35).

40. Abraham Joshua Heschel, *God in Search of Man: A Philosophy of Judaism* (New York: Noonday Press, 1955), 136.

41. For a beautiful discussion of the rhetoric and politics of war in Saint Paul's epistles, see Gil Anidjar, "The Theological Enemy," in *The Jew, The Arab: A History of the Enemy* (Stanford: Stanford University Press, 2003), 3–39.

42. Kant's practical reason is the culmination of this logic, to the extent that it revolves around the example of the holy will of God that is itself bound by the moral law. "Now this principle of morality, just on account of the universality of the lawgiving that makes it the formal supreme determining ground of the will regardless of all subjective differences, is declared by reason to be at the same time a law for all rational beings insofar as they have a will. . . . It is, therefore, not limited to human beings but applies to all finite beings that have reason and will and even includes the infinite being as the supreme intelligence." Immanuel Kant, *Critique of Practical Reason*, trans. Mary Gregor (Cambridge: Cambridge University Press, 1997), 27. Carl Schmitt, on the contrary, who is an anti-Kantian if not a Hegelian, attempts to exhume a divine triumphalism that excepts itself from the law, thus effecting a reterritorialization of the enemy. In this respect, I would disagree with Giorgio Agamben who, in *Homo Sacer,* tends to make Kant into a thinker of what Schmitt calls the "state of exception," and, further, identifies the state of exception with the fulfillment of the law. See Giorgio Agamben, *Homo Sacer: Sovereign Power and Bare Life,* trans. Daniel Heller-Roazen (Stanford: Sanford University Press, 1998), 52–53.

43. The original French text has been lost. The version in *The Declared Enemy* has been retranslated from the English translation published in the *Evergreen Review.* See Jean Genet, "A Salute to 100,000 Stars," trans. Richard Seaver, *Evergreen Review,* no. 61 (December 1968).

3. MAYHEM

1. Hannah Arendt, *On Revolution* (New York: Penguin Books, 1963), 11.

2. This statement was originally cited in Edward Epstein's article for the *San Francisco Chronicle,* "Success in Afghan War Hard to Gauge" (March 23, 2002).

3. Sigmund Freud, *The Standard Edition of the Complete Psychological Works of Sigmund Freud,* ed. and trans. James Strachey, 24 vols. (London: Hogarth Press, 1953–74), vol. 4, 289. Hereafter SE followed by volume number.

4. Adi Ophir, *The Order of Evils: Toward an Ontology of Morals,* trans. Rela Mazali and Havi Carel (New York: Zone Books, 2005).

5. See www.iraqbodycount.org/about/.

6. William Tecumseh Sherman, *Memoirs* (New York: Library of America, 1990), 601. Sherman is also credited with coining the famous slogan "War is hell."

7. On another level, the malediction of war is inseparable from the cardinal military virtue: courage. In the dialogue on the subject of courage in Plato's *Laches*, Socrates and his interlocutors distinguish between true courage and rashness, impulsiveness, or madness. "By no means . . . do I call courageous wild beasts or anything else that, for lack of understanding, does not fear what should be feared. Rather I would call them rash or mad" (Plato, *Laches and Charmides*, trans. Rosamond Kent Sprague [New York: Hackett, 1992], 42–43). Analogous statements recur throughout the modern writing on war. For example, Sherman (again) seems to rediscover Plato's definition when he writes (much more colorfully than Plato): "There is, of course, such a thing as individual courage, which has a value in war, but familiarity with danger, experience in war and its common attendants, and personal habit, are equally valuable traits, and these are the qualities which we usually have to deal with in war. All men naturally shrink from pain and danger, and only incur their risk from some higher motive, or from habit; so that I would define true courage to be a perfect sensibility of the measure of danger, and a mental willingness to incur it, rather than the insensibility to danger of which I have heard far more than seen" (Sherman, *Memoirs*, 886). All courage worthy of the name implies knowledge and foresight, a just estimation of the danger at hand. There is no courage, in other words, without prudence, if not jurisprudence. The malediction whereby a subject explicitly articulates and assumes responsibility for knowledge of war and its horrors would thus be essential to courage—essential to the sober calculation at the heart of courage as an ethical position and to any biographical or autobiographical "profile in courage."

8. See Francisco Goya y Lucientes, *The Disasters of War*, with a new introduction by Philip Hofer (New York: Dover, 1967). It is also important to note that the Chapman brothers produced what they called a "rectified" version of Goya's entire series of etchings, which they titled *Insult to Injury*. In a gesture akin to Robert Rauschenberg's *Erased de Kooning Drawing*, the artists purchased a mint edition of the etchings—specifically, the edition printed in 1937 under the auspices of the anti-Fascist resistance during the Spanish Civil War—and proceeded to paint (surprisingly apposite) razor-toothed clown, puppy, and Mickey Mouse heads over the faces of the victims in every single image. As the title suggests, the artists liken their own practice to the violence that Goya represents in *¡Grande hazaña! ¡Con muertos!* By defacing and ridiculing the postmortem representation of victims within all of Goya's scenes of violence, the Chapman brothers place each of Goya's etchings themselves in the position of the corpses within this one exemplary image. This image thereby becomes their *ars poetica*—and even their *ars politica*. See Jake Chapman and Dinos Chapman, *Insult to Injury* (Göttingen: SteidlMACK, 2003).

9. Susan Sontag, *Regarding the Pain of Others* (New York: Picador, 2004), 45.

10. Ibid.

11. See the following "absurd" dream from *The Interpretation of Dreams*: "A man who had nursed his father during his last illness and had been deeply grieved by his death, had the following senseless dream some time afterwards. *His father was alive once more and was talking to him in his usual way, but* (the remarkable thing was that) *he had really died, only he did not know it*" (Freud, SEV, 430).

12. Maurice Blanchot, *The Instant of My Death*, trans. Elizabeth Rottenberg (Stanford: Stanford University Press, 2000), 7.

13. In the second volume of his work on cinema, Gilles Deleuze calls "visionary" any "purely optical and sound situation that does not extend into action," a situation that is defined by the encounter with something intolerable or unbearable. "A purely optical and sound situation does not extend into action, any more than it is induced by an action. It makes us grasp, it is supposed to make us grasp, something intolerable and unbearable. Not a brutality as nervous aggression, an exaggerated violence that can always be extracted from the sensory-motor relations in the action-image. Nor is it a matter of scenes of terror, although there are sometimes corpses and blood. It is a matter of something too powerful, or too unjust, but sometimes also too beautiful, which henceforth outstrips our sensori-motor capacities. . . . Romanticism had already set out this aim for itself, grasping the intolerable or the unbearable, the empire of poverty, and thereby becoming visionary, to produce a means of knowledge and action out of pure vision." Gilles Deleuze, *Cinema 2: The Time-Image*, trans. Hugh Tomlinson and Robert Galeta (Minneapolis: University of Minnesota Press, 1989), 17–18.

14. Ian Baucom, "*The Disasters of War*: On Inimical Life," *Polygraph* 18 (2006): 187.

15. "Goya n'a pas de lumière, il n'a qu'un éclairage." André Malraux, *Le triangle noir* (Paris: Gallimard, 1970), 85.

16. Of the many references to Goya's *Disasters of War* in scholarly literature on war and violence, I find none more suggestive than the geographer Kenneth Hewitt's remarks at the opening of his paper on "place annihilation" because of his emphasis upon violence that aims at *places* rather than *people*. If Goya's images teach us something about the wars of the twentieth and twenty-first centuries, this prophetic power lies in their insight about the vast, "place annihilating" scope of human violence. "There is no more apt introduction to my subject than the etchings of Francisco Goya. . . . Sharing my concerns here, he depicts mainly the plight of noncombatants: the impact of war on the old, children, women, ordinary men made destitute, mutilated, or summarily executed. . . . Goya's choice of material also prefigures the now-common notion of war as a threat to ecological or biological existence. Moreover, his vision is prophetic. Its message transcends the events he saw in Napoleon's Peninsular War. Whatever the changes in armies and weaponry, the atrocities he portrays could equally have come from more recent wars, including the bombed out cities described below. In turn, the immediate

significance of bombing casualties and urban devastation in World War II lies in its prophetic relation to the thermonuclear threat." Kenneth Hewitt, "Place Annihilation: Area Bombing and the Fate of Urban Places," *Annals of the Association of American Geographers* 73, no. 2 (June 1983): 257.

17. Arjun Appadurai, "Dead Certainty: Ethnic Violence in the Era of Globalization," *Development and Change* 29, no. 4 (1998): 918. This indispensable essay revolves around precise descriptions of atrocities. The sexualized intimacy of such violence is what makes it heterogeneous with killing and death. "Eating the liver or heart of the exposed 'class enemy' is surely a horrible form of intimacy, and one does not have to make recourse to deeper structural theories about 'friendly' cannibalism to see that eating the enemy is one way of securing a macabre intimacy with the enemy who was so recently a friend. Making one prisoner bite off the genitals of another is an even more grotesque war of simultaneously inflicting deep pain, injury, and insult while imposing a brutal sort of intimacy between enemy bodies" (918). Serious consideration of such violence should invalidate once and for all careless clichés about the relationship between sex and death. The sexuality of this violence, to my reading, clearly entails a disregard for the limits of death. Moreover, Appadurai is careful to avoid reducing the specificity of these horrific acts of violence to the suffering that they inflict or even to the category of violence itself. Each act has a specific shape and meaning that must be confronted and understood: "it becomes clear that even the worst acts of degradation—involving feces, urine, body parts; beheading, impaling, gutting, sawing, raping, burning, hanging, suffocating—have macabre forms of cultural design and violent predictability" (909). And yet, by the end of Appadurai's discussion, it becomes clear that "the worst" remains synonymous with "death" and that "death" now encompasses the whole range of violence that he addresses. The phrase that gives the essay its title, "dead certainty," also provides its final words: "Together, these forms of uncertainty call for the worst kind of certainty: dead certainty" (922–23). The way in which Appadurai equates "ethnic violence" with "ethno*cidal* violence" effectively closes off a necessary series of questions. What is violence—acts of dismemberment, for example—that attacks the body without necessarily taking aim at its life? Violence whose *telos* is not death? Is this violence at all? Or rather, is it the height (or depth) of violence? Does such violence allow us to glimpse the violent core of violence, the violence of violence? How do we measure the violence of violence if it does not lead to death? Does such violence have a place within history or politics? Further, what is the relationship of death and dying to such acts of violence? If a victim dies after another victim bites off his genitals, for instance, does saying he was "killed" provide an adequate description of this violence? Alternately, does it suffice to claim that such dismemberment is a form of death? Is there not a more complicated relationship, in this case, between dismemberment and death?

18. "with, prep., adv., and conj.: The prevailing senses of this preposition in the earliest periods are those of opposition ('against') and of motion or rest in proximity ('towards', 'alongside'), which are now current only in certain traditional collocations or specific applications. These notions readily pass

into uses denoting various kinds of relations, among which those imply-
ing reciprocity are at first prominent . . . . 1. Denoting opposition and derived
notions (separation; motion toward): a) In a position opposite to; over
against: = AGAINST . . . Chiefly in adverbial phrases with repeated noun,
as face with face, where *to* is now used. 2. Of conflict, antagonism, dispute,
injury, reproof, competition, rivalry, and the like: in opposition to, adversely
to: = AGAINST. 3. Of resistance, defense, protection, warning, caution: =
AGAINST. 4) Of separation or deliverance: = FROM."

19. Sigmund Freud, "The Antithetical Meaning of Primal Words," in
SEXI, 155–61. In this brief essay, Freud explains how the work of the nineteenth-century philologist Karl Abel—which he discovered in 1909—helped
to reveal an aspect of the dream-work that he described in *The Interpretation of Dreams* but did not fully understand when he wrote the seminal treatise: the way in which dreams disregard oppositions. The logic of this disregard, Freud now concludes thanks to Abel, lies in the history and structure
of language itself. The essay bears the same title as one of the philologist's
pamphlets, and it largely consists in a review or even merely a report on this
pamphlet, citing the conclusions but not the examples. But Freud does retain
a few examples, including the English word *without*. "Even today the Eng-
lishman in order to express *ohne* says *without* (*mitohne* in German), and the
East Prussian does the same. The word *with* itself, which corresponds to the
German *mit*, originally meant *without* as well as *with*, as can be recognized
from *withdraw* and *withhold*" (160). Needless to say, I am arguing that the
English *with* functions in the same manner—although less clearly marked
within the body of the word itself—in relation to *against*.

20. Carl Schmitt, *Theory of the Partisan*, trans. A. C. Goodson, *New
Centennial Review* 4, no. 3 (Winter 2004), electronic supplement (www.
msu.edu/journals/cr/schmitt.pdf), 5.

21. Heinrich von Kleist, *Penthesilea*, trans. Joel Agee (New York: HarperPerennial, 2000), 8–9.

22. Carl von Clausewitz, *On War*, trans. Michael Howard and Peter Paret
(Princeton: Princeton University Press, 1976), 77.

23. W. G. Sebald, *On the Natural History of Destruction*, trans. Anthea
Bell (New York: Modern Library, 2004), 27–28.

24. Étienne Balibar, *Politics and the Other Scene* (New York: Verso
Books, 2002), 136.

25. Ibid., 136–37.

26. On the question of history as the conversion of violence, see Étienne
Balibar, *Violence and Civility and Other Lectures on Political Philosophy*,
trans. James Swenson (New York: Columbia University Press, 2013).

27. "We have often heard it maintained that sciences should be built up
on clear and sharply defined basic concepts. In actual fact no science, not
even the most exact, begins with such definitions. . . . They must at first necessarily possess some degree of indefiniteness; there can be no question of
any clear definition of their content. . . . A conventional basic concept of this
kind, which at the moment is still somewhat obscure but which is indispensable to us in psychology, is that of an 'instinct' [*Trieb*]." Freud, SEXIV, 116.

28. Such a reading bears witness to the powerful legacy of the Marquis de Sade. In order to restore the death drive to its inherently disruptive potentiality, then, Lacan insisted on reading Sade with Kant and vice versa. See Jacques Lacan, "Kant avec Sade," trans. James Swenson, *October* 51 (Winter 1989): 55–75.

29. Joan Copjec, *Imagine There Is No Woman: Ethics and Sublimation* (Cambridge, MA: MIT Press, 2002), 29.

30. Freud, SE XVIII, 36.

31. I am not entirely convinced, for example, that Copjec does not fall into this trap in spite of the subtlety of her reading of the Freudian and Lacanian theories of the drive. Her entire argument revolves around the opposition between a theory of the drive that privileges death and a theory that supposes the drive to be constitutively sexed. Her emphases upon the inhibition of the death drive as a "positive activity" and, likewise, upon the failure of the drive to reach its putative object as an opening are both predicated upon the claim that sex emerges as a problem and a horizon where death proves impossible. The very articulation and affirmation of sex in such terms, for Copjec, seems not only to bear witness to the impossibility of death but also to break from it. She does not consider the possibility that sublimation itself might open new forms of violence and destruction, that the confrontation with the impossibility of death functions to reopen rather than resolve the question of the relationship between the death drive and violence. In his later work, Freud examines the close relationship between sublimation and what he calls the "desexualization" of the drive; and this transformation favors the displaced return of the death drive in the form of "merciless violence" directed against the ego. Rather than merely a further vicissitude of the drive, desexualization, we might say, constitutes a vicissitude of sublimation itself. Although Copjec astutely identifies sublimation as the defining vicissitude or "destiny" of the drive, she does not consider the possibility that it would itself be subject to transformation. Her readings of Freud and Lacan and of Sophocles's *Antigone* are thus imbued with the palpable hope that sublimation—properly conceived—is the name for a kind of incorruptible opening or desire; and Antigone becomes the embodiment of this opening. That said, it seems to me that Copjec's insistence upon the relationship between sublimation and sexual difference might open a host of questions about "sex and violence" that can no longer be conceived in terms of sadism and masochism.

32. In his 1915 essay on war and death, for example, Freud confronts the ways in which the outbreak of World War I dashed the hopes and ideals underlying the project of European civilization: "We had expected the great world-dominating nations of white race upon whom the leadership of the human species has fallen, who were known to have worldwide interests at their concern, to whose creative powers were due not only our technological progress [*die technischen Fortschritte*] towards the control of nature but the artistic and scientific standards of civilization [*die künstlerischen und wissenshaftlichen Kulturwerte*]—we had expected these peoples to succeed in discovering another way of settling misunderstandings and conflicts of interest" (Freud, SE XIV, 276). From the perspective of the European citizen of the

world, the outbreak of the war came as an unwelcome surprise—and Freud the European feigns surprise as well. From the perspective of Freud the psychoanalyst, however, the war confirmed what he had learned about human nature from analytic experience. What is surprising to the citizen is not to the psychoanalyst. Whence the irony that weighs upon Freud's largely sympathetic projection of the former's hopes. The analyst knows that no technological progress will ever succeed in controlling nature. He knows that "artistic and scientific standards of civilization" will never tame the drive once and for all. Against the hopes and ideals of civilization, then, Freud demands that we respect the indomitable force of nature. Such a reading of Freud finds further confirmation in the second section of this same essay when he aligns the drive with a primitive will to murder. What is missing from this essay—which we encounter in Freud's later words—is any reflection on the discontents of civilization, that is, any attempt to distinguish civilization from its civilization function; to distinguish technology, art, and science from the ideal that they claim to embody.

33. Freud, SEXIX, 53.

34. On this point, see André Green's careful analysis of the relationship between sublimation and the death drive in *The Work of the Negative* (New York: Free Association Books, 1999).

35. Jacqueline Rose, "Deadly Embrace," *London Review of Books*, November 4, 2004.

36. For a broader meditation on the concept of suicide as weapon, see Ian Hacking, "The Suicide Weapon," *Critical Inquiry* 35, no. 1 (Autumn 2008): 1–32.

37. Adriana Cavarero, *Horrorism: Naming Contemporary Violence*, trans. William McCuig (New York: Columbia University Press, 2009), 2.

38. Catherine Malabou, *The New Wounded: From Neurosis to Brain Damage*, trans. Steven Miller (New York: Fordham University Press, 2012).

39. Cavarero, *Horrorism*, 2.

40. Ibid., 20–21.

41. Ibid., 31.

42. Ibid., 5.

43. Ibid., 11.

44. Ibid., 8.

45. Ibid.

46. Ibid., 30.

47. Ibid., 31–32.

48. Ibid., 32.

49. Ibid., 8.

50. Ibid., 21.

51. Ibid., 23.

52. Gilles Deleuze, *Essays Critical and Clinical*, trans. Michael A. Greco and Daniel W. Smith (Minneapolis: University of Minnesota Press, 1997), 133.

4. WAR, WORD, WORST

1. *Huffington Post*, May 26, 2012. www.huffingtonpost.com/2012/05/26/syria-massacre-over-90-pe_n_1547533.html. Accessed July 9, 2012.

2. *New York Times*, October 1, 2004. http://select.nytimes.com/gst/abstract.html?res=F70711F6395C0C728CDDA90994DC404482. Accessed July 9, 2012.

3. *Mail and Guardian*, June 14, 2012. http://mg.co.za/article/2012-06-14-burma-unrest/. Accessed July 9, 2012.

4. *Guardian*, March 30, 2007. www.guardian.co.uk/world/2007/mar/30/1?INTCMP=SRCH. Accessed July 9, 2012.

5. *Guardian*, September 4, 2002. www.guardian.co.uk/uk/2002/sep/05/northernireland.rosiecowan?INTCMP=SRCH. Accessed July 9, 2012.

6. *Mail and Guardian*, May 3, 2012. http://mg.co.za/article/2012-05-03-egypt-clashes-see-worst-violence/. Accessed July 9, 2012.

7. BBC News Europe, February 12, 2012. www.bbc.co.uk/news/world-europe-17008476. Accessed July 9, 2012.

8. Bloomberg Business Week, January 15, 2012. www.businessweek.com/news/2012-01-15/kazakhs-vote-for-new-parliament-after-worst-violence-in-20-years.html. Accessed July 9, 2012.

9. *Atlantic Cities*, January 31, 2012. www.theatlanticcities.com/neighborhoods/2012/01/5-us-cities-worst-gang-violence/1095/. Accessed July 9, 2012.

10. *France24 International*, October 16, 2011. www.france24.com/en/20111016-rome-faces-million-dollar-damage-bill-protest-violence-occupy-wall-st-economy-debt-italy. Accessed July 9, 2012.

11. David Rieff, "The Maimed," *New York Times Magazine*, July 18, 2004.

12. Theodor Adorno, *Notes to Literature II*, trans. Shierry Weber Nicholson (New York: Columbia University Press, 1991), 262.

13. For Beckett, Adorno writes, modernism is synonymous with obsolescence. "For Beckett, culture swarms and crawls, the way *Jugendstil* ornamentation swarmed and crawled for the avant-garde before him: modernism as what is obsolete in modernity. Language, regressing, demolishes this obsolete material" (Adorno, *Notes to Literature II*, 241).

14. Samuel Beckett, *Nohow On: Company, Ill Seen Ill Said, Worstward Ho* (New York: Grove Press, 1996), 89.

15. See Elaine Scarry, *The Body in Pain* (Oxford: Oxford University Press, 1985). My evocation of Scarry is less a direct citation than a kind of mash-up of her keywords and phrases.

16. Beckett, *Nohow On*, 90.

17. Ibid., 91.

18. Samuel Beckett, *The Complete Short Prose, 1929–1989*, ed. S. E. Gontarski (New York: Grove Press, 1995), 202].

19. Ibid., 116.

20. Alexander Garcia-Düttmann, "The Potentiality of the Worst," *World Picture* 7 (Autumn 2012); www.worldpicturejournal.com/WP_7/Duttmann.html.

21. See Andrew Renton, "*Worstward Ho* and the End(s) of Representation," in *The Ideal Core of the Onion: Reading Beckett Archives*, ed. John Pilling and Mary Bryden (Reading, UK: Beckett International Foundation, 1992), 99–135.

22. Ibid., 89.

23. Ibid., 90.

24. Ibid., 99.

25. Samuel Beckett, *All Strange Away* (London: John Calder, 1979), 3.

26. J. L. Austin, *How to Do Things with Words* (Cambridge, MA: Harvard University Press, 1975), 16.

27. Vladimir Ilych Lenin, "On Slogans," trans. Stephan Apresyan and Jim Riordan, in *Revolution at the Gates: Selected Writings of Lenin from 1917*, ed. Slavoj Žižek (New York: Verso, 2002), 62.

28. See Deleuze and Guattari's brief but decisive analysis of Lenin's text on slogans, "November 20, 1923: Postulates of Linguistics," in *A Thousand Plateaus*, trans. Brian Massumi (Minneapolis: University of Minnesota Press, 1987), 75–110. This chapter includes an extremely interesting discussion of speech-act theory that has been unjustly ignored in most recent discussions of performative language.

29. Lenin, "On Slogans."

30. Hannah Arendt, "What Remains? The Language Remains? A Conversation with Günther Gaus," in *Essays in Understanding*, ed. Jerome Kohn (New York: Harcourt, Brace, 1994), 1–23.

31. Paul Celan, *Collected Prose*, trans. Rosemarie Waldrop (Riverdale-on-Hudson: Sheep Meadow Press, 1986), 34.

32. J. L. Austin, "The Meaning of a Word," in *Philosophical Papers* (Oxford: Oxford University Press, 1961), 68.

33. Beckett, *Nohow On*, 82.

34. Ibid., 94.

35. Ibid., 100.

36. Ibid.

37. Ibid., 101.

38. Ibid., 99.

39. Alain Badiou, *Handbook of Inaesthetics*, trans. Alberto Toscano (Stanford: Stanford University Press, 2005), 100. On Beckett's poetics of ill saying, see also Bruno Clément, *L'Œuvre sans qualités* (Paris: Seuil, 1994).

40. Austin, *Philosophical Papers*, 67–68.

41. Ibid., 69.

42. Ibid., 68.

43. Ibid., 56.

44. Ibid., 67.

45. Ibid., 68–69.

5. THE TRANSLATION OF A SYSTEM IN DECONSTRUCTION

1. Wilhelm von Humboldt, *On Language: On the Diversity of Human Language Construction and its Influence on the Mental Development of*

the Human Species, ed. Michael Losonsky, trans. Peter Heath (Cambridge: Cambridge University Press, 1999). See also Paul Ricoeur, *On Translation,* trans. Eileen Brennan (New York: Routledge, 2006); and Antoine Berman, *The Experience of the Foreign: Culture and Translation in Romantic Germany,* trans. S. Heyvaert (Albany: SUNY Press, 1992).

2. Walter Benjamin, "The Task of the Translator," in *Illuminations: Essays and Reflections,* trans. Harry Zohn (New York: Schocken Books, 1968), 77.

3. Roman Jakobson, "On the Linguistic Aspects of Translation," in *The Translation Studies Reader,* ed. Lawrence Venuti (New York: Routledge, 2000), 113–18.

4. Such translation is clearly described by Nietzsche in "On Truth and Lie in an Extra-Moral Sense" as the formation of a primordial sociolinguistic contract that makes it possible for the human race to make the transition from the war of all against all that constitutes the state of nature to a peaceful society founded upon the supposition of truth and good will. "From boredom and necessity, man wishes to exist socially and with the herd; therefore, he needs to make peace and strives accordingly to banish from his world at least the most flagrant *bellum omni contra omnes.* This peace treaty brings in its wake something which appears to be the first step toward acquiring that puzzling truth drive: to wait, that which shall count as 'truth' from now on is established. That is to say, a uniformly valid and binding designation is invented for things, and this legislation of language likewise establishes the first laws of truth." Friedrich Nietzsche, *Philosophy and Truth,* ed. and trans. Daniel Breazeale (Amherst, NY: Humanity Books, 1990), 81.

5. Marc Crépon, "Deconstruction and Translation: The Passage into Philosophy," *Research in Phenomenology* 36, no. 1 (2006): 304.

6. Ibid., 308.

7. Benjamin, "The Task of the Translator," 74.

8. Jacques Derrida, "Des Tours de Babel," in *Acts of Religion,* ed. Gil Anidjar (London: Routledge, 2001), 111.

9. Jacques Derrida, "What Is a 'Relevant' Translation?," trans. Lawrence Venuti, *Critical Inquiry* 27, no. 2 (Winter 2001): 176.

10. Derrida, "Des Tours de Babel," 104.

11. Jacques Derrida, "Two Words for Joyce," trans. Geoffrey Bennington, in *Post-Structuralist Joyce: Essays from the French,* ed. Derek Attridge and Daniel Ferrer (Cambridge: Cambridge University Press, 1985), 155–56.

12. Derrida, "Des Tours de Babel," 110.

13. In other words, language in deconstruction—rather than language *tout court*—is the object of translation. Commentators on Derrida— including Derrida himself—have often observed that the theory and practice of translation is central to his work. Why is this the case? My own commentary suggests the following conclusion. The translator is the *Dasein* of deconstruction. The translator is the reader for whom deconstruction becomes an issue. The task of the translator discloses deconstruction in action.

14. Derrida, "Des Tours de Babel," 104.

15. If each language is a body, then this incompletion might well be understood as a fragmentary state, as if the body of language were shattered or lacking key pieces. The task of the translator would then be to reconcile, if not actually make whole, what has been set asunder. In "The Task of the Translator," for example, Benjamin uses such a metaphor: "Fragments of a vessel which are to be glued together must match one another in their smallest details, although they need not be like one another. In the same way a translation, instead of resembling the meaning of the original, must lovingly and in detail incorporate the original's mode of signification, thus making both the original and the translation recognizable as fragments of a greater language, just as fragments are part of a vessel" (in *Illuminations*, 78). For Derrida, however, the tower of Babel is *more than fragmentary*—perhaps even more than radically fragmentary. It is not incomplete merely because it has been felled or broken, but rather because it is *incapable of being finished*. The Babel event institutes nothing less than what Derrida calls "an internal limit to formalization."

16. In the opening paragraphs of "The Theater of Cruelty and the Closure of Representation," Derrida explores the way in which Artaud's theater affirms and reactivates a purely hypothetical theater that was repressed at the origin of Western theater. "Indeed, the eve of the origin of this declining, decadent, and negative Western theater must be reawakened and reconstituted in order to revise the implacable necessity of affirmation on its Eastern horizon. This is the implacable necessity of an as yet inexistent stage, certainly, but the affirmation is not to be elaborated tomorrow, in some 'new theater.' Its implacable necessity operates as a permanent force." Jacques Derrida, *Writing and Difference*, trans. Alan Bass (Chicago: University of Chicago Press, 1978), 233. Both in Derrida's reading of Artaud and in his reading of the Babel myth, he repeats and subtly displaces Artaud's affirmation and reawakening of the archaic moment.

17. Paris, for example, is defined by the Commune, the Occupation, and the events of May '68; Berlin, by the Blitz. In this sense, the Babel narrative— much like but also much more than other biblical narratives—is uncannily modern. On this point and many others in the present discussion, Jean-Luc Nancy's essay, "In Praise of the Melee: For Sarajevo, 1993," has much to offer. "In order to live in Sarajevo, there was no need to identify it. From this point on, however, those who die in Sarajevo will die the death of Sarajevo itself; they will die of the militarily imposed possibility of identifying this name with some substance or some presence that measures up to the 'nation' or the 'state,' some bodily symbol erected precisely in order to body forth and symbolize what was only a place and a passage." Jean-Luc Nancy, *A Finite Thinking*, trans. Simon Sparks et al. (Stanford: Stanford University Press, 2004), 278.

18. Derrida, "Des Tours de Babel," 105.

19. Ibid., 110.

20. Rarely in his reading of the Babel narrative does Derrida mention "the tongue of Genesis" by its proper name: Hebrew. He mostly refers to this language in terms of its formal traits: "One should never pass over in silence the

question of the tongue in which the question of the tongue is raised and into which a discourse on translation is translated. . . . First: in what tongue was the tower of Babel constructed and deconstructed? In a tongue within which the proper name of Babel could also, by confusion, be translated by 'confusion.' The proper name Babel, as a proper name, should remain untranslatable, but, by a kind of associative confusion that a unique tongue rendered possible, one thought it translated in that very tongue, by a common noun signifying what *we* translate as confusion" (Ibid., 104–5).

21. Ibid., 109.

22. Accordingly, there is an essential relationship between the proper name and the papers—passports, identity cards, driver's licenses, etc.—that are most often borne in a concealed place (pocket, wallet, handbag) as close as possible to the body. In *Paper Machine*, Derrida offers these reflections on the *wallet* that in French is called *une portefeuille*. "When its 'figure' does not designate a set of documents authenticating an official power, a force of law (the ministerial portfolio), *portefeuille* names this pocket within a pocket, the invisible pocket that you carry [*porte*] as close as possible to yourself, carry on your person, almost against the body itself. Clothing under clothing, an affect among other effects. This pocket is often made of leather, like the skin of a parchment or the binding of a book. More masculine than feminine, let's think about it, a wallet gathers all the 'papers,' the most precious papers, keeping them safe, hidden as close as possible to oneself. They attest to our goods and our property. We protect them because they protect us (the closest possible protection: 'This is my body, my papers, it's me . . . ')." Jacques Derrida, *Paper Machine*, trans. Rachel Bowlby (Stanford: Stanford University Press, 2005), 188 n. 29.

23. Derrida, "Des Tours de Babel," 110; my emphasis.

24. Ibid., 109–10.

25. Jacques Derrida, *Of Grammatology*, trans. Gayatri Spivak (Baltimore: Johns Hopkins University Press, 1998), 6–7.

26. Derrida, "What Is a Relevant Translation?," 177.

27. In "Force and Translation; Or, The Polymorphous Body of Language," *philoSophia* 3, no. 1 (Winter 2013): 1–18, Elissa Marder examines Lawrence Summers's claim—included in his six-point program for reforming the U.S. education system—that the study of foreign language might no longer be a " universally worthwhile" undertaking. Since English has emerged as a global language and machine translation has become more accurate and efficient, he concludes, it is no longer necessary for each and every American student to spend time learning languages. Beyond underscoring the imperialist hubris in Summers's claim that English might have achieved the status of the universal language into which all other languages are translated, thereby rendering the task of the translator obsolete, Marder notes that he completely ignores the very existence of foreign literatures: "Here I would like to pause briefly to point out that in his haste to explain why foreign language study would be unnecessary in the American university of the future, Summers's doesn't even bother to mention the very existence of foreign literature as a potential object of study presumably because of the inherently limited return

on such an investment of energy and resources" (3). Literature, for Marder, embodies something—the polymorphous body of language itself—that remains insuperably foreign. I would add—in somewhat different terms— that Summers can ignore the study of literature because, strangely, literature has both everything and nothing to do with language. As I have been exploring through Derrida's reading of Babel, no literary work is strictly speaking written "in" a given language. The "language of Genesis" is not Hebrew; the language of *Finnegans Wake* is not English. Instead, the writing of the literary work by definition—by virtue of its *economy* rather than its *foreignness*—poses intransigent problems for the reader and the translator. It is this inherently problematic dimension of the literary work that Derrida calls "war."

28. Benjamin, "The Task of the Translator," 69.

29. Ibid., 71.

30. Derrida, "Des Tours de Babel," 114.

31. Ibid., 74–75.

32. Benjamin, "The Task of the Translator," 76.

33. Ibid., 76.

34. Derrida, "Two Words for Joyce," 145–46.

35. Ibid., 152.

36. Ibid., 154.

37. Ibid; translation modified in accordance with the published French version of the text in *Ulysse Gramophone* (Paris: Galilée, 1987).

38. This is the crux of Schmitt's critique of liberalism. In "The Counterrevolutionary Philosophy of the State," he writes: "Just as liberalism discusses and negotiates every political detail, so it also wants to dissolve metaphysical truth in discussion. The essence of liberalism is negotiation, a cautious half measure, in the hope that the definitive dispute, the decisive bloody battle, can be transformed into a parliamentary debate and permit the decision to be suspended forever in an everlasting discussion." Carl Schmitt, *Political Theology: Four Chapters on the Concept of Sovereignty*, trans. George Schwab (Cambridge, MA: MIT Press, 1985), 63.

39. Ibid., 155.

40. Paul de Man, "The Rhetoric of Temporality," in *Blindness and Insight* (Minneapolis: University of Minnesota Press, 1983), 225.

41. Despite his usual emphasis upon the paradoxes of metaphor, de Man himself ultimately insists upon translating the word *translation* as metaphor. Arguably, this decision is a function of his linguisticism, his insistence that translation is a relation from language to language. In his lecture on Benjamin's "Task of the Translator," he writes: "The translation is not a metaphor of the original; nevertheless, the German word for translation, *übersetzen*, means metaphor. *Übersetzen* translates exactly the Greek *metaphorein*, to move over, *übersetzen*, to put across. *Übersetzen*, I should say, *translates* metaphor—which, asserts Benjamin, is not at all the same. They are not metaphors and yet the word means metaphor. The metaphor is not a metaphor, Benjamin is saying. No wonder translators have difficulty. It is a curious assumption to say that *übersetzen* is not metaphorical, *übersetzen* is not

based on resemblance, there is no resemblance between the translation and the original. Amazingly paradoxical statement, metaphor is not metaphor." Paul de Man, *Resistance to Theory* (Minneapolis: University of Minnesota Press, 1986), 83.

42. Jacques Derrida, *Resistances—Of Psychoanalysis*, trans. Pascale-Anne Brault and Michael Naas (Stanford: Stanford University Press, 1998), 11.

43. Ibid., 15.

44. Derrida, "What Is a 'Relevant' Translation?," 179–80.

45. Derrida, "Two Words for Joyce," 156.

46. Étienne Balibar, "What's in a War? (Politics as War, War as Politics)," *Ratio Juris* 21, no 3 (September 2008): 368.

47. Ibid., 369.

48. It is significant that Balibar's prime example both of war not recognized as war and of war that doesn't exactly correspond to the concept of war is the so-called Algerian War: "The spectacular case of what is now known (at least in France) as La guerre d'Algérie: during the war itself, and long after, it was never officially called a war (although the participant soldiers would certainly consider it such), because it was supposed that the Algerian people were part of the French nation and the Algerian Resistance (the *Mujahadin*, in Arabic) were gangs of rebels, terrorists, and criminals. . . . It is very rare that a war that is not named as such does not, indeed, receive one or several other names, which function as denials or play a role in avoiding drawing some of the usual political or legal consequences from the fact that one is waging a war either from the point of view of internal politics or from the point of view of international law, such as treating captives as 'prisoners of war,' concluding a peace treaty, and so on" ("What's in a War?," 369). It could very well be the case that every time Derrida ("the Arab, the Jew"— as Gil Anidjar has written in his beautiful introduction to *Acts of Religion*) names war he is also naming without naming this war without a name. In any event, there is no question that the specter of colonial and postcolonial violence, the conflictual relation between poly- and monolinguism, haunts all of Derrida's writings on translation. See, for the most exemplary example, *The Monolingualism of the Other*, trans. Patrick Mensah (Stanford: Stanford University Press, 1998). Perhaps not accidentally, this latter is also the work in which Derrida most explicitly traces the persistent hyperbolism of his thinking:

For, naturally, the hyperbolic taste for the purity of language is something that I also contracted at school. I am not unaware of that, and it is what needed to be demonstrated. The same goes for hyperbole in general. An incorrigible hyperbolite. A generalized hyperbolite. In short, I exaggerate. I always exaggerate. . . . No revolt against any discipline, no critique of the academic institution could have silenced what in me will always resemble some last will, the last language of the last word of the last will: speak in good French, in pure French, even at the moment of challenging in a million ways everything that is allied to it, and sometimes everything that inhabits it. Without a doubt I contracted this hyperbolism ('more French than the

French,' more 'purely French' than was demanded by the purity of the purists even while I am from the very beginning attacking purity and purification in general, and of course the 'ultras' of Algeria). . . . But as I have just suggested, this excessiveness was probably more archaic in me than the school. Everything must have begun before preschool; it should remain then for me to analyze it closer to my own distant past, but I still feel incapable of this. Nevertheless, I need to think back to that preschool past in order to account for the generality of the 'hyperbolism' which will have invaded my life and work. Everything that proceeds under the name of 'deconstruction' arises from it, of course; a telegram would suffice for that here, beginning with the 'hyperbole' (it's Plato's word) that would have ordered everything, including the reinterpretation of *khora*, namely, the passage to the very beyond of the passage of the Good or the One beyond being (*hyperbole . . . epekeina tes ousias*), excess beyond excess: impregnable. (48–49)

49. Derrida, "Two Words for Joyce," 147.

50. In *Technics and Time*, vol. 1: *The Fault of Epimetheus*, trans. Richard Beardsworth and George Collins (Stanford: Stanford University Press, 1998), Bernard Stiegler considers the possibility of a technical device that would break the "time barrier" and speculates on the nature of the "boom," the "shock" that would accompany this transition. "A supersonic device, quicker than its own sound, provokes at the breaking of the barrier a violent sonic boom, a sound shock. What would be the breaking of a time barrier if this meant going faster than time? What *shock* would be provoked by a device going faster than its 'own time'? Such a shock would in fact mean that speed is older than time. For either time, with space, determines speed, and there could be no question of breaking the time barrier in this sense, or else time, like space, is only thinkable in terms of speed (which remains unthought)" (15).

51. Cathy Caruth, *Unclaimed Experience: Trauma, Narrative, History* (Baltimore: Johns Hopkins University Press, 1996), 4.

52. In *Moses and Monotheism*, Freud explicates the structure of traumatic neurosis with the example of a train collision: "It may happen that someone gets away, apparently unharmed, from the spot where he has suffered a shocking accident, for instance a train collision. In the course of the following weeks, however, he develops a series of grave psychical and motor symptoms, which can be ascribed only to shock or whatever else happened at the time of the accident. This appears quite incomprehensible and is therefore a novel fact" (Cited in Caruth, *Unclaimed Experience*, 16).

53. Derrida, "Two Words for Joyce," 147.

54. Ibid., 146–47.

55. Friedrich Nietzsche, *Genealogy of Morality*, ed. Kieth Ansell-Pearson, trans. Carol Diethe (Cambridge: Cambridge University Press, 2007), 38.

56. Derrida, "Two Words for Joyce," 147.

57. Benjamin, "The Storyteller," in *Illuminations*, 84.

58. Cited in Derrida, "Two Words for Joyce," 152–53.

59. Ibid., 153.

60. For a commentary on this passage that overlaps in many respects with Derrida's and my own, see John Bishop, *Joyce's Book of the Dark* (Madison: University of Wisconsin Press, 1986), 288–96.

61. Ibid., 156.

AFTERWORD

1. On the role of teletechnology in war and its impact on the concept of the political, see David Wills, "Raw War: Teletropological Effects of a Divided Front," *Oxford Literary Review* 31, no. 2 (2009): 133–52.

2. Alain Badiou, *Handbook of Inaesthetics*, trans. Alberto Toscano (Stanford: Stanford University Press, 2005), 113.

3. Jean Genet, *The Declared Enemy: Texts and Interviews,* trans. Jeff Fort (Stanford: Stanford University Press, 2004), 1. Translation modified.

4. See David Zucchino, "U.S. Troops Posed with Body Parts of Afghan Bombers," *Los Angeles Times*, April 18, 2012.

5. Jacques Derrida, "Faith and Knowledge," in *Acts of Religion*, ed. Gil Anidjar (New York: Routledge, 2002), 89.

6. Ruth Seifert, "War and Rape: A Preliminary Analysis," in *Mass Rape: The War against Women in Bosnia-Herzegovina*, ed. Alexandra Stiglmayer (Lincoln: University of Nebraska Press, 1994), 58.

7. Ibid., 63–64.

8. Alexandra Stiglmayer, "The Rapes in Bosnia-Herzegovina," in *Mass Rape*, 95.

9. Rhonda Copelon, "Resurfacing Gender: Reconceptualizing Crimes against Women in Time of War," in *Mass Rape,* 200.

Adorno, Theodor. *Notes to Literature II.* Translated by Shierry Weber Nicholson. New York: Columbia University Press, 1991.

Agamben, Giorgio. *Homo Sacer: Sovereign Power and Bare Life.* Translated by Daniel Heller-Roazen. Stanford: Stanford University Press, 1998.

Alter, Robert. *The Five Books of Moses: A Translation and Commentary.* New York: W. W. Norton, 2004.

Anidjar, Gil. *The Jew, The Arab: A History of the Enemy.* Stanford: Stanford University Press, 2003.

Appadurai, Arjun. "Dead Certainty: Ethnic Violence in the Era of Globalization." *Development and Change* 29, no. 4 (1998): 905–25.

Arendt, Hannah. *Between Past and Future: Eight Exercises in Political Thought.* New York: Penguin Books, 1954.

———. *The Life of the Mind.* New York: Harcourt Brace Jovanovich, 1971.

———. *On Revolution.* New York: Penguin Books, 1963.

———. "Truth and Politics." In *Between Past and Future: Eight Exercises in Political Thought.* New York: Penguin Books, 1954.

———. "What Remains? The Language Remains? A Conversation with Günther Gaus." In *Essays in Understanding,* edited by Jerome Kohn. New York: Harcourt, Brace, 1994.

Ascherson, Neal. "'Heritage Terrorism' Is a Way of Sticking Two Fingers Up at West." *Guardian Unlimited,* March 13, 2001.

Austin, J. L. *How to Do Things with Words.* Cambridge, MA: Harvard University Press, 1975.

———. *Philosophical Papers.* Oxford: Oxford University Press, 1961.

Badiou, Alain. *Abrégé de métapolitique.* Paris: Seuil, 1998.

———. "Against Political Philosophy." In *Metapolitics,* translated by Jason Barker. New York: Verso Books, 2005.

———. *Handbook of Inaesthetics*. Translated by Alberto Toscano. Stanford: Stanford University Press, 2005.

Balibar, Étienne. *Politics and the Other Scene*. Translated by Christine Jones, James Swenson, and Chris Turner. New York: Verso Books, 2002.

———. *Violence and Civility and Other Lectures on Political Philosophy*. Translated by James Swenson. New York: Columbia University Press, 2013.

———. *Violence et civilité*. Paris: Gallimard, 2010.

———. "What's in a War? (Politics as War, War as Politics)." *Ratio Juris* 21, no. 3 (September 2008): 365–86.

Baucom, Ian. "*The Disasters of War*: On Inimical Life." *Polygraph* 18 (2006): 166–90.

Beckett, Samuel. *All Strange Away*. London: John Calder, 1979.

———. *The Complete Short Prose, 1929–1989*. Edited by S. E. Gontarski. New York: Grove Press, 1995.

———. *Imagination Dead Imagine*. London: Calder and Boyars, 1966.

———. *Nohow On: Company, Ill Seen Ill Said, Worstward Ho*. New York: Grove Press, 1996.

Benjamin, Walter. "Theses on the Philosophy of History." In *Illuminations: Essays and Reflections*. Translated by Harry Zohn. New York: Schocken Books, 1969.

Benslama, Fethi. "La dépropriation." *Lignes* 24 (February 1995): 34–61.

Bergeron, Danielle. "Ethics and the Consequences of the Act." Unpublished manuscript. Keynote address delivered at "Narrative, Act, Ethics," Buffalo, NY, March 1, 2012.

Bermond, Daniel. "Entretien avec Gérard Genette." *L'Express*, January 9, 2002.

Berman, Antoine. *The Experience of the Foreign: Culture and Translation in Romantic Germany*. Translated by S. Heyvaert. Albany: SUNY Press, 1992.

Bishop, John. *Joyce's Book of the Dark*. Madison: University of Wisconsin Press, 1986.

Blanchot, Maurice. *The Instant of My Death*. Translated by Elizabeth Rottenberg. Stanford: Stanford University Press, 2000.

Burke, Jason. "Idols Are Reduced to Rubble." *Observer*, March 4, 2001.

Caruth, Cathy. *Unclaimed Experience: Trauma, Narrative, History*. Baltimore: Johns Hopkins University Press, 1996.

Cavarero, Adriana. *Horrorism: Naming Contemporary Violence*. Translated by William McCuig. New York: Columbia University Press, 2009.

Celan, Paul. *Collected Prose*. Translated by Rosemarie Waldrop. Riverdale-on-Hudson: Sheep Meadow Press, 1986.

Chapman, Jake, and Dinos Chapman. *Insult to Injury*. Göttingen: Steidl-MACK, 2003.

Clausewitz, Carl von. *On War*. Translated by Michael Howard and Peter Paret. Oxford: Oxford University Press, 2007.

Copelon, Rhonda. "Resurfacing Gender: Reconceptualizing Crimes against Women in Time of War." In *Mass Rape: The War against Women in Bosnia-Herzegovina*, edited by Alexandra Stiglmayer. Lincoln: University of Nebraska Press, 1994.

Copjec, Joan. *Imagine There Is No Woman: Ethics and Sublimation*. Cambridge, MA: MIT Press, 2002.

Crépon, Marc. "Deconstruction and Translation: The Passage into Philosophy." *Research in Phenomenology* 36, no. 1 (2006): 299–313.

Crossette, Barbara. "Taliban: War for War's Sake." *New York Times*, March 18, 2001.

Deleuze, Gilles. *Cinema 2: The Time-Image*. Translated by Hugh Tomlinson and Robert Galeta. Minneapolis: University of Minnesota Press, 1989.

———. *Essays Critical and Clinical*. Translated by Michael A. Greco and Daniel W. Smith. Minneapolis: University of Minnesota Press, 1997.

Deleuze, Gilles, and Félix Guattari. *A Thousand Plateaus*. Translated by Brian Massumi. Minneapolis: University of Minnesota Press, 1987.

de Man, Paul. *Allegories of Reading: Figural Language in Rousseau, Nietzsche, Rilke, and Proust*. New Haven: Yale University Press, 1979.

———. *Blindness and Insight*. Minneapolis: University of Minnesota Press, 1983.

———. *Resistance to Theory*. Minneapolis: University of Minnesota Press, 1986.

Derrida, Jacques. *Archive Fever*. Translated by Eric Prenowitz. Chicago: University of Chicago Press, 1996.

———. *Chaque fois unique, la fin du monde*. Edited by Michael Naas and Pascale-Anne Brault. Paris: Galilée, 2003.

———. "Des Tours de Babel." In *Acts of Religion*, edited with an introduction by Gil Anidjar. New York: Routledge, 2001.

———. "Faith and Knowledge." In *Acts of Religion*, edited with an introduction by Gil Anidjar. New York: Routledge, 2001.

———. *Mémoires: for Paul de Man*. Translated by Eduardo Cadava et. al. New York: Columbia University Press, 1986.

———. *The Monolingualism of the Other*. Translated by Patrick Mensah. Stanford: Stanford University Press, 1998.

———. *Of Grammatology*. Translated by Gayatri Spivak. Baltimore: Johns Hopkins University Press, 1998.

———. *Paper Machine.* Translated by Rachel Bowlby. Stanford: Stanford University Press, 2005.

———. "Psychoanalysis Searches the State of Its Soul." In *Without Alibi,* edited and translated by Peggy Kamuf. Stanford: Stanford University Press, 2002.

———. Resistances—Of Psychoanalysis. Translated by Pascale-Anne Brault and Michael Naas. Stanford: Stanford University Press, 1998.

———. "Two Words for Joyce." Translated by Geoffrey Bennington. In *Post-Structuralist Joyce: Essays from the French,* edited by Derek Attridge and Daniel Ferrer. Cambridge: Cambridge University Press, 1985.

———. "What Is a Relevant Translation?" Translated by Lawrence Venuti. *Critical Inquiry* 27, no. 2 (Winter 2001): 174–200.

———. *Writing and Difference.* Translated by Alan Bass. Chicago: University of Chicago Press, 1978.

Derrida, Jacques, and Elisabeth Roudinesco. *For What Tomorrow . . . : A Dialogue.* Translated by Jeff Fort. Stanford: Stanford University Press, 2004.

The Dictionary of War. www.dictionaryofwar.org. Accessed June 15, 2012.

Durham, Scott. *Phantom Communities: The Simulacrum and the Limits of Postmodernism.* Stanford: Stanford University Press, 1998.

Else, Gerald Frank. *Aristotle's* Poetics: *The Argument.* Cambridge, MA: Harvard University Press, 1967.

Epstein, Edward. "Success in Afghan War Hard to Gauge." *San Francisco Chronicle,* March 23, 2002.

The English Bible, King James Version: The Old Testament. Edited by Herbert Marks. New York: W. W. Norton, 2012.

Freud, Sigmund. "The Antithetical Meaning of Primal Words." In *The Standard Edition of the Complete Psychological Works of Sigmund Freud,* 24 vols., edited and translated by James Strachey, vol. 11, 153–62. London: Hogarth Press, 1953–74. Hereafter SE and volume number.

———. *Beyond the Pleasure Principle.* In SE XVIII, 1–64.

———. *The Ego and the Id.* In SE XIX, 1–63.

———. "Mourning and Melancholia." In SE XIV, 237–58.

———. *The Interpretation of Dreams.* SE IV.

———. *Three Essays on the Theory of Sexuality.* In SE VII, 123–246.

———. "Thoughts for the Times on War and Death." In SE XIV, 273–302.

———. "Why War?" SE XII, 197–215.

Garcia-Düttmann, Alexander. "The Potentiality of the Worst." In *World Picture* 7 (Autumn 2012). www.worldpicturejournal.com/WP_7/Duttmann.html.

Gellhorn, Martha. *The Face of War.* New York: Atlantic Monthly Press, 1988.

Genet, Jean. *The Blacks: A Clown Show.* Translated by Bernard Frechtman. New York: Grove Press, 1994.

———. *Un captif amoureux.* Paris: Gallimard, 1986.

———. *The Declared Enemy: Texts and Interviews.* Translated by Jeff Fort. Stanford: Stanford University Press, 2004.

———. *Prisoner of Love.* Translated by Barbara Bray. Middletown, CT: Wesleyan University Press, 1992.

Genette, Gérard. Paratexts: Thresholds of Interpretation. Translated by Jane E. Lewin. Cambridge: Cambridge University Press, 1997.

Green, André. *The Work of the Negative.* Translated by Andrew Weller. New York: Free Association Books, 1999.

Gourgouris, Stathis. "A Lucid Drunkenness (Genet's Poetics of Revolution)." *South Atlantic Quarterly* 97, no. 2 (Spring 1998): 413–56.

Goya y Lucientes, Francisco. *The Disasters of War.* With a new introduction by Philip Hofer. New York: Dover, 1967.

Guattari, Félix. "Genet retrouvé." *Revue d'études palestiniennes* 21 (1986): 27–42.

Hacking, Ian. "The Suicide Weapon." *Critical Inquiry* 35, no. 1 (Autumn 2008): 1–32.

Hägglund, Martin. "Radical Atheist Materialism: A Critique of Meillassoux." In *The Speculative Turn,* edited by Levi Bryant, Nick Srnicek, and Graham Harman. Victoria, Australia: Re-press, 2011.

Halliwell, Stephen. *The "Poetics" of Aristotle: Translation and Commentary.* Chapel Hill: University of North Carolina Press, 1987.

Hankins, Jérôme. "Entretien avec Leila Shadid." In *Genet à Shatila,* edited by Jérôme Hankins. Paris: Solin, 1992.

Harding, Luke. "Fury as Army Attacks Buddhist Relics." *Guardian Unlimited,* March 2, 2001.

———. "Taliban Blow Apart 2000 Years of Buddhist History." *Guardian Unlimited,* March 3, 2001.

Hegel, G. W. F. *Phenomenology of Spirit.* Translated by A. V. Miller. Oxford: Oxford University Press, 1979.

Heidegger, Martin. *Being and Time.* Translated by Joan Stambaugh. Albany: SUNY Press, 1996.

Heschel, Abraham Joshua. *God in Search of Man: A Philosophy of Judaism.* New York: Noonday Press, 1955.

Hewitt, Kenneth. "Place Annihilation: Area Bombing and the Fate of Urban

Places." *Annals of the Association of American Geographers* 73, no. 2 (June 1983).

Hilton, Isabel. "Blaming the Breakers of Statues." *Guardian Unlimited,* March 4, 2001.

Humboldt, Wilhelm von. *On Language: On the Diversity of Human Language Construction and Its Influence on the Mental Development of the Human Species.* Edited by Michael Losonsky. Translated by Peter Heath. Cambridge: Cambridge University Press, 1999).

Huyssen, Andreas. *Present Pasts: Urban Palimpsests and the Politics of Memory.* Stanford: Stanford University Press, 2003.

Hyppolite, Jean. *Logic and Existence.* Translated by Leonard Lawlor and Amit Sen. Albany: SUNY Press, 1997.

Idzerda, Stanley. "Iconoclasm and the French Revolution." *American Historical Review* 60, no. 1 (October 1954): 13–26.

Iraq Body Count. www.iraqbodycount.org/. Accessed June 15, 2012.

Jakobson, Roman. "On the Linguistic Aspects of Translation." In *The Translation Studies Reader,* edited by Lawrence Venuti. New York: Routledge, 2000.

James, Henry. "The Art of Fiction." In *Literary Criticism,* vol. 1: *American Writers & European Writers.* New York: Library of America, 1985.

Kant, Immanuel. *Critique of Practical Reason.* Translated by Mary Gregor. Cambridge: Cambridge University Press, 1997.

———. *Practical Philosophy.* Edited by Mary J. Gregor. Translated by Allen Wood. Cambridge: Cambridge University Press, 1996.

———. *Toward Perpetual Peace and Other Writings on Politics, Peace, and History.* Edited with an introduction by Pauline Kleingeld. Translated by David L. Colclasure. New Haven: Yale University Press, 2006.

———. "What Is Enlightenment?" In *Political Writings,* edited by Hans Reiss. Cambridge: Cambridge University Press, 1991.

Kierkegaard, Søren. "By a Graveside." In *Three Discourses on Imagined Occasions,* edited and translated by Howard V. Hong and Edna H. Hong. Princeton: Princeton University Press, 1993.

Kleist, Heinrich von. *Penthesilea.* Translated by Joel Agee. New York: HarperPerennial, 2000.

Klossowski, Pierre. "Protase et Apodose," *L'Arc,* no. 43 (1970).

———. *Roberte et Gulliver.* Paris: Fata Morgana, 1987.

Lacan, Jacques. *Écrits: The First Complete Edition in English.* Translated by Bruce Fink. New York: W. W. Norton, 2007.

———. "Kant avec Sade." Translated by James Swenson. *October* 51 (Winter 1989): 55–75.

Lacoue-Labarthe, Philippe, and Jean-Luc Nancy. *Le retrait du politique*. Paris: Galilée, 1983.

Latour, Bruno. *On the Modern Cult of the Factish Gods*. Durham, NC: Duke University Press, 2010.

———. *We Have Never Been Modern*. Translated by Catherine Porter. Cambridge, MA: Harvard University Press, 1993.

Latour, Bruno, and Peter Weibel, eds. *Iconoclash*. Cambridge, MA: MIT Press, 2002.

Lenin, Vladimir Ilych. *Revolution at the Gates: Selected Writings of Lenin from 1917*. Edited by Slavoj Žižek. New York: Verso Books, 2002.

Lévinas, Emmanuel. *Totality and Infinity*. Translated by Alphonso Lingis. Pittsburgh: Duquesne University Press, 1969.

Lyotard, Jean-François. *Soundproof Room: Malraux's Anti-Aesthetics*. Translated by Robert Harvey. Stanford: Stanford University Press, 2001.

MacAskill, Ewen. "Afghan Buddhas Lost Forever." *Guardian Unlimited*, March 12, 2001.

MacCannell, Juliet Flower. "Fascism and the Voice of Conscience." In *The Hysteric's Guide to the Future Female Subject*. Minneapolis: University of Minnesota Press, 1999.

Malabou, Catherine. *The New Wounded: From Neurosis to Brain Damage*. Translated by Steven Miller. New York: Fordham University Press, 2012.

Malraux, André. *Le triangle noir*. Paris: Gallimard, 1970.

Marker, Chris. *Commentaires 1*. Paris: Seuil, 1961.

Matsuura, Koichiro. "Les crimes contre la culture ne doivent pas rester impunis." *Le Monde*, March 16, 2001.

McNulty, Tracy. "Klossowski, ce soir." *Journal of Culture and the Unconscious* 1, no. 1 (Spring 2000): 81–103.

Milianti, Alain. "Le fils de la honte: Notes sur l'engagement politique de Jean Genet." *Revue des études palestiniennes*, no. 42 (Winter 1992): 205–12.

Nagel, Thomas. "War and Massacre." *Public Affairs* 1, no. 2 (Winter 1972): 123–44.

Nancy, Jean-Luc. *A Finite Thinking*. Translated by Simon Sparks et. al. Stanford: Stanford University Press, 2004.

———. "L'Idôlatrie des Taliban." *Libération*, March 13, 2001.

———. *Le regard du portrait*. Paris: Galilée, 2000.

Nietzsche, Friedrich. *Genealogy of Morality*. Edited by Keith Ansell-Pearson. Translated by Carol Diethe. Cambridge: Cambridge University Press, 2007.

———. *Philosophy and Truth*. Edited and translated by Daniel Breazeale. Amherst, NY: Humanity Press, 1990.

Obama, Barack, "A Just and Lasting Peace." www.nobelprize.org/
nobel_prizes/peace/laureates/2009/obama-lecture_en.html.

OllieGarkey. "UC Berkeley Purchases Armored Personnel Carrier." *Daily
Kos*, July 3, 2012. www.dailykos.com/story/2012/07/03/1105732/-UC-
Berkeley-Purchases-Armored-Personnel-Carrier. Accessed July 3, 2012.

Ophir, Adi. *The Order of Evils: Toward an Ontology of Morals*. Translated
by Rela Mazali and Havi Carel. New York: Zone Books, 2005.

Patterson, Orlando. *Slavery and Social Death*. Cambridge, MA: Harvard
University Press, 1985.

Plath, Sylvia. "Words." In *The Collected Poems*, edited by Ted Hughes. New
York: HarperPerennial, 2008.

Plato. *Laches and Charmides*. Translated by Rosamund Kent Sprague. New
York: Hackett, 1992.

Rad, Gerhard von. *Holy War in Ancient Israel*. Translated by Marva J.
Dawn. Grand Rapids, MI: Eerdmans, 1991.

Renton, Andrew. "*Worstward Ho* and the End(s) of Representation." In *The
Ideal Core of the Onion: Reading Beckett Archives*, edited by John Pilling
and Mary Bryden. Reading, UK: Beckett International Foundation, 1992.

Reuters News Agency. "Islamist Militants in Mali Continue to Destroy
Shrines." *New York Times*, July 1, 2012.

Ricoeur, Paul. *On Translation*. Translated by Eileen Brennan. New York:
Routledge, 2006.

Rose, Jacqueline. "Deadly Embrace." *London Review of Books,* November
4, 2004.

———. *Why War?* London: Wiley-Blackwell, 1993.

Rumsfeld, Donald H. "A New Kind of War." *New York Times*, September
27, 2001.

Santner, Eric. *The Psychotheology of Everyday Life: Reflections on Freud
and Rosenzweig*. Chicago: University of Chicago Press, 2001.

Sassen, Saskia. "Anti-war." http://dictionaryofwar.org/node/891.

Scarry, Elaine. *The Body in Pain*. Oxford: Oxford University Press, 1985.

Schmitt, Carl. *The Concept of the Political*. Translated by George Schwab.
Chicago: University of Chicago Press, 2007.

———. *The Crisis of Parlimentary Democracy,* Translated by Ellen Ken-
nedy. Cambridge, MA: MIT Press, 1984.

———. *The Nomos of the Earth*. Translated by G. L. Ulmen. New York:
Telos Press, 2003.

———. *Political Theology: Four Chapters on the Concept of Sovereignty*.
Translated by George Schwab. Cambridge, MA: MIT Press, 1985.

———. *Theory of the Partisan*. Translated by A. C. Goodson. *New*

Centennial Review 4, no. 3 (Winter 2004): electronic supplement (www. msu.edu/journals/cr/schmitt.pdf).

Sebald, W. G. *On the Natural History of Destruction.* Translated by Anthea Bell. New York: Modern Library, 2004.

Seely, Hart. *Pieces of Intelligence: The Existential Poetry of Donald Rumsfeld.* New York: Free Press, 2009.

Seifert, Ruth. "War and Rape: A Preliminary Analysis." In *Mass Rape: The War against Women in Bosnia-Herzegovina,* edited by Alexandra Stiglmayer. Lincoln: University of Nebraska Press, 1994.

Sherman, William Tecumseh. *Memoirs.* New York: Library of America, 1990.

Sontag, Susan. *Regarding the Pain of Others.* New York: Picador, 2004.

Stiegler, Bernard. *Technics and Time,* vol. 1: *The Fault of Epimetheus.* Translated by Richard Beardsworth and George Collins. Stanford: Stanford University Press, 1998.

Stiglmayer, Alexandra. "The Rapes in Bosnia-Herzegovina." In *Mass Rape: The War against Women in Bosnia-Herzegovina,* edited by Alexandra Stiglmayer. Lincoln: University of Nebraska Press, 1994.

Tarski, Alfred. "The Concept of Truth in Formalized Languages." In *Logic, Semantics, and Metamathematics.* Oxford: Clarendon Press, 1956.

Tasso, Torquato. *Jerusalem Delivered.* Translated by Anthony Esolen. Baltimore: Johns Hopkins University Press, 2000.

UNESCO. *Convention Concerning the Protection of World Cultural and Natural Heritage.* http://whc.unesco.org/archive/convention-en.pdf.

Virno, Paolo. "Virtuosity and Revolution: The Political Theory of Exodus." In *Radical Thought in Italy: A Potential Politics,* edited by Paolo Virno and Michael Hardt. Minneapolis: University of Minnesota Press, 1996.

Warminski, Andrzej. "Facing Language: Wordsworth's First Poetic Spirits." *Diacritics* 17, no. 4 (Winter 1987): 18–31.

Weber, Samuel. *Targets of Opportunity.* New York: Fordham University Press, 2005.

Weil, Simone, and Rachel Bespaloff. *War and the "Iliad."* Translated by Mary McCarthy. New York: NYRB Classics, 2005.

Weizman, Eyal. *The Least of All Possible Evils.* New York: Verso Books, 2011.

Wills, David. "Teletropological Effects of a Divided Front." *Oxford Literary Review* 31, no. 2 (2009): 133–52.

INDEX

Page numbers in italics refer to figures.